PROBLEMS OF THE MODERN ECONOMY

The Urban Economy

PROBLEMS OF THE MODERN ECONOMY

General Editor: EDMUND S. PHELPS, *Columbia University*

Each volume in this series presents
prominent positions in the debate of
an important issue of economic policy

AGRICULTURAL POLICY IN AN AFFLUENT SOCIETY

THE BATTLE AGAINST UNEMPLOYMENT

CHANGING PATTERNS IN FOREIGN TRADE
AND PAYMENTS

THE CRISIS OF THE REGULATORY COMMISSIONS

DEFENSE, SCIENCE, AND PUBLIC POLICY

THE GOAL OF ECONOMIC GROWTH

INEQUALITY AND POVERTY

LABOR AND THE NATIONAL ECONOMY

MONOPOLY POWER AND ECONOMIC PERFORMANCE

POLLUTION, RESOURCES, AND THE ENVIRONMENT

PRIVATE WANTS AND PUBLIC NEEDS

THE UNITED STATES AND THE DEVELOPING ECONOMIES

THE URBAN ECONOMY

The
Urban
Economy

Edited with an introduction by

HAROLD M. HOCHMAN

CITY UNIVERSITY OF NEW YORK

NEW YORK
W · W · NORTON & COMPANY · INC ·

Copyright © 1976 by W. W. Norton & Company, Inc. All Rights Reserved.
Published simultaneously in Canada by George J. McLeod Limited, Toronto.
First Edition

Library of Congress Cataloging in Publication Data
Main entry under title:
The Urban economy
   (Problems of the modern economy)
   Bibliography: p.
   1. Urban economics—Addresses, essays, lectures. 2. Cities and
towns—United States—Addresses, essays, lectures, 3. United States—
Economic policy—1961–   —Addresses, essays, lectures. I. Hochman,
Harold M.
HT321.U33   330.9′173′2   75–29036
ISBN 0–393–05537–X
ISBN 0–393–09243–7 pbk.

Printed in the United States of America
1   2   3   4   5   6   7   8   9   0

Permission to use copyright materials from the following sources is hereby acknowledged:

"Urbanization," by Kingsley Davis, translated from *Encyclopedia Universitas,* volumes 67/68, January 18 and 25, 1973, published by Salvat Editores, S.A. Reprinted by permission of the author and the publisher.

"The Nature of Urban Areas," by Edwin S. Mills, adapted from Chapter 1 of his book, *Urban Economics,* published by Scott, Foresman and Company, 1972. Reprinted by permission of the author and the publisher.

"The Functions of the City," by Robert Dorfman, from *Thinking about Cities: New Perspectives on Urban Problems,* edited by Anthony H. Pascal, pp. 32–40. Copyright © 1970 by Dickenson Publishing Company, Inc., Encino, California. Reprinted by permission of the author, the publisher, and The Rand Corporation.

"Financing Urban Government," by Dick Netzer. Reprinted by permission of the publishers from James Q. Wilson, ed., *The Metropolitan Enigma,* Chapter 3, "Financing Urban Government," pp 72–88, published by Harvard University Press. Copyright © 1967 by the Chamber of Commerce of the United States of America; copyright © 1968 by the President and Fellows of Harvard College.

"The Cost Disease of the Personal Services and the Quality of Life," by William J. Baumol and Wallace E. Oates. Reprinted by permission from the 1972/2 *Quarterly Review,* Skandinaviska Enskilda Banken, Stockholm, Sweden.

"The City as a Distorted Price System," by Wilbur Thompson. Reprinted by permission from *Psychology Today* magazine, August 1968. Copyright © Ziff-Davis Publishing Company.

"Understanding Urban Government: Metropolitan Reform Reconsidered," by Robert L. Bish and Vincent Ostrom. Adapted from Chapters 2 and 3 of *Understanding Urban Government: Metropolitan Reform Considered,* by Robert L. Bish and Vincent Ostrom, published by the American Enterprise Institute for Public Policy Research, Washington. Copyright © 1973 American Enterprise Institute. Reprinted by permission of the authors and the publisher.

Contents

Introduction

ALL COMMUNITIES, whether urban or not, encounter difficulties in the management of collective resources; most suffer the waste of human resources implicit in poverty and discrimination; and inadequacies in housing, transportation, and provision of social services are common.

What, then, is the uniquely urban dimension? It is the compounding and intensification of these problems as population density increases. When individuals concentrate, responding to economic forces, interactions multiply, generating social and economic costs and ample opportunity for conflict. Moreover, the concentration of poor and disadvantaged minorities in central cities reinforces problems of urban resource allocation.

In the late 1960s, American cities experienced alienation and aggression on a wide scale, reflected in urban riots and seemingly rampant crime. To many, the urban situation seemed nothing short of a crisis. For those who could afford it, "flight to the suburbs" was an apparent escape. Meanwhile the poor continued to migrate from rural areas to the central cities of metropolitan areas. The resulting changes in population composition made the urban prospect even bleaker. All levels of government—federal, state, and local—faced new demands for remedial public programs, largely defined in terms of the conventional functional fields—housing, transportation, social services, and the like—and directed, with minimal delay, to the amelioration of urban problems.

Though efforts to meet these demands, fueled by political incentives that favor short-run over lasting impact, seemed, in the early 1970s, to relieve the crisis, many of the root problems remained as real as they were a half-decade before, despite some improvement in minority incomes and a decline in the incidence of crime-prone age groups in the central city population. Dissatisfaction with imbalances in social and economic development, though moderated, smolders on. The poor and the nonpoor alike remain disillusioned—no happier for the failure of Congress to enact meaningful welfare reform and other corrective programs. Most of all, many cities, New York foremost among them, seem crippled by their financial obligations. These are, in part, a result of economic recession. But, in significant part, they are the residue of the programmatic responses of urban governments to the crisis of the 1960s, giving rise to a pervasive and uneasy feeling that the apparent respite of a year or two ago implied only that the short run had been salvaged at the expense of the long.

Several factors, peculiar to the social and political setting of present-day America, make it likely that urban problems will continue to be more difficult for the United States to resolve than for other developed countries. The first is the ethnic and racial heterogeneity of the people who live in our major urban centers. In most metropolitan areas, central cities contain rival minorities, which differ in preferences and are often in conflict. The provision of public services and the maintenance of a stable social environment are thus far more complicated than in the cities of Western Europe, where ethnic differences are less distinct and minorities must accept rules and institutions that are suited to the majority culture and majority preferences. A second factor is the more decentralized character of our metropolitan areas. Aside from a few exceptions, such as London and Tokyo, our metropolitan areas tend to be more extensive. This sharpens the dimensions, psychic and physical, that separate the disparate minorities that make up our urban populations.

Our legal tradition is a third factor. Reform is difficult to enact because property rights, once in force, are protected from arbitrary change. Most inequalities, however uncomfortable, derive from activities that are legal. Efforts to alter the distributional effects of social arrangements encounter formidable resistance, not because men are perverse, but because the expectations that will be disappointed by changes in the effective constitution are considered to be legitimate. Moreover, no matter how broad their geographic and political boundaries may seem, cities have fundamentally open economies, making it likely that local fiscal efforts to relieve distributional imbalances will prove self-defeating.

PART ONE: URBAN STRUCTURE AND FUNCTIONS

The three essays in Part One, dealing with the structure and functions of urban communities, set the frame of reference for the subsequent discussion of urban public policy.

In the first essay, Kingsley Davis, a sociologist and demographer, discusses the urbanization of human societies, tracing the process from ancient times to the present. He points out that the major breakthrough in urbanization, "an increase either in the *number* of people in towns or cities or in the *proportion* dwelling in such places," "came only with the enormous growth in human productivity made possible by the use of inanimate energy and machinery." Urbanization has, therefore, been a by-product of industrialization, historically concentrated in the last century.

In its initial stages rural migration to urban centers was a fundamental factor in urbanization. But Davis argues that the accelerated growth of cities since 1850 primarily reflects an acceleration in the growth of the world's population, attributable to changing birth rates and mortality. Looking ahead, Davis finds this a matter of serious concern, and fears for a future in which man will have "a termite-like existence in cities of tens or hundreds of millions." If this Malthusian prospect and the "ceaseless search for space" it entails are to be avoided, he argues, modern societies must face up to the realities of human multiplication and take effective steps to curb population growth.

In the second selection, Edwin Mills presents a careful introduction to the economic characteristics of urban areas. He defines urban areas as places where population density is much higher than elsewhere. Then, in a discussion that is founded on "central place theory," Mills describes the fundamental economic forces that determine the locational characteristics and spatial dimensions of the urban economy. Mills sees the urban concentration of economic activities as an efficient response, by utility-seeking households and profit-motivated firms, to economies of scale and agglomeration. He also stresses comparative advantage, both in consumption and in production, arising, for example, from access to natural resources. What sets the limits to urban scale, he then points out, is the fact that these advantages of urban location are finite, as reflected in the costs of the congestion that accompany increasing density.

A primary issue of urban policy, perhaps the primary issue, is that of determining whose interests the city is to serve—current or future residents, taxpaying residents, residents of the metropolitan area, etc.—then finding ways for the community to resolve conflict. Robert Dorfman's essay points out that "a city can be regarded from four points of view"—as "a very elaborate physical, technological, and spatial layout"; "a governmental or political entity"; "an economic unit," serving "as the communication center, or market, for some industries"; or "a social unit." But Dorfman devotes most of his attention to the final category, the city as a social unit, a nexus for human interaction and the value-reinforcing life experience which is produced by identification with a social group. Dorfman stresses the dependence of urban life on neighborhoods and the significance of population clustering on the basis of ethnic and income similarities.

To Dorfman, deficiencies in the "social health" of the black minority are not attributable to the weakness of their economic base. Instead, he argues that the basic problem for blacks is the lack of sufficient success models within their identification group. For Dorfman the importance of a sense of neighborhood or community justifies the rejection of total integration, "cultural homogenization of the population," as undesirable as well as infeasible. He argues, rather, in favor of "strengthening the positive, constructive satisfactions of life within the ethnic neighborhoods so as to reduce the emotional importance of the hostility relations among them."

PART TWO: URBAN FINANCE AND GOVERNANCE

Public policy operates through two media. One is fiscal action, which includes public expenditures and taxation, as well as other means of raising public revenues. The second is the complex of rules and institutions that comprise the system of governance, which defines propery rights and regulates private and public transactions. Distinctions between finance and governance, however, are more a matter of convenience than substance. On both fronts, government is not only concerned with the provision of

tangible services, but with assuring that community characteristics are those its constituents desire.

In the urban context such questions are bound up, inextricably,
with the status of the central city in its metropolitan area and,
in an overarching sense, with the full complex of intergovernmental relationships that characterizes the federal system. Indeed,
were the full costs of public education to be assumed by state
governments or the burdens of welfare spending transferred to
the national government, the purely fiscal element in the crisis of
most central cities would very likely disappear. Similarly, the
introduction of area-wide or metropolitan government, or any
other changes in the tenor of interjurisdictional arrangements,
would alter public service demands.

In the first selection in Part Two, Dick Netzer, seeking the
sources of the urban fiscal dilemma, points to two determinants
of public service demand. The first is the attractiveness of urban
centers to the poor and the demands for social services to which
their migration gives rise. The second is the effect of suburbanization on the demand for an urban infrastructure and on the fiscal
capabilities of the central cities.

Cities rely on the property tax as their primary source of
revenue. Netzer sees this tax as an excise on housing, which raises
rents, inducing out-migration of the very households that cities
have a fiscal interest in retaining and discouraging the maintenance and rehabilitation of low-income housing. For the poor,
concentrated in the least desirable areas of the central cities, the
effect is to reduce the supply and increase the cost of housing.

The paper by William Baumol and Wallace Oates suggests
another reason why urban fiscal problems are severe. Because
many urban services, such as education and cultural activities, are
labor-intensive, they are, on average, less susceptible to productivity improvement than most privately produced output. Taken
with the inelasticity of citizen demands for urban services and the
monopolistic characteristics of their supply—consider, for example, the effects of strikes by garbage collectors and school-
teachers—this gives rise to uncomfortable pressures on urban
government budgets.

Wilbur Thompson, in the next essay, considers "The City as a
Distorted Price System," seeking the efficient allocation of the

location-specific resources that characterize it as an urban center. But, in examining urban priorities, he points out that cities often treat not only tax-financed public services but the amenities that determine the character of urban life as "free goods." Urban resources, however, are scarce, and such price systems, whether for street repair or social services, are not only defective as rationing mechanisms but also in distributional terms. This is most clear where use patterns vary with the economic status of users or in terms of peak versus off-peak differences in the timing of consumption. Consequently, Thompson argues for the introduction of more explicit prices or user charges, not just to raise nontax revenue, but because this will itself improve urban resource allocation.

In the field of urban public finance, much attention has been directed to spillovers of tax burdens and public service benefits across jurisdictional boundaries. Such spillovers, which occur because the geographical distribution of costs and benefits differs from the political assignment of responsibilities, pose both efficiency and equity problems, sometimes of serious proportions. The next two selections discuss some of the responses to these problems.

Henry Aaron's essay contains an incisive survey of the characteristics of revenue sharing, enacted in October 1972. The ostensible purpose of such revenue sharing—"the New Federalism"—was to remand some state and local responsibilities for revenue-raising to the national government, while permitting lower-level authorities—local, metropolitan, and regional—to retain decision-making authority for public programs. It is, of course, too soon to evaluate the effects of revenue sharing on the quality of urban governance. But Aaron's argument was quite critical of its ability to foster fiscal equalization and neutralize the disparities in fiscal capacity that are so important a symptom of the urban dilemma.

Through most of the twentieth century, Robert Bish and Vincent Ostrom remind us, "respectable" students of urban government and public administration supported metropolitan consolidation, along with professional, as opposed to political, administration of public service programs. In recent years, however, the glamor of metropolitan reform has worn thin, giving way to a renewed interest in "community control" and compromise two-tier (metropolitan and local) or multitier systems that retain the advantages of polycentric government.

Bish and Ostrom, taking the public choice paradigm (which derives from the work of Anthony Downs, James Buchanan and Gordon Tullock, and Mancur Olson, among others) as their conceptual basis, see responsiveness to constituent preferences as the paramount concern in local governance. They argue that local governments should adopt allocative mechanisms that are capable of recognizing public service demands and put into effect supply arrangements that simulate the market mechanism. The strength of their approach, in this context, is that it offers a theoretical basis for compromise between the arguments for polycentric and consolidated local government.

PART THREE: THE ECONOMY OF THE CENTRAL CITY

In Part Three, the emphasis shifts from the public to the private sector. The papers focus on the dynamic relationships between the central city, as a location for private sector activities, and the twin processes of urban growth and development.

The nature of these relationships and what they imply in terms of the assets and liabilities of the central city, in effect, its balance sheet, is the subject of Benjamin Chinitz's essay. To Chinitz, the centrality of the city is one of its major assets, because firms wish to minimize freight costs and maximize access to labor supply. But, to some extent, this locational advantage is offset by urban rents and urban congestion.

For Chinitz, the primary problem of the central city economy is an increasing mismatch between urban jobs and urban labor supply, resulting from a decrease in the availability of low-skill jobs and disproportionate in-migration of this type of labor. Moreover, urban practices in housing and welfare spending transfer high-value space to the "poverty market" and discourage the poor from seeking residences outside the center. In Chinitz's view, policies that "contribute to the automatic or natural resolution of the problem" have simply not been chosen "over policies which perpetuate or even exacerbate [it]."

There are many similarities between this argument and the

view of urban problems found in the essay by Jay Forrester. Forrester, however, goes well beyond Chinitz. His paper stresses the limits of technical change and recommends that ctities adopt explicit defensive policies, capable of stemming or altering the composition of migration flows.

To Forrester, cities must closely control their growth, both rate and composition, to guard against ever-deepening fiscal and social difficulties. His thesis is that the costs of growth are bound to rise faster than its benefits, because resources and the capacity for technical change are limited, thus assuring ever-diminishing returns. Morover, the "attractiveness principle," producing migration in response to economic advantage, gives rise to undesirable demographic changes, creating problems of public management that technical change cannot reconcile.

Despairing, perhaps, of constructive cooperation, Forrester focuses on the policy options open to the central cities themselves, as independent political entities. He suggests that "a valid goal for urban leadership is to focus on improving the quality of life for residents already in the city, while at the same time protecting against growth that would overwhelm the gains . . . [thus maintaining] the attractiveness for the present residents while decreasing the attractiveness to those who might inundate the system from the outside." To do this, cities must control their population composition, adopting measures that assure them the fiscal capacity to finance and provide the public services their current residents desire—regardless, seemingly, of cost in terms of ethical and constitutional controversy. What this amounts to, in brief, is a prescription to discourage and even limit the in-migration of the poor.

The computer simulation model from which Forrester's inferences are drawn, comprising behavioral relationships and ecological and technological conditions, contains myriad assumptions, all fair game for the wary critic. In the next selection, John Kain contends that many of these assumptions are narrow and unrealistic, and that different policy implications would follow if they were modified. For example, Forrester's assumption that the interjurisdictional structure of governance in metropolitan areas is fixed and immutable precludes such remedies as political reorganization or intergovernmental cooperation. In a rejoinder to

Kain, Forrester assesses the advantages and pitfalls of formal modeling as a means of increasing our understanding of urban systems.

In the next paper, William Alonso examines the efficacy of local efforts to control population size and composition. Alonso is concerned, in particular, with the local no-growth policies that have received substantial currency in recent years. Alonso has little sympathy with the policies he is evaluating—and, it would seem, for good cause. In the first place, local (and certainly metropolitan) efforts to control population are unlikely to be effective. Moreover, when they are effective they are regressive and counterproductive in terms of social well-being. Their effect, if based, say, on fiscal criteria, is simply to exclude the poor.

The contrast between Alonso's position and Forrester's is marked. It is clearly Alonso's view that one's status as a current member of a particular political community confers no entitlement to the kind of monopoly of location that Forrester commends. But Alonso is also critical of local no-growth policies on positive grounds. To him, local population growth depends largely on the migration patterns of the young, and, in this respect, he suggests that the demographic implications of local no-growth policies may well be both unattractive and unstable. Indeed, since local no-growth implies a demographic shift toward an older population, such a policy may simply be a preface to economic decline.

The final paper in Part Three, by John Kain and John Meyer, deals with the delivery of public services in a particular functional area, urban transportation. Kain and Meyer argue that modern systems of urban transportation, which focus on travel to the central city from outlying areas, have "almost certainly caused a *relative* deterioration in the access to job opportunities enjoyed by a significant fraction of the poor." Though many, if not most, of the poor continue to live within the urban core, "new job opportunities have grown more swiftly *outside* this central business district." Thus, Kain and Meyer argue that new and more flexible modes of transportation must be developed if urban transportation systems are to serve the poor more effectively.

The transportation problems of the urban poor, as described by Kain and Meyer, are exacerbated by the difficulties, associated

with financial constraints and discrimination, which confront
blacks who wish to move closer to suburban employment opportunities. Nor are such moves, when they do occur, an unmixed
blessing, for their effects on neighborhood cohesiveness within
the city are bound to be adverse. It is, after all, the employable
residents who are likely to be most important to the social health
of the urban center.

PART FOUR: THE FUTURE OF THE INNER CITY

Many of the selections in the first three parts allude to the
problems that the concentration of disadvantaged· (in particular,
racial) minorities in central cities pose for the community-at-
large. In Part Four there is a modest shift in emphasis. The
discussion turns to the effects of public policy on core-city residents, and what government can and should do to improve them.

The papers by Anthony Downs, John Kain and Joseph Persky,
and Joel Bergsman, taken together, comprise a debate on the
future of the urban ghetto. In each paper, the primary concern
is whether it is appropriate for the larger community, in planning
for the future of the core cities, to pursue a policy of "ghetto
gilding" or "ghetto enrichment," through local development programs; to encourage integration through "ghetto dispersal"; or to
adopt mixed or compromise strategies. The final selection in this
part, by Andrew Brimmer and Henry Terrell, contains a critical
evaluation of black capitalism, as a means of advancing the economic well-being of the Negro population.

The themes that recur in the debate on the ghetto are familiar.
Dominant, of course, is the tension between the interests of the
nonpoor, whose objectives are controlling in Forrester's analysis,
and the interests of the disadvantaged. One relevant conflict is
between the objective of integration and the case for social and
cultural differentiation, as earlier stated, in a different setting, by
Bish and Ostrom. Another is between the short-run interests of
ghetto residents and the long-run well-being of the ethnic
minorities to which they belong.

After defining the "urban ghetto" in strictly racial terms, Downs
focuses on the population dynamics within it. He attributes the

emergence of ghettos to a "law of cultural dominance." This, he claims, derives from a belief, common to all racial groups, that everyday life should primarily be value reinforcing rather than value-altering, an argument similar to Dorfman's. Since the normal process of residential choice is governed by such preferences, Downs argues, racial tipping occurs, producing the urban ghettos with which he is concerned in his essay.

Having set the scene, Downs discusses three policy strategies: the "present-policies" alternative, which he considers untenable; "enrichment-only," or "ghetto-gilding"; and "enrichment-plus-dispersal." Downs gives "several reasons why dispersal of at least future increases in Negro population through major metropolitan areas would be desirable." One, which mirrors the Kain and Meyer argument, is that the suburban areas are where new jobs seem to be appearing. Second, the suburbs, not the central cities, are where the vacant land needed to build new and better housing is available. Third, perhaps most important, dispersal of the ghetto is the only way of avoiding the "continuance of two separate and unequal societies in the United States and of giving members of both races more real opportunity to learn to live with each other."

Downs is frankly troubled by present policies that bear on the urban ghetto. These, in his view, involve continuing segregation in housing and schools, concentration of Negro population growth in central cities, and "the continued failure of society to transfer any really large economic aid to the most deprived portions of the central cities." Pursued to its logical conclusion, Downs believes, the present-policies alternative will not only bankrupt many of the older central cities, but, substituting rhetoric for real change, it will leave the disadvantaged even more disillusioned than they are now.

The alternative strategies of enrichment and dispersal are considered, in even more detail, in the paper by Kain and Persky. These authors, like Downs, argue that "central cities are poor largely because they are black, and not the converse." To Kain and Persky, as to many of the other writers in this volume, living patterns in the urban ghetto have little redeeming virtue. In their eyes, the existence of the ghetto is "responsible for, or seriously aggravates, the most visible problems of urban Negroes"; they see the ghetto itself as a serious impediment to real improvements in the economic status of the black population. Thus, dispersal is essential, and gilding of the ghetto involves self-defeating—and morally objectionable—programs that distort metropolitan growth and, by impeding locational adjustment, reduce economic efficiency.

Bergsman's evaluation of the alternative strategies is more eclectic. Whereas both Downs and Kain-Persky argue from the perspective of the community-at-large, Bergsman probes into the consistency of these strategies with the objectives of various economic, social, and political subgroups. He turns out to be more sympathetic to a program mix in which measures designed to improve conditions in the ghetto have a significant role, in part because he does not consider large-scale dispersal to be a viable option. But he also stresses the favorable impact on values and behavior of the examples set by successful black entrepreneurs, with whom ghetto residents can identify.

In their essay on "black capitalism," Andrew Brimmer and Henry Terrell make skillful use of evidence obtained in the OEO Survey of Economic Opportunity. To Brimmer and Terrell, black capitalism, defined specifically as investment in black-owned businesses in urban ghettos, must be viewed as an alternative to investment in human capital or to other strategies directed to improving the well-being of the minority population.

Brimmer and Terrell point out that active discussion of black capitalism rests largely on its "intuitive appeal to varying shades of political opinion. To the black militant it is appealing because it promises community ownership of property and an end to 'exploitation' by outside merchants. . . . to white conservatives because it stresses the virtues of private enterprise capitalism as the path to economic advancement instead of reliance on government expenditures, especially for public welfare." They argue, however, that the foundations of this appeal in economics are shaky indeed. Employment potential in the ghetto, they believe, is highly limited. The ghetto, inherently, is not conducive to investment in businesses of types that serve the national economy. Deficiencies in its capital endowment make the job opportunities black capitalism might foster less attractive in terms of wage potential than jobs in industries with more general markets. And the ghetto is heavily reliant on self-employment, which is a "rapidly declining factor in our modern economy because the rewards to employment in salaried positions are substantially greater."

Brimmer and Terrell present the main thrust of their argument in straightforward economic terms. Only in their conclusion do they address the sociological argument for black capitalism, the suggestion that the introduction of dynamic elements into the ghetto will provide individuals who see themselves excluded from the prosperity of middle-class society with motivation and opportunity. But Brimmer and Terrell do not seem to share this optimistic perspective. Indeed, they claim to be troubled by "black economic development through black capitalism . . . [because it] may *substitute* [emphasis mine] for efforts in vital areas which are of the utmost importance to the Negro population." They argue, thus, that "the pursuit of black capitalism [in the long run] may retard the Negro's economic advancement by discouraging many from the full participation in the national economy with its much broader range of challenges and opportunities."

PART FIVE: URBAN CRISIS AND URBAN PROSPECT

The selections in Part Five draw from all of the arguments represented in the previous selections, asking how and whether public policy directed to the sources of urban crisis might brighten the urban prospect.

Selections from the writings of Edward Banfield, taken from a *Daedalus* essay and *The Unheavenly City*, are the point of departure. This is followed by a dialogue, consisting of two reviews of *The Unheavenly City*, by Russell Murphy and Theodore Marmor, and a paper by Worth Bateman and Harold Hochman, which presents a different interpretation of the urban crisis and the extent to which public policy might play a constructive role in alleviating it.

Few books of current topical interest have been as controversial

—or provoked so much animus, indeed intolerance—as *The Unheavenly City*. For the views it presents, its author, Edward Banfield, distinguished political scientist and conservative critic of interventionist social policy, has been both applauded and condemned. To be sure, Banfield's interpretation of the nature and future of our urban crisis is, in some respects, cantankerous. It is marked, above all, by trenchant criticism of current policies and a set of iconoclastic policy recommendations, all of which seem to deny the productivity of good intentions and to sanction actions which might, in the eyes of some students of public policy, infringe intolerably on individual liberties.

In his focus on sociological factors, emphasizing distinctions in social class and the class imperative, Banfield's diagnosis of the urban crisis differs considerably from the perspective represented by many of the other authors. Despite this, however, much common ground exists. Banfield argues that most of the "problems" that are generally supposed to constitute the urban crisis "could not conceivably lead to disaster," for they have to do with "comfort, convenience, amenity, and business advantage . . . [rather than] the essential welfare of individuals or what may be called the good health of the society." In his eyes, it is not the journey to work, inadequate urban housing, or the decline of the central business district that is the real issue, but whether "the society [can] maintain itself as a 'going concern.'" He argues that this depends on "its ability to produce desirable human types," something which is, in his interpretation, a matter of class culture.

To Banfield, conventional public programs, operating through increased levels of public service provision, are foredoomed to failure. On the one hand, such programs, which reflect middle- and upper-class values, give rise to unreasonable expectations. On the other, they do not come to grips with the class imperative and the psychological sources of the problems engendered by the lower-class component of the urban population. The lower class, according to Banfield, is so present-oriented that its members cannot be expected to be responsive to the kinds of programs which the well-intentioned or altruistic middle and upper classes are likely to design on their behalf—assuming, optimistically, that these programs are consistent with lower-class interests. While

Banfield, in discussing these questions, is careful to separate the issues of class and race, the demographic composition of core cities makes it all too simple to draw such a correlation.

What, then, is Banfield's counsel? It is, it would appear, patience. Urban problems, like the biblical poor, will always be with us, and care must be taken that remedial programs do not actually run counter to intention.

These arguments, with the definition of class and the class imperative that are central to them, are evaluated by Russell Murphy and Theodore Marmor. Whether a lower class, with the characteristics Banfield attributes to it, can be defined; whether the social condition of its members does, in fact, render them immune to treatment; and whether Banfield's views on the appropriate content of public policy are correct are among the issues discussed in their reviews of *The Unheavenly City*.

There is one major difference between Banfield's thesis and the argument developed in the essay by Harold Hochman and Worth Bateman. Whereas Banfield attributes deficiencies in "essential welfare" to the inherent characteristics of people, and, by and large, eschews positive action, Bateman and Hochman associate urban dissatisfaction with the system of rules and institutions under which these people live and ask what changes in these institutions might dissipate such dissatisfaction. They maintain that it is a pervasive sense of "distributive injustice, coupled with the urban concentration of those who are most dissatisfied," rather than the present-orientedness of the lower classes, "that is what the urban crisis is all about." The crisis is triggered by "a judgment that the structure of rights to property, income, and political power, and the institutions and rules determining the way in which these rules are established and enforced, are in-equitable and unlikely to change," and it is reinforced by re-peated frustration of attempts to change them.

The implication of this view is that social reform must be directed to the rules of the game. Such reform, altering the real structure of rights and the determinants of economic status and political power, will engender distributional change. For Bate-man and Hochman, it is the political majorities who must be future-oriented enough to adopt constitutional reforms, not only for the benefit of the lower classes, but because such reforms will also serve their own long-term self-interest.

CONCLUDING REMARKS:

To some readers, the selections may appear cynical. Too often for comfort, they suggest that the effects of past efforts to improve urban life through government programs may have been perverse. But in public policy, critical evaluation is a positive and essential factor in choice. Rejection of the dubious panacea, the redirection of attention from the appealing but simplistic short-run approach, not only prevents deception and dispels naïve trust, but husbands resources and redirects the social effort to more productive measures. In no way, however, do the readings, whatever their cast, imply that inaction is the appropriate policy. To retreat, doing nothing, permitting events to evolve as they may, is just as likely to fail as misguided action. In urban affairs as elsewhere, the future cannot be guaranteed by deferring tomorrow's problems to yesterday.

Whether any or all of the essays in this book contain a correct definition of the urban crisis, much less a correct prescription, is moot. It is for the reader, as student and citizen, to determine which of the interpretations are correct, and what they offer in the way of constructive policy guidance. It seems beyond question, however, that a meaningful approach to our urban problems and the relationships among our cities and their metropolitan neighbors must probe the processes of urbanization themselves. Policies based on bureaucratic convenience and historical precedent, adhering strictly to the well-defined functional structure that characterizes government at all levels, do not describe the most promising path to a brighter urban prospect.

Part One   Urban Structure and
Functions

Urbanization

KINGSLEY DAVIS

*Kingsley Davis is one of our most distinguished students of urban
demography and sociology. He is Ford Professor of Sociology and
Comparative Studies and Director of International Population and
Urban Research at the University of California (Berkeley). The
source of this selection, which discusses the meaning of urbanization and the historical process through which cities have
evolved, is an article in the Spanish encyclopedia* Universitas.

In ordinary usage the term *urbanization* has no exact meaning.
Sometimes, especially in Spanish, it means the spread of urban
settlement over a particular territory; but it may mean an increase either in the *number* of people in towns and cities or in
the *proportion* dwelling in such places. These meanings are all
distinct and should not be confused.

The fundamental distinction is that between an urban and a
rural settlement. An urban settlement is one that contains a sizable population in a small area. It therefore has a density too
high for the practice of agriculture within the settled area and a
population too big to be mainly engaged in agriculture in the
surrounding area. A rural settlement, on the other hand, is
sparsely settled. Each individual household may be separated
from others by a substantial amount of open land (as on ranches
and farms in Argentina and the United States); or the households may be clustered in villages so small that the villagers can
nearly all practice agriculture on the surrounding land.

For statistical purposes, an urban place is usually defined in terms of both population and territory. Demographically, a frequent practice is to call urban any settlement above a certain minimum size. This minimum varies from one country to another. In 1950 and 1960, it was found that in 73 countries for which a definition could be found, 59 (representing 40 per cent of the world's population) had a minimum definition that fell somewhere between 2,000 and 7,500 inhabitants. Only 11 countries designated as urban a town with fewer than 2,000 inhabitants, and only 3 required the number to be more than 7,500. In 122 countries, however, no minimum was stated, and in 19, no urban data was provided.[1] In some countries, instead of having a minimum size, an urban unit is defined as one that has a town "government"; or one that is the "capital of a province"; or one that "has urban characteristics."

With respect to territory, the boundaries of each urban place should ideally include only the area of actual urban settlement, but usually political boundaries are accepted—boundaries of either discontinuous or continuous units. Discontinuous political territories are those which are separated from one another by other types of territories; continuous units are those that are not so separated. For instance, in the United States the entire national territory is divided into states; there is no "nonstate" area. The corporate towns and cities, however, are distinct units which do not divide up the national territory; accordingly, there is normally territory outside of cities and towns separating one city or town from the next one. Some nations do not designate towns and cities as discontinuous areal units, but instead report data on continuous local units such as *municipios, communes,* or *Shi.* These are broad territories which generally include both rural and urban districts. To designate some of these units as urban, the statistical office often adopts a minimum population. Thus, in Japan, the entire country is divided into local units that resemble English counties or Spanish *municipios.* When considered urban, these are called *Shi,* and when rural, *Gun.* In the United Nations *Demographic Yearbook, 1970,* Japan is shown as having 63.5 per cent of its population urban

1. Kingsley Davis, *World Urbanization, 1950–1970,* vol 1 (Berkeley, California: Institute of International Studies, University of California, 1969), p. 13.

according to the census of 1960. When one looks in the Japanese census of 1960,[2] one finds that this is the percentage of the Japanese population living in *Shi*. The *Shi*, however, include far more rural than urban territory, and the *Gun* include some urban territory. When the population in what the census calls "densely inhabited districts" is separated out within the *Shi* and *Gun*, it comes to only 43.7 per cent of the Japanese population in 1960. These districts contain only 1 per cent of the nation's total territory; their density of settlement is 10,563 per square kilometer, whereas the rest of Japan's population—both in *Shi* and *Gun*—lives at an average density of only 144 per square kilometer. Clearly, the proportion that is urban in Japan is exaggerated by using the *Shi* and *Gun* as units.

When the territories of towns and cities are defined as discontinuous units, there is less probability of "overbounding" (i.e., including rural districts). However, the other problem— "underbounding" (exclusion of urban inhabitants)—is more likely, because normally the boundary of the political entity— the town or city proper—is used. In periods of population growth, the population living in an urban center tends, in time, to expand beyond any fixed political boundary. Although the boundary may be enlarged from time to time through annexation, it usually does not keep up with the movement of people. Consequently, with respect to bigger urban centers, many countries now either try to determine the actual boundaries by putting together local political units which surround the central city and which meet certain criteria of being urban. The first approach gives Urbanized Areas; the second gives Metropolitan Areas, Urban Agglomerations, Urban Complexes, etc.

Although lack of strict comparability inevitably introduces error into international and historical comparisons, it does not entirely vitiate them. The problem that receives most attention —the lack of agreement on a minimum population qualifying a place as urban—is actually one of the least important. In most countries the proportion of the urban population living in places of 2,000 to 7,500 is not large; therefore, it makes little difference which point in this range is taken as the minimum size for an

2. Bureau of Statistics, Office of the Prime Minister, *Population of Japan, 1960: Summary of the Results* (Tokyo, 1963), p. 280.

urban place. Actually, one can adopt one's own cut-off point and deal only with places 10,000+, 20,000+, or even 100,00+. More serious is the question of delimiting the boundaries of urban units. In the past (e.g., in the United States until 1950), the larger urban places tended to become progressively more underbounded; it came to make a big difference whether the political boundary or the actual urbanized area was taken. For instance, by 1970 the New York Metropolitan Area had more than twice as many inhabitants as New York City proper. Here are 4 census figures for New York in 1970:[3]

City Proper	7,894,862
Standard Metropolitan Statistical Area	11,571,899
Standard Consolidated Area	16,178,700
Urbanized Area	16,206,841

Similarly, in 1969 Tokyo had 9,005,000 people in the City Proper and 11,454,000 in the Urban Agglomeration.[4] It follows that comparisons must be based on a knowledge of what is being compared.

WHEN DID TOWNS AND CITIES ARISE?

Throughout some 99 per cent of its history, the human species lived exclusively in nomadic tribes or tiny settlements. This zero urbanization was not a matter of preference but of necessity, because local sustenance was not sufficient to maintain towns. The first urban settlements (towns) arose as soon as they were technologically possible. They emerged from Neolithic farm villages in the Near East and possibly in Southeast Asia some 6,000 to 7,000 years ago. By 3000 B.C. certain places were big enough to be called cities, but they were very small cities by modern standards. Babylon, approximately 3.2 square miles, perhaps housed 50,000 people. Thebes, at its height as Egypt's capital near 1600 B.C., had a reputed circumference of 14 miles; it may have contained 225,000, fewer than Bilboa today. Urban centers arose independently but somewhat later in the New

3. Bureau of the Census, *Census of Population, 1970,* "Number of Inhabitants: United States Summary," PC(1)-A1, pp. 81, 116, 175, 179.
4. United Nations, *Demographic Yearbook, 1970,* p. 455.

World. One of the largest was Chanchan, capital of the Chimu empire on the Peruvian coast, the ruins of which cover 8 square miles and may have housed between 100,000 and 200,000 people.

Both in the Old and New Worlds, the earliest cities were small relative to their hinterlands. They depended directly on agriculture. The agriculture was rich in per-acre productivity because—at least in areas capable of supporting towns and small cities—it was practiced on alluvial soil that was irrigated and bathed by a tropical sun. The productivity per man, however, was low, because cultivation was mainly by muscle, the digging stick being the principal tool (wielded by hand in the New World, sometimes drawn by animals in the Near East). The rich soil and labor-intensive cultivation caused the hinterlands to be densely settled, but the low human productivity meant that probably 50 to 150 farmers were required to support 1 city inhabitant. The low proportion of the regional population living in cities is illustrated by Tenochtitlan (now Mexico City). Estimated by Borah and Cook to have had approximately 235,000 inhabitants when the Spaniards arrived, it was itself agricultural, for most families apparently cultivated their own *chiampas* with rich soil and irrigation scooped up from the lake. Even so, the city at its zenith constituted only some 2 per cent of the total population of its region, estimated at 10.9 million.

The earliest cities—those of the Near East and Southeast Asia—were repeatedly overrun and eventually exterminated by rural, often nomadic invaders. As a consequence, the societies where they arose regressed to virtually zero urbanization. The regimes in the cities were at best semiliterate, theocratic, and grossly superstitious. They did not develop a technology capable of solving problems of salination and erosion, of labor productivity and defense. They were incapable of indefinitely protecting their hinterland and themselves from marauding rural invaders.

THE ANCIENT WORLD

The next step in urban evolution was taken in another region, the Greco-Roman world. Here the agricultural base was less favorable, but greater reliance was placed on commerce and shipping in the Mediterranean. Helped by the use of bronze, iron, alphabetic writing, and coinage, the cities were larger and the proportion of the regional population living in them was greater. However, one should not exaggerate the gains. Athens at its peak in the fifth century B.C. had only between 120,000 and 180,000 inhabitants. Something like three-fourths of the citizens owned farm land, and there were enough people outside Athens to make Attica itself predominantly rural. Sparta comprised separate villages on a plain of less than 3 square miles with a population probably never more than 25,000; yet the immediate hinterland in Laconia and Messenia contained hundreds of thousands. Syracuse and Carthage, both centers of seaborne trade, may have exceeded Athens in size, but not by much.

Later, by virtue of superior military and political organization, extensive seaborne commerce and plunder, Rome possibly became the first city to reach a million inhabitants. However, Mark Jefferson, finding that the Aurelian wall enclosed a space of 4.5 square miles, pointed out that if Rome had been as densely settled as the Paris of 1901, it would have contained only 400,000 people. Even with allowance for suburbs, Jefferson gave Rome a population of less than 500,000. Similarly, although Constantinople's size in the eleventh century has been estimated at nearly a million, the statistics of 1885 give only 390,000 for Istanbul (the area of Constantinople in the Middle Ages). In any case, since the tributary regions of these two cities were enormous, it appears unlikely that the population of either city represented more than 2 or 3 per cent of the total. Both cities were conquered by essentially rural folk and their regions reduced to lesser urbanization. The Romans, like their predecessors, had a static view of production. Wealth was a matter of trade and conquest; economic improvement was the expansion of cultivation and handicraft by known techniques in the hands of workers of low status. A conscious effort to improve the technology of manufacture and agriculture, and to upgrade the skills rather than the number of the population, was out of the question.

MEDIEVAL TOWNS AND THE BEGINNING OF
MODERN URBANIZATION

The place where major urbanization finally arose—northwestern Europe—was far less auspicious than the other regions. Cold, cloudy, heavily forested, and remote, this part of Europe was so completely rural after the Roman debacle that modern minds find it hard to comprehend. The Roman towns had all but disappeared except as ruins. Marseilles was entirely depopulated. Rome became a fortified village, eventually almost uninhabited. Northwestern Europe was so rural that even the emperors, kings, princes, bishops, and other feudal aristocracy lived in the countryside.

Perhaps this clean slate was the guarantor of ultimate city success. Two seemingly adverse conditions may have presaged the age to come—one the low productivity of medieval agriculture in both per-acre and per-man terms, the other the feudal social system. The first meant that the towns, once they began, could not survive on the basis of local agriculture alone but had to trade at a distance and had, consequently, to manufacture something at home with which to trade. The second condition, the feudal system itself, meant that the medieval towns could not gain political dominance over their hinterlands and thus become self-defeating city-states. The old cities of the ancient world so dominated the rural inhabitants of their rich hinterland that they gained sustenance by tribute rather than by service and trade, but the medieval towns had to take their place as only one among several forces in the society, their authority generally restricted to the town walls. The towns thus specialized in commerce and manufacture, and evolved local institutions suited to this role. Craftsmen were housed in the towns, for there the merchants could regulate quality and cost. Competition among towns stimulated local specialization and technological innovation. The need for literacy, accounting, and geographical knowledge caused the towns to invest in secular education. This emphasis on technique in industry and commerce was, of course, the hallmark of the later industrial revolution.

The nature of medieval towns bears out this interpretation.

They were small in size and yet, over the whole region, rather numerous. The biggest town in eleventh-century England was London, with about 16,000 inhabitants, but there were several others under 5,000. Of the numerous towns in Germany by 1500, probably none exceeded 30,000. By 1400 the present territory of Switzerland comprised more than 100 towns, but most of them had less than 1,000 inhabitants. This is what one would expect of towns that had arisen in the interstices of a feudal order and had to fend for themselves. The contrast with Rome is clear. Despite the number of towns, their combined population was small in relation to the rural population. Russell's data indicate that in England in 1086 the proportion of people living in boroughs of more than 3,200 inhabitants was 3.3 per cent; by 1377 hardly more than 4 percent lived in towns as distinct from villages. The continent may have been somewhat more urbanized, but its character was still that of overwhelming agrarianism.

After centuries of city-building, the breakthrough in urbanization came only with the enormous growth in human productivity made possible by the use of inanimate energy and machinery. Until then, despite the favorable beginning made by medieval towns and the conquest of the New World, the progress of urbanization in Europe was barely perceptible. Population estimates at 2 or more dates for 33 towns and cities in the sixteenth century, 46 in the seventeenth, and 61 in the eighteenth yield an average rate of growth during 3 centuries of less than .6 per cent per year. Estimates of the growth of the continent's total population between 1650 and 1800 work out to slightly more than .4 per cent. If only the cities of 100,000 or more inhabitants are taken, one finds that in 1600 their combined population comprised 1.6 per cent of the estimated population of Europe; in 1700, 1.9 per cent; and in 1800, 2.2 per cent.

With industrialization, the subsequent transformation was astounding. Already by 1801 nearly one-tenth of the people of England and Wales lived in cities of 100,000 or more. As Figure 1 shows, this proportion doubled in forty years and doubled again in another 60 years. By 1900 England and Wales was an "urbanized society"—one in which a majority of inhabitants live

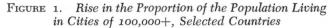

FIGURE 1. *Rise in the Proportion of the Population Living in Cities of 100,000+, Selected Countries*

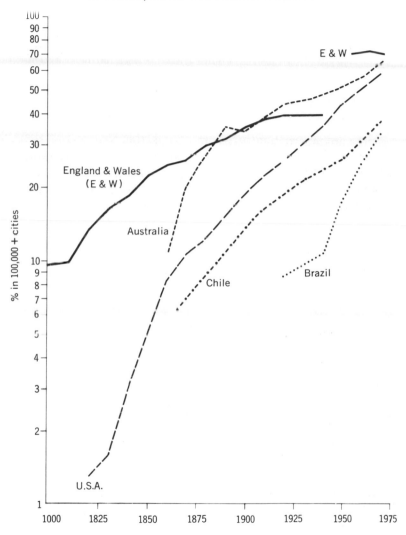

The separate line for 1950, 1960, and 1970 on the chart is for the entire United Kingdom rather than England and Wales, and it is based on metropolitan areas rather than cities proper.

in urban places—the first such society in the world. Since industrial technology, once invented, did not have to be reinvented in each country but could be borrowed, the process of urbanization was generally speedier the later it occurred. The change from 10 to 30 per cent in cities of 100,000 and over required about 79 years in England and Wales, 66 in the United States, 48 in Germany, 36 in Japan, and 26 in Australia.

THE LAST STAGES IN THE PROCESS OF URBANIZATION

The close association between urbanization and economic development has persisted. Data for 1970 (see Table 1) show a strong relationship between per capita income and the proportion of the population urban. Yet when urbanization is measured in terms of some such proportion—that is, as the urban or city population divided by the total population—the rise in urbanization must eventually come to a halt. The limit of such a fraction is unity; as a nation approaches that limit, the rate of increase in the proportion slows down. The process of urbanization is thus a cycle through which nations move as they industrialize. When charted, this cycle describes an attenuated "S," or logistic, curve, with an inflection point that characteristically comes at an early stage. As the proportion urban climbs above 50 per cent, the curve begins perceptibly to flatten out, and as the proportion reaches 70 to 80 per cent, its course falters or even declines. What is happening at these advanced levels?

When a society becomes advanced enough to have a high degree of urbanization, it can also afford an extreme amount of suburbanization and "fringe" settlement. Its population continues to be increasingly concentrated in urbanized areas, but the part of these areas that expands most rapidly is the fringe, or area around the central city. Many of the fringe inhabitants are classified as rural despite the fact that they are economically and socially connected with the urban complex. As a result, the proportion of the rural population engaged in agriculture declines steadily. In Spain, for example, 4.59 million people were engaged in primary production in 1900. These constituted 30.5

TABLE 1.   *Relation Between Degree of Urbanization and Per Capita Income*

Average per capita income * 1968	Number of countries	Average per cent urban 1970
Under 100	7	12.51
100–200	16	25.97
200–400	19	39.61
400–800	13	61.52
800–1600	11	64.74
1600 +	12	72.52

* U.S. dollars.

per cent of the population living in places of less than 50,000 inhabitants. By 1960, the workers in primary production —4.85 million—represented only 24.9 per cent of the inhabitants in places of less than 50,000. In the latest stage of urbanization, the proportion of people engaged in agriculture becomes very small. In Sweden, for example, the economically active workers in agriculture, fishing, and forestry combined had sunk, by 1960, to 13.8 per cent of all active workers, and the population dependent on these industries was only 38 per cent of the rural population. In Australia, by 1961, the share of economically active workers in agriculture, forestry, and fishing had dropped to 10.9 per cent of all workers.

It is sometimes assumed that as a society becomes urbanized, the density in cities increases. This impression seems to be a mistaken conclusion drawn from two true propositions: First, the density of settlement for the population at large increases. (This, however, is because more of the people are living in urban places, not because the urban places are becoming more densely settled.) Second, the larger the city, the higher, in general, is the density. (This rank-order can hold, however, regardless of what is happening to the average density of all cities.) These facts would not be so likely to lead to the false conclusion that urban density is rising if it were not for the inveterate habit of measuring urban growth only in terms of population. Either by design or by assumption, the territorial boundary is held fixed. Obviously, however, urban aggregations grow in territory as well as population. Since urbanization and economic development go together, technology increasingly makes it possible for urban dwellers to spread out and enjoy more space per person and still remain a part of the metropolitan complex. In other words, urban settlements tend to increase faster in territory than in population, with a resulting decline in density. Evidence to prove this trend is scarce, because it requires data on the actual moving boundary of urban settlement, a kind of information that, as already mentioned, few countries provide. In the United States an effort has been made since 1950 to determine the territory covered by the Urbanized Areas. The average density of these entities has declined as follows:

	Persons per square mile
1950	5,408
1960	3,837
1970	3,376

Characteristically, the central city grows slowly or even declines in resident population while the surrounding area, the suburbs and fringe, increase rapidly. As technology improves, the fringe extends ever farther from the central city. Beginning near the central city, suburban density is high, but it declines gradually with distance out.

THE WORLD'S URBANIZATION

In 1970, 39 per cent of the world's people were urban and 61 per cent rural. (See Table 2.) Thus the earth is not yet highly urbanized. It has reached about the point that the United States had reached in 1900. The human species is still devoting most of its energy to meeting the elementary needs for food and natural fiber through agriculture. Yet the percentage urban today, modest as it is, is very recent. Prior to 1850 no country had as large a proportion urban as the whole world does today.

There are two ways of projecting the future rise in the urban percentage. One is to assume that the recent rate of rise in the

TABLE 2.   *Per Cent of World Population Rural and Urban,
1950 and 1970, with Rate of Change*

	Percentage		Relative change (per cent) 1950–70
	1950	1970	
World total	100.0	100.0	
Rural	71.8	61.4	− 14.4
Urban	28.2	38.6	36.6
Cities 100,000 +	16.2	23.6	45.8
Cities 1,000,000 +	7.2	12.3	69.8

SOURCE: Kingsley Davis, *World Urbanization, 1950–1970*, vol. 2 (Berkeley: International Population and Urban Research, University of California, 1972).

proportion will continue. The other is to assume that the urban percentage will change from its current level just as it did in the past of some individual country that has already gone through the urban transition. For the second approach, for several reasons, the United States affords a good model. The first method yields a high projection, the second method a low one.

According to the first method, the world will be 50 per cent urban by 1987 and 100 per cent urban in 2032. By 2023, half the human species—and by 2050 all human beings—will be living in cities of over a million. According to the second method, the world will be 50 per cent urban in 1991, half in cities of 100,000+ in 2025. By the end of the present century, the projected proportions are as follows:

	Projected percentage in the year 2000	
	First projection	Second projection
Rural	38.5	45.5
Urban	61.5	54.5
Cities 100,000 +	41.5	38.8
Cities 1,000,000 +	27.1	29.5

What happens to these proportions is of course different from what happens to the absolute populations; changes in the urban fraction tell us nothing about changes in the urban or rural pop-

ulations considered separately. The recent growth in the town
and city population has been spectacular. Here are the figures:

| | Population (millions) | | Increase, 1950 to 1970 | |
	1950	1970	Absolute (millions)	Per cent
World total	2,502	3,628	1,126	45.0
Rural	1,796	2,229	433	24.1
Urban	706	1,399	693	98.1
Cities 100,000 +	405	855	450	111.4
Cities 1,000,000 +	181	442	261	144.6

In two decades the entire urban population rose by 98 per cent,
the city population by 111 per cent. More than half a billion
people were added to the earth's urban population, and more
than a fourth of a billion to the cities of a million or more. These
were the fastest growth rates ever shown by the world's urban
population.

The rate of growth of the world's urban population between
1950 and 1970 was more than twice the rate of rise in the fraction of humanity who live in urban places. The reason for this is
that rapid growth characterized not only the urban population
but also the rural. In 1950–70 the rural population increased at
a rate about a fourth as high as the urban rate. This was fast
enough to double the world's rural population in 63 years. When
growth in the last two decades is compared with that during
the first half of the century, the acceleration was greater for the
rural population than for the urban.

An important conclusion emerges: The accelerated growth of
cities in the world since 1950 is not due to an acceleration in the
shift from rural to city residence. It is due, rather, to an acceleration in the growth of the world's total population. This increased
total must go somewhere; in fact, it goes into both the rural
and the urban sectors.

In the future, for the world as a whole, the rural population
should increase for a while and then start declining, whereas
the growth of the urban population should continue to increase
to a fantastic degree. According to high and low projections,
the population in 2000 will change from 1970 as follows:

	Actual population (millions)	Projected population (millions) 2000	
	1970	High	Low
World total	3,628	6,335	5,231
Rural	2,229	2,436	2,380
Urban	1,399	3,899	2,851
Cities 100,000 +	855	2,627	2,035
Cities 1,000,000 +	442	1,691	1,543

According to the high projection, by the end of the century the urban population will exceed today's entire human population, and the population living in cities of a million or more will exceed today's entire urban population. These projections, of course, rest on the assumption that the world's development during the next 30 years will follow a smooth course, without earth-shaking catastrophes; but the results they yield cast doubt on the validity of that assumption. The projected figures show how difficult it will be for the earth to follow a smooth course for even 30 years.

If the city population increases, so will the size of the largest cities. It has been found that the rank-size distribution of the world's cities maintains a fixed shape; hence the tip of the pyramid must rise as the number of cities composing the pyramid increases. The projections just described imply that by the end of the century there will be 1 city of over 100 million, 2 of more than 60 million, 5 of more than 30 million, and 9 of more than 16 million. The largest city today, New York (the urbanized area, not the city proper), with approximately 16 million, has grave problems. Even if cities of 30 million or more should prove technically feasible, there is no ground for believing they will prove socially acceptable; yet, unless human population growth is stopped, such cities will very likely come into being.

THE SOURCES OF URBAN POPULATION INCREASE

To reach a better understanding of the interrelation between urbanization and population growth, one needs to see how the sources of city growth have changed. In the past history of the now developed countries, the main factor in the growth of towns and cities was rural-urban migration. Death rates were high in cities, because the means for controlling mortality were ineffective and the presence of large numbers in one place allowed infectious diseases to spread easily. On the other side, birth rates were low, partly because of sterility and partly because of unfavorable conditions and competing motivation. As a result, deaths exceeded births; if the cities had not grown by rural-urban migration, they would not have grown at all. For instance, over a period of 140 years, from 1721 to 1861, the average annual excess of deaths over births in Stockholm was 10.8 per 1,000. The average net migration per year, however, was 17.2 per 1,000. This left an average annual growth rate of 6.4 per 1,000, which was fairly rapid for that period. After 1861 Stockholm's death rate dropped rapidly, while net migration continued at about the same rate; births exceeded deaths, and the city's growth speeded up.

In underdeveloped countries today this history is not being repeated. The reason is that the means of mortality control, which had to be gradually invented in the West during the two centuries preceeding 1950 can now be applied quickly in the most backward areas of the world, particularly in cities. Further, mortality control has come so quickly and with such little change in the old institutional system that urban birth rates have remained much higher than they were historically in the cities of the now industrialized nations. As a result, the extremely rapid growth of cities in the contemporary underdeveloped world is due as much to the natural increase of the city population itself as to the influx of peasants. In three Latin American countries (El Salvador, Mexico, and Panama) the average vital rates in 1966–68 were as follows:

	Birth rate	Death rate	Natural increase
Urban	41.8	9.1	32.7
Rural	42.7	8.1	34.6

The urban population in these three countries was growing at an average rate of approximately 4.5 per cent per year. Since the urban natural increase was 3.3 per cent per year, it was responsible for about 70 per cent of the urban population growth. In other words, if all international migration were stopped, cities in today's underdeveloped countries would be growing rapidly.

In today's third world it is not only the cities that have a great excess of births over deaths, but also the countryside. In the past, a substantial share of rural increase was drawn off by migration to towns and cities, but now a lesser share is drawn off, because the cities can supply their own labor by their own excess of births over deaths. As a consequence, the rural population of less-developed countries is growing faster than any rural population ever increased before. In some of these countries, the supply of agricultural land is expanding as fast as, or faster than, the rural population, but in others, especially the poorest of the underdeveloped countries, the supply of land is not being augmented sufficiently to prevent a rapidly rising agricultural density. This rising density delays the modernization of agriculture and contributes to underemployment, rural poverty, and political unrest.

When the social and economic problems of large cities and the distress of overcrowded rural areas are both taken into account, the present unprecedented growth of the world's population is seen as the main factor making the urban transformation of the entire world seem doubtful. If economic development were not complicated and impeded by the sheer multiplication of human beings, we could envision an earthly regime in which the population would be nearly all urban but living in reasonably sized cities with vast rural areas as recreational parks and modernized food-growing areas. Instead, it looks as though only a major world catastrophe will save the species from a termitelike existence in cities of tens or hundreds of millions.

The Nature of Urban Areas

EDWIN S. MILLS

Edwin Mills is the Gerald L. Phillippe Professor of Urban Studies at Princeton University and Editor of the Journal of Urban Economics. *In recent years, he has written extensively on urban density and the urban environment. This selection is adapted from the first chapter of his* Urban Economics, *one of the leading textbooks in its field.*

WHAT IS A CITY?

LIKE MANY WORDS, *city* is used in several distinct but related senses. Legally, a city is a political subdivision, usually created by a state, provincial, or national government. It can be distinguished from other subdivisions, such as counties, boroughs, towns, and villages. But the practice in designating cities varies widely from country to country and from state to state in the United States. What is designated a city in one state may be designated a town in another state. More important, the part of an urban area included in a city varies from place to place and from time to time. The city of Boston contains 23 per cent of the people in the Boston metropolitan area, whereas the city of Des Moines contains 70 per cent of the people in its metropolitan area.

To the political scientist studying local government, the legal definition of the city is of primary importance. But to the urban economist, it is secondary. For the most part, we can assume that the boundaries of the legal city were chosen for historical and political reasons, and are exogenous to the urban economic system.

Much more fundamental for the urban economist than legal designations is the variability in the density of population and employment from one place to another. At any point in time, a country contains a number of people and a number of square miles of land. The ratio of the two is the country's average pop-

ulation density. In the United States in 1970, the average population density was about 60 per square mile. It is conceivable
that every square mile in the country might have about the
same number of people. The beginning of urban economics is
the observation that population density varies enormously from
place to place.

There are about 230 places in the United States where population density reaches extremely high levels relative to the average, and relative to the level a few miles away. In New York
City, for example, the 1960 population density was about 24,700
per square mile. Fifty miles away in Sussex County, New Jersey,
it was 93. A less dramatic, but instructive, example is Wichita,
Kansas. In 1960, its population density was 4,900 people per
square mile, whereas twenty miles away in Butler County,
Kansas, the density was 27. Such places are clearly urban areas.
They contain more than half the residents of the nation, and
they constitute the popular image of a metropolitan area. But
they do not exhaust the list of urban areas. Outside of these 200
or so areas, there are hundreds of small cities and towns, many
of which have population densities that exceed those in the
surrounding area by a factor of 100 or 200. They are also urban
areas.

Thus, an urban area is fundamentally a place with a much
higher population density than elsewhere. At least a few such
places have existed since the beginning of recorded history, and
they are now found in every country in the world. For many
purposes, this crude definition is perfectly adequate. But for
purposes of data collection and analysis, ambiguities arise,
and some warnings are in order.

First, an urban area is a relative concept. A place with a population density of 2,000 per square mile might be thought of
as an urban area in a country in which the average density is
50, but not in a country in which the average density is 500. In
fact, this is rarely a problem because variations in density within
countries are large relative to variations in average densities
between countries.

Second, although in most cases the data make it clear whether
or not a place is an urban area, it is not certain that the same
theoretical analysis will apply to all urban areas. Miami, Florida,

Washington, D.C., and Flint, Michigan, are all large urban areas, but quite different theories may be required to explain their existence, functions, and structure.

Third, urban areas come in a continuum of sizes, and there is inevitable ambiguity in the designation of small areas. The problem exists, regardless of the definition used. Official statistics necessarily employ an arbitrary population cutoff, of, say, 2,500 to 50,000 in presenting data on urban areas.

Fourth, what happens when two formerly separate urban areas grow together? Suppose there are two places, separated by thirty or forty miles, where population densities are much higher than in the surrounding areas. Draw a straight line through the two places, compute population density along the line at two points in time, and suppose the results to be as shown in Figure 1. Earlier, they were clearly two separate urban areas. But what about later? Should they be called one or two? The answer is that we cannot decide without additional criteria.

Possible criteria might involve the amount of movement of people and freight between the two centers. For many purposes, it does not matter much whether the two places are designated as one or two urban areas. For almost all purposes, the kinds of relationships that exist between the places are much more important than the numbers game of counting urban areas. Several formerly separate urban areas have in fact grown together in the United States. The New York/northeastern New Jersey and Chicago/Gary areas are the most prominent examples.

Figure 1

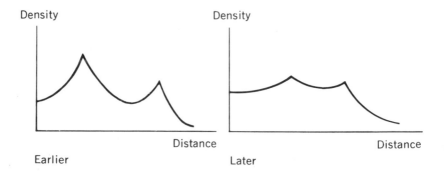

WHY URBAN AREAS?

If the urban area is to be defined by dramatically high population densities relative to those found elsewhere, the next question is, "Why do we have urban areas?" In fact, there is no single answer. Historians, geographers, sociologists, political scientists, and economists tend to emphaize somewhat different sets of factors in explaining the existence of urban areas. But we can begin with the proposition that urban areas exist because people have found it advantageous to carry on various activities in a spatially concentrated fashion.

Most of the differences of opinion about the reasons for urban areas result from the fact that these activities may be of very different kinds: military activities, religious practice or religion administration, government, and production and distribution of goods and services. At various times in history, many urban areas had defense as their major function. It was simply more economical and effective to defend a large group of people if they were spatially concentrated. The word *was* is used intentionally, because weapons technology in the nuclear age may make it easier to defend a dispersed than a concentrated population. In such urban areas, people commuted out of the city to carry on the predominant economic activity, farming. Some urban areas began as cathedral towns or centers for religion administration. Finally, some cities grew because they were seats of civil government. Washington, D.C., is the most obvious U.S. example.

However, most urban areas do not owe their existence or size to military, religious, or governmental activities. In countries where economic decisions are mainly privately made, the sizes of most urban areas are mainly determined by market forces. Households have found that income and employment opportunities, and prices and availability of consumer goods, are more favorable in urban than in other areas. And business firms have found that returns are higher on investments made in urban than in rural areas.

In the United States, seats of government are almost the only substantial exceptions to the determination of urban sizes by market forces. Washington, D.C., is a clear exception. So, to some extent, are most state capitals. But most state capitals were intentionally located in small towns away from major centers, and many have remained small towns. European national capitals, such as London, Paris, and Rome, are harder to classify. They certainly owe part of their size to their being seats of government. But the opposite is also true. They were made seats of government partly because they were major cities.

People unsympathetic to economic location theory sometimes claim that historical, rather than economic, forces have determined the locations of major urban areas. They claim, for example, that a certain urban area is where it is because some settlers happened to land there first. But this idea assumes that settlers, or other founders, were unresponsive to the advantages and disadvantages of alternative locations. Much more important, the map is dotted with places where settlers happened to settle. Some became major urban centers, but most remained just dots on the map, despite elaborate local plans and efforts to make them metropolitan centers. Those that developed into major centers did so because their economic potential induced thousands of people and institutions to decide to work, live, and produce there. The best assumption is that economic factors affect location decisions to about the same extent that they affect other types of decisions, such as pricing by firms, and demand for goods and services by consumers.

Scale Economies · How do market forces produce urban areas? We have said that most urban areas arise mainly because of the economic advantages of large-scale activities. The economist's term for this phenomenon is *indivisibilities* or, more generally, *scale economies*. General price theory says that a firm's production function displays scale economies if a proportionate change in all inputs leads to a greater proportionate change in output.

What is the relationship between scale economies and spatial concentration? Economists usually assume that most scale economies are realized within a plant, which is usually a contiguous set of production facilities. But even if they are contiguous, they may be more or less concentrated; that is, the ratios of capital or other inputs to land may be high or low. Which ratio entails lower costs?

In some cases, the mechanism by which proximity provides scale economies is clear. When a raw material is subject to several processing stages, greater spatial separation of the stages entails more movement of the material. This is particularly significant for cases where material must be at extreme temperatures during processing: to move molten steel over substantial distances would be highly impractical. But contiguity does not always seem to be a requirement for scale economies. It is easy to imagine that a firm with two plants might find it economical to provide a service facility, such as maintenance, for its plants and that it might therefore have lower average costs than a firm with one plant that either bought maintenance services from another firm or produced them itself. Although examples are easy to come by, economists have paid to date relatively little attention to the spatial aspects of scale economies.

Scale economies are important for the existence of urban areas. Consider a simple model of a country in which there are no scale economies. In the economy, a finite, but possibly large, number of different goods is produced. Inputs in each industry are: the outputs of other industries; a single kind of labor, which is mobile; and a single nonproduced natural resource, which is distributed uniformly over the total land area. Suppose that all input and output markets are competitive, and that there are neither economies nor diseconomies of scale at any output in any industry. Thus production can take place on however small a scale is necessary to meet local demands. There is no loss of efficiency, so no need for transportation from one area to another. Each small area would contain the same mix of production and mix of people with different tastes. Markets would be in equilibrium because population and employment densities were uniform, with all demands satisfied by local production.

The density of population or employment in any one area could not be greater than elsewhere: competition for land in a high-density area would drive its land values above the land values in areas of lower density, so households and businesses in the high-density area would move to an area of lower density with lower land costs. They would not be held back by lower production costs or lower prices of consumer goods and services resulting from economies of scale in the high-density area.

The crux of the argument here is that, if there are no scale economies, production can take place on a very small scale near each consuming location, and population and production density—and land values—will thus be uniform.

Now change the model by supposing that one industry (S) does have scale economies, at least at small outputs. Now it pays to concentrate spatially the production of industry S in order to obtain a lower average cost. The amount produced in one place depends on the extent of the scale economies, on the nature of demand, and on transportation cost. In addition, workers in industry S live near their place of work to avoid commuting costs. Moreover, it is advantageous to other industries, without scale economies, to locate nearby if they sell their products to industry S or to its employees. It is also advantageous to their employees to live nearby. Again, the same advantages apply to industries selling to these industries and their employees; and so on.

The process produces a spatial concentration of economic activity that legitimately can be called an urban area. Although the process makes it appear that everything might end up in one urban area, at some size the advantages of proximity are balanced by high transportation and land costs, and the urban area's growth ceases. Thus there will be several urban areas, each of which has one firm of industry S. In addition, the urban areas do not trade with each other, although industry S may export its output to the surrounding countryside. Each urban area satisfies its own demands for the product of industry S and for the products of all industries without scale economies. So there is as yet no specialization among urban areas.

Specialization of a kind results from the next step toward reality in our model. Economists tend to think of scale economies mainly in manufacturing. In terms of absolute scale, that may be appropriate. In a manufacturing plant, scale economies may not be exhausted until employment numbers in the hundreds. But scale economies are pervasive in all industries, at least at low levels of output. In retailing, wholesaling, and services, scale economies also exist, but may be exhausted when employment reaches only a dozen or a few dozen. It is not the absolute scale at which economies are exhausted, but rather *the scale relative to market demand* which determines whether there can be one, two, or a hundred firms in an industry. Many service industries, for example, are highly specialized and have extremely low per capita demands. Scale economies may preclude such industries from locating in towns and small cities, or may permit so few firms that they have substantial monopoly power. Thus, large urban areas provide specialized cultural, legal, medical, financial, and other services that are not available in small urban areas.

The fact that scale economies exist in all industries rather than in just one, and that scale economies may be exhausted at different levels of output or employment in different industries, greatly enriches our hypothetical landscape. All industries tend to concentrate spatially to some extent, and transportation costs can be kept low if they concentrate near each other. Thus, it is now possible to account for variety among urban-area sizes, and for a certain kind of trade between large and small urban areas. The small urban areas would contain only those industries whose scale economies were exhausted by the demands of small populations. The larger urban areas would contain, in addition to small-scale industries, industries whose scale economies were exhausted only by the demands of a larger population. The larger urban areas would supply such products not only to their own residents but also to residents of small urban areas. The largest urban areas would contain all types of industries, and would be the only urban areas to contain those industries whose scale economies required the demands of the largest population to exhaust them.

Thus, urban areas of a given size would export to urban areas of smaller sizes, but there would be no other kind of trade between urban areas. In particular, it is not yet possible to account for mutual trade, in which one urban area both exports to and imports from another.

Agglomeration Economies • So far, the existence of urban areas has been explained entirely in terms of scale economies in production, a concept that economists understand relatively well.

Urban economists also often refer to the *agglomeration economies* of urban areas. In part they mean by the term the advantages of spatial concentration resulting from scale economies. Of course, it must be remembered that scale economies exist not only in the private sector, but also in mixed public/private or regulated sectors, such as transportation, communication, and public utilities. Also, scale economies may exist in such public-sector activities as education, police protection, water supply, and waste disposal.

Urban economists also use the term *agglomeration economies* to refer to the advantages of spatial concentration that result from the scale of an entire urban area but not from the scale of a particular firm. The most important of such agglomeration economies is statistical in nature, and is an application of the law of large numbers. Sales of outputs and purchases of inputs fluctuate in many firms and industries for random, seasonal, cyclical, and secular reasons. To the extent that fluctuations are imperfectly correlated among employers, an urban area with many employers can provide more nearly full employment of its labor force than can an urban area with few employers. Likewise, a firm with many buyers whose demand fluctuations are uncorrelated will have proportionately less variability in its sales than a firm with few buyers. It can therefore hold smaller inventories and employ smoother production scheduling.

A second agglomeration economy is complementarity in labor supply and in production. Different kinds of labor are to some extent supplied in fixed proportions. Industries with large demands for female workers are attracted to areas where women live because of their husbands' workplaces. Complementarity in production works the same way. If two commodities can be produced more cheaply together than separately, then users of both commodities will be attracted to areas where they are produced.

A third agglomeration economy has been emphasized by Jane Jacobs. Although her argument is complex, it is based on the contention that spatial concentration of large groups of people permits a great deal of personal interaction, which in turn generates new ideas, products, and processes. She views urban areas generally as the progressive and innovative sector of society. Hers is a fascinating theory, which ties in with economists' interest in sources of technical progress, and deserves careful attention.

Other types of agglomeration economies have been claimed, but on analysis they usually turn out to be special cases of the mechanisms just described.

Comparative Advantage · The foregoing analysis has assumed a single, uniformly distributed natural resource. It accounts for large and small urban areas, but for trade between urban areas of only a very special kind. Thus the last step in our argument is to recognize that regions have comparative advantage for certain products because of the variability of available natural resources. Land is a natural resource used in all economic activity, but its qualities vary from place to place. Although fertility is not important for most urban activities, other qualities are, such as drainage, grade, and the nature of subsoil formations.

In addition, most manufacturing and to some extent other industries directly or indirectly process mineral or other natural resources. The uneven occurrence of such resources produces regional comparative advantage for particular products. A characteristic of much technical progress is the increase in the number of processing stages to which natural resources are subjected. Presumably, proximity to the natural resource thereby becomes gradually less important relative to the other locational factors already discussed. At the same time, increases in population and per capita income make greater demands on certain replenishable natural resources, especially air and water. The availability of pure air and water becomes increasingly important as a determinant of comparative advantage.

A final factor in comparative advantage is climate. Temperature and humidity affect heating, air conditioning, and construction costs. Rainfall affects drainage and water supply in complex ways, but is otherwise unimportant. Snowfall makes most kinds of transportation expensive, slow, and dangerous.

There is an obvious similarity between the factors that determine comparative advantages among urban areas and those that determine comparative advantages among countries. International trade specialists usually list differences in technology, costs and skills of labor, and costs and availability of capital, in addition to natural resources, as determinants of international comparative advantage. The state of technology obviously varies much less within than between countries, but recent studies of production functions have shed little light on regional differences in technology within the United States. Labor is obviously much more mobile within than between countries. Within the United States, regional differences in wage rates and education of the labor force have become smaller over time. But they are not negligible, and they have persisted for long periods. Much existing physical capital is nearly immobile—although there are notable exceptions, such as airplanes and trucks. Investment of new capital, however, responds quickly to regional differences in rates of return, and such differences are therefore small in a growing economy. Thus, differences in natural resources are much more important, relative to other factors, in determining the comparative advantage of regions within a country than between countries.

Another factor that determines urban size and location is proximity to economical interurban transportation. The transportation way may be man-made—a road, railroad, or airport, for example—or it may be of natural origin—a navigable river or an ocean port. The argument is that, other things being equal, goods for interurban shipment are produced near interurban transportation terminals to avoid extra unloading and reloading of goods. This argument must be used with care, however. Transportation access is a determinant of urban area size and location if there is some reason for interurban trade, but it is not itself a reason for interurban trade. In the absence of regional comparative advantage or other reasons for such trade, proximity to interurban transportation would be irrelevant. In fact, almost all large U.S. urban areas are located on navigable bodies of water, which is evidence not only that navigable waterways permit profitable interurban trade, but also that regional differences in comparative advantage are strong. Furthermore, if there are international differences in comparative advantage, there will be international trade, providing a reason for urban areas at major ports of entry and exit. Most large urban areas on the eastern seaboard of the United States owe their prominence to international differences in comparative advantage.

Up to this point, the discussion of natural resources has been concerned entirely with their direct effects on comparative advantage in production. But natural resources may also have direct effects on people's welfare, and hence indirect effects on production costs. Suppose that climate, topography, and other natural conditions cause workers and their families to prefer to live in some areas rather than others. Labor costs would be lower in the more desirable areas and production would concentrate there. It has been claimed by Perloff that these "amenity resources" have become increasingly important in recent decades, as industry has become less tied to location near natural resources and therefore more "footloose." Those parts of the country claimed to have the most amenity resources are Florida and the southwest, and these have indeed been among the most rapidly growing parts of the country since World War II. (Amenity resources can also be used to account, in part, for the decentralized structure of the Los Angeles area. The amenity resources there are presumably climate, topography, and proximity to ocean beaches, which more or less pervade the basin and generate no need for an urban area with a high central density. Unfortunately, man-made disamenities, such as smog, also pervade the Los Angeles basin)

To what extent do regional comparative advantages pertain directly to production, and to what extent indirectly by their effects on people's welfare? The question is answerable but unanswered. It is necessary to know to what extent firms in, for example, the southwest have lower costs than they would have elsewhere because of lower labor costs and to what extent because of lower nonlabor costs. It does not answer the question to point out that the southwest is a high-wage area. Many of the industries that have been attracted there demand highly skilled labor. One of the reasons firms have located there so rapidly is that highly skilled workers are more mobile than others.

In summary, regional comparative advantages occur for a variety of reasons, mostly related to natural resources. Regional comparative advantage accounts for mutual interurban trade, and for the tendency of major urban areas to be located near economical interurban transportation.

LIMITS TO URBAN SIZE

So far the discussion has been entirely in terms of the reasons for the existence of urban areas. Only incidentally have the limits to the size of large urban areas been mentioned. One limit to urban area size is the demand for the products in which it specializes. In other words, an urban area's size may be limited by the demand for its exports. Another limit is the natural resources which provide its comparative advantage; if they run out, the comparative advantage disappears. Even if they are not depleted, their rate of extraction may be subject to diminishing returns. Alternatively, if natural resources are not extracted, they may be subject to congestion. Only so many ships can be handled economically by a port, and only so many people can live comfortably in the Los Angeles basin. Even replenishable resources, such as clean air and water, are limited in supply—as we are now becoming painfully aware—and if they are over-used, they deteriorate.

Some writers have speculated that there is also an intrinsic limit to urban size in the sense that the entire urban area is subject to diminishing returns, at least beyond some point. Suppose that an entire urban area is in equilibrium. No change in the location or level of any activity can increase either consumer welfare or producer profits. Suppose that all industries, including local transportation, have constant returns to scale at outputs greater than those that exist. Suppose the output of each industry in the urban area is to be doubled. Can that be done by doubling the urban area's population, and the labor and other inputs in each industry? To double inputs in all industries efficiently requires that floors be added to some buildings and that others be demolished to make way for increased transportation.

Doubling inputs in the transportation system will produce twice as many passenger-miles and ton-miles of transportation services. However, transportation per person and per ton of output will be unchanged, since population and output have also doubled. Is this enough transportation for the larger urban area? The land area has doubled, so it seems reasonable to assume that trip lengths must increase. If so, transportation must grow faster than the urban area's population, and real income and output per capita must fall. Whether trip lengths increase, and diminishing returns therefore occur, depends on precisely how spatial arrangements change as urban areas grow. At present, too little is known to decide whether or not increased trip lengths are a significant cause of diminishing returns to urban size. But the theoretical case seems persuasive.

Even if this analysis is correct, it does not imply that traffic congestion is inevitably worse in large than in small urban areas. Some congestion is desirable in large urban areas. In addition, some congestion occurs in large urban areas because, as traffic increases, not enough land is taken from buildings and other uses to handle the increased transportation without increased congestion. But failure to tear down buildings for more transportation is not perfidy on the part of public officials. It results from the fact that, once buildings have been put in place, it is often prohibitively expensive to tear them down. Thus, one reason for downtown congestion is the historical fact that the land-use decisions for structures and transportation were made in an earlier era when transportation needs were slight.

As this fact illustrates, many urban problems are made more serious and complex by the fact that structures have long lives, and thus urban spatial relationships are strongly influenced by decisions made long ago.

The Functions of the City

ROBERT DORFMAN

Robert Dorfman, Professor of Economics at Harvard University, contributed this essay on urban functions to the Workshop on Urban Programs at the RAND Corporation, conducted in 1967 and 1968. The papers presented at this workshop, which RAND and the Ford Foundation jointly sponsored, were published in Thinking about Cities: New Perspectives on Urban Problems, *edited by Anthony H. Pascal.*

A CITY can be regarded from four points of view. First, it is *a very elaborate physical, technological, and spatial layout.* From this aspect a city is a complex of buildings, wires, pipes, wireless communications, ventilation facilities, surface and subsurface means of access, and so on. It is a large and complicated machine for housing, maintaining, and transporting its population and for storing and transporting the materials they use and disposing of their wastes. In contrast with most other machines, a city comes into being by growth rather than by design and construction. As a result, the parts are not well designed to fit each other; they are in varied states of disrepair and obsolescence, and they are replaced and modernized seriatim. Blighted areas and slums are a normal characteristic of a city just as obsolete components are a normal part of a large factory. In short, the physical aspect of a city is that of a great machine in a perpetual state of construction and chronic inadequacy; but, as Parkinson observed long before me, physical inadequacy is a sign of growth and vitality.

From a second point of view a city can be regarded as *a governmental or political entity.* From this point of view an American city is a fantastically complicated and unwieldly institution, a circumstance from which many of its difficulties flow. A survey of Cook County disclosed that there are more than 1,300 governmental jurisdictions, legally independent of each other, each of which discharges some governmental functions within the county. This situation is typical: our overlay of state, federal, municipal, county, sewage district, school district, and other jurisdictions guarantees it. Coordination among all these units is, of course, impossible. In fact, coordination within any one of them, say the municipal government itself, is difficult because many of the officials are independently elected and have independent constituencies and authorities that render them only partially subject to the control of the mayor or other titular head. In short, governmentally, as well as physically, a city is a jumble of poorly integrated parts.

The foregoing two aspects of the city are, however, subsidiary and instrumental. The city as physical facilities and as governmental organization exists to serve the city's other two aspects: the city as *an economic unit* and the city as *a social unit*. It is to these two aspects, and particularly the second, that we have to pay the most attention. I shall argue that much of the complexity of city life results from the conflicting demands made upon the city by its economic and social functions.

The primary economic function of the city is to house one or more markets. A city is not a good place for a farm or a mine or even a factory. But for those economic activities that depend upon numerous contacts and flows of information, location in the right city is practically indispensable. In spite of all the marvels of electronics, it remains true that the everyday conduct of business requires quick, cheap, informal, and intimate communication between a business firm and its suppliers, customers, and even rivals. This kind of communication is going on all the time in the city, in its employment offices, its restaurants, its display rooms, its stores, its streets, its conference rooms. Telephones and jet travel are all very well; but frequently in large affairs, and almost always in the multitude of small ones, it pays to be on the spot. Economists refer to the advantages of close contact as "economies of agglomeration." If you want to cast a TV serial, you had better be in Hollywood, where the actors are; and if you are an actor, you had better be there also because that is where the producers expect to find you. If you want buyers to see your dressers, you had better have a New York showroom. And so on.

Economically speaking, each city is a center or market of one sort or another, and the particular industries it serves define its primary economic functions. Or, in slightly different words, each city specializes in providing quick, cheap, day-to-day communication facilities for the firms in one or a few of the nation's economic sectors.

The economic function of the city is, therefore, to serve as the communication center, or market, for some industries. The size and character of the city are dictated to a large extent by the size and physical requirements of the markets it houses. Not only must it provide working space and communications for its industries, but it must provide living space, public utilities, protective services, and logistic support of every sort for the industries and for the people who staff them.

From the economic point of view the city is a market place and its population is the staff of the market and of the firms that participate in it. The inhabitants of the city are, therefore, in close day-to-day contact with each other in the course of performing their economic functions, and these contacts disregard, very largely, the social likes and dislikes of the people involved. These social likes and dislikes are, however, the essence of the fourth aspect of the city, its aspect when regarded as a social entity.

The most superficial glance at an American city will disclose that it includes a wide variety of people who sort themselves out into neighborhoods largely on the basis of ethnic affinity and socioeconomic similarity. These neighborhoods have neither economic nor administrative nor legal signficance. They are social entities purely, and they discharge most of the social functions of the city insofar as they are discharged at all.

This clustering on grounds of ethnic and income similarity is the contemporary expression of one of mankind's most deep-seated urges: the need to be a loyal member of a well-defined and somewhat exclusive social group. I mention below some of the specific psychological satisfactions derived from such membership, but the central fact, which probably requires no further analysis, is that a man needs to attach himself emotionally to some tribe, clan, or community, and feels lost, isolated, and meaningless when he cannot do so. Once upon a time, I suppose, this trait had important survival value, for the ability of the clan to prey upon its competitors and resist their depredations depended upon the loyalty of its members. Nowadays the antagonistic aspect of group indentification is disfunctional, though it persists and accounts for many of the characteristics of the American city. The constructive, communal-minded aspect remains essential.

The need for identification with a group accounts for the subdivision of the city into homogeneous neighborhoods. A group is a group of allies. It cannot be all-inclusive, for the vitality and solidarity of the alliance depend on the existence of potential enemies. As James Stephens once said, there cannot be an inside without an outside. Moreover, this same need explains why the neighborhoods must stand in very complicated relationships to one another. Overt and unmitigated enmity cannot be tolerated, but some amount of distrust, hostility, and xenophobia is part of the cement that solidifies the group.

The group or neighborhood provides other satisfactions to its members in addition to the general feeling of belonging to something and of purpose in life (namely, promoting the general welfare of the group). One of these is the comfort and security that comes from being among people who share rather than challenge our presuppositions, tastes, and values. This particular satisfaction dictates the formation of neighborhoods on the basis of similarity of ethnic and cultural backgrounds and also explains why virtually all of an individual's social life may be lived within the confines of his ethnic community.

In the second place, the group provides the anonymous individual with vicarious feelings of significance and accomplishment through his identification with talented or influential members of his group. And we should not overlook that the ethnic group provides a safe and socially accepted channel for expressing aggression. We all experience more frustrations and more occasions for rage than we can respond to under the conditions of modern urban life. Frustration cannot be bottled up indefinitely, but it can be displaced. When, for example, we should like to beat our wife or insult our boss, we can gain considerable relief from our necessarily suppressed rage by calumniating the members of some other social group. Under extreme provocation, we can even join a riot.

In short, there are real and important psychological needs —for identification, for approval and support, for discharge of hostility—that can be met by belonging to an appropriate social group. In a small and homogeneous town, the whole community may coalesce into such a group. In a large and diverse city, the populace divides itself into ethnically oriented neighborhoods (primarily) in its attempt to satisfy these needs. These neighborhoods are generally too amorphous and unstable, I should think, to provide much sense of communal effort or purpose. They do provide the security of being among people of similar beliefs and tastes, and they do provide outlets for deflected aggression, which are all the more important because of the feebleness of the positive, constructive satisfactions.

The functions mentioned so far all follow from perceiving a neighborhood or social group as one of a number of associated and competitive groups that occupy the same living space. There is another vital social function that any community must discharge, irrespective of the presence of competing groups: it must socialize its members, particularly its young. This is done by inculcating the traditions and culture of the community (including, importantly, loyalty to it) and by providing a sufficient variety of models of desirable behavior and of social roles so that an individual can find adequate scope for self-expression and personal development within the confines of his community. In our cities part of the task of social indoctrination is carried on by the city as a whole (for example, through its formal educational system) and part, less formally, by the ethnic neighborhoods which otherwise would atrophy. Models of personal development, however, have to be provided almost entirely by the ethnic communities because young people do not have sufficient contact with outsiders, nor can they, simply because they are outsiders, identify with them. It should be remarked at once that Negro communities are particularly deficient in models of social behavior and development.

From these considerations there emerges a simplified model of an American city. It consists of a cluster of ethnically distinguished neighborhoods whose members collaborate in staffing

the firms, markets, and other economic and political organizations of the city. Economic cooperation brings the members of
the diverse ethnic communities into intimate and daily contact
with each other. Social predilections separate them at the end
of the day. There emerges a delicate balancing of economic and
social forces. On the one hand, the demands of economic life
render the diverse groups dependent upon each other and enforce cooperation among them. On the other hand, competition for economic opportunity creates an arena for the virulent
expression of social antagonism. The economic life of the city
depends upon moderating the diverse tendencies, while social
vitality reinforces them.

The tensions just described are mitigated, to an extent, by
carrying over into economic life the ethnic divisions of social
life. Certain occupations and industries become segregated, just
as neighborhoods are. It would be surprising if it were otherwise. People wish to work, as to live, among people with whom
they feel most at ease. Some aspects of economic performance
are transmitted in the cultures of the groups, as emphasis on
scholarliness and bookishness among Jews. Wherever markets
are imperfect, the tendency of members of any group to favor
their fellows draws them together, just as the suspiciousness,
prejudice, and competitiveness of members of each group
against outsiders drives them apart. And, finally, just because
personal contacts are much richer within groups than between
them, the flows of information, which are an important part of
markets and of city life, facilitate economic relationships within
groups more than among them.

The consequence is that the diverse ethnic groups within the
city come to dominate different industries and occupations.
Though this fact has its regrettable side from the viewpoint of
individualistic and egalitarian standards, it contributes to the
viability of the city and to the stability and health of the social
groups. It diminishes the tensions of the economic life of the
city by reducing the frequency and intimacy of contacts between members of alien groups, that is, it extends to economic
life some of the coziness of social life. But I attach more importance to its impact on the vitality of the ethnic groups which
provide most of the social satisfactions of the city. The esteem

and status of the group is derived in substantial part from its contribution to the economic life of its city, and in particular from the industries in which it plays a dominant role. Thus, the specialization of ethnic groups to industries is an important support to their self-regard and to their feelings of security and belongingness in the city as a whole. Furthermore, through this means the structure of economic status in the city as a whole is duplicated within its ethnic communities. The models of personal conduct and development that were mentioned above as one of the requisites for a healthy community are a by-product of this industrial specialization. They could be created without the specialization to be sure, and sometimes are; but their vividness and effectiveness are reinforced by the circumstance that the career pattern is part of the group culture and tradition, is contained largely within it, and includes some elements of exploitation of alien groups.

The economic and social functions of the city thus impinge very forcefully upon each other. The economic functions provide the city's unity and define the opportunities for the ethnic groups that comprise it. The social functions create the city's diversity and strongly influence all aspects of behavior, including economic.

This vision, or image, of the nature of the American city has implications for our understanding of what is wrong with it today and what can be done about it. In the first place, it maintains that many of the important social functions of the city depend upon the vitality of the ethnic communities and neighborhoods within it. Integration, in the sense of cultural homogenization of the population, is not in the field of possibility in the visible future and may not even be desirable if, as this analysis suggests, a man needs to be a member of a psychologically manageable subgroup less diverse and overwhelming than an entire city. It suggests, indeed, that the neighborhoods and subgroups in American cities are less vital and coherent than they should be if they are to provide their members with meaningful social satisfactions. It suggests, furthermore, that since subgroups will persist, so will tensions among them. If the social development of the cities can be influenced at all by conscious planning, which is doubtful, emphasis should be placed on strengthening the positive, constructive satisfactions of life within the ethnic neighborhoods so as to reduce the emotional importance of the hostility relations among them.

More specifically, it should be noted that the quality of housing has not come up in this discussion. Improvement of housing may well be desirable on various grounds, but this analysis implies that it is not one of the critical elements in our urban problem. Perhaps this is the reason public housing schemes have not had the beneficent social effects expected from them. Improvement of housing is an attractive social expedient because we know how to accomplish it simply by spending money; but it should not, for that reason, be made the centerpiece of our attack on the problem of the cities if the problem actually lies elsewhere.

Formal education, also, has played only a small role in this analysis, which perhaps is fortunate because it is so terribly difficult to improve. The Coleman Report indicates that the success of formal education depends more on the cultural environment of the students than the other way round, which is a conclusion that this analysis tends to also. This, again, implies that the strategic focus of our attack should not be on the formal educational system.

Jobs are important as everyone knows, but this analysis indicates that not any old jobs will contribute to a lasting solution of our urban problems. Specifically, developing employment opportunities in the lowest occupational levels of scattered industries may contribute more to perpetuating exploitative and hostile relationships among ethnic groups than to enhancing the integrity of the disadvantaged ones.

The positive implication of this discussion is that the social health of the ethnic groups that comprise a city is strongly influenced by their roles in the economic life of the city. In particular, the social health of a group seems to require that there be some significant markets in which its members occupy influential, if not dominant, positions. Surely the Negroes are distinguished from the other ethnic groups in precisely this regard: that they have no such economic bases of power, status, and social mobility. If this be so, effort should be concentrated on creating such economic foundations for social health for the Negro communities. I am well aware of the difficulties of this enterprise, and I am struck also that none of the major programs with which I am acquainted are pointed in this direction, which may be the essential one.

PART TWO   Urban Finance
and Governance

Financing Urban Government

DICK NETZER

Dick Netzer is the author of Economics and Urban Problems, *a widely read and thoughtful treatment of the major issues in urban public policy, published in 1970. He is Dean of the Graduate School of Public Administration at New York University and Chairman of the Committee on Urban Economics, a group of research scholars, supported by the Ford Foundation, that concerns itself with monitoring and disseminating research results in its field. This essay, despite its date, continues to be the best over-all summary of issues in the field of urban public finance. It first appeared in 1965, as a chapter in* The Metropolitan Enigma, *edited by James Q. Wilson of Harvard University.*

SOME RECENT TRENDS

IN RECENT YEARS, as throughout the twenty years following World War II, local (and state government) public expenditures have been increasing substantially more rapidly than has the nation's total output and income (see table).[1] Public expenditures in urban areas have always been significantly higher, in relative terms, than those in nonurban areas and recently have been increasing slightly faster, in dollar terms, within the urban areas. This difference is to be expected, since nearly all the nation's population growth has been occurring in urban areas. But urban population growth alone does not explain the rate of increase in public spending. Indeed, the increase in *per capita*

1. The dates used here are related to data availability. A Census of Governments was conducted in 1962 and in 1957; the preceding Census of Governments occurred in 1942.

41

Percentage Increases in Nonfederal Public Expenditures,
1957–1962 and 1957–1963/64

	Percentage increase	
Expenditure item	1957–1962	1957–1963/64
Gross national product[a]	27	43
Total expenditures		
All state and local governments	48	70
All local governments	46	65
Local governments in metropolitan areas [b]	47	—
Central city governments in large cities[c]	31	45
Per capita expenditures[d]		
All state and local governments	36	51
All local governments	34	47
Local governments in metropolitan areas	30	—

SOURCE: Adapted from various publications of the U.S. Bureau of the Census, Governments Division.

[a] For calendar years 1957–1962 and 1957–1964.

[b] For identical collections of metropolitan areas in 1957 and 1962.

[c] Includes only the municipal governments per se (that is, excluding overlapping but separate county, school district, and special district governments); for the 42 cities with a 1960 population of more than 300,000, excluding Honolulu.

[d] Based on estimated 1957, 1962, and 1964 populations.

local government expenditures in metropolitan areas has been more rapid than the increase in *aggregate* gross national product.

What is perhaps most striking, public expenditures in the larger central cities have been climbing steeply, despite their losses or slow growth in population. In the most recent seven-year period for which data are available, expenditures of municipal governments in the larger cities rose by 45 percent (see table), about two-thirds as rapidly as expenditures of all other local governments combined. Consider the twelve largest metropolitan areas (1964 population over 1.8 million). In the eight-year period, 1957 to 1965, property tax revenues (used here as a partial proxy for local expenditures) rose by 86 percent for these entire areas. In their central portions, property tax revenues rose by 69 percent.[2] But there has been little population growth in the central portions—less than half the rate of the entire areas

2. "Central portions" are the counties that include the central cities. In five of the twelve areas, the "central portions" and central cities are substantially identical. In 1960, the central cities' population was 74 percent of that of the "central portions."

between 1960 and 1964.

To be sure substantially more external aid to central cities in the provision of public services has been forthcoming in recent years. State and federal aid to central city governments has risen considerably more rapidly than have central city expenditures. Also, the *direct* role of state governments in the provision of public services in and for the central cities has expanded considerably. Since the passage of the Interstate Highway Act in 1956, the states have been far more active in the construction of central city highways than previously. In a growing number of states, the state government is directly involved in urban mass transportation, in park and open space activities, and in housing programs. In some states in the northeast, expansion of state higher education programs has had an important effect on central city populations. But despite all this, the taxes imposed by central city governments, collected from static populations and slowly growing central city economies, continue to rise sharply.

THE PURPOSES OF URBAN GOVERNMENT

The explanation for rising public expenditures in urban areas is not hard to find. In the central cities, local-tax-financed outlays for services directly linked to poverty (in the health and welfare fields) have not been static; the central cities of the twelve largest metropolitan areas account for an eighth of the country's population, but nearly 40 percent of health and welfare outlays financed from local taxes. For central city governments, the problems associated with poverty and race are by far the most urgent of public problems.

Neither poverty nor racial disabilities can be eliminated solely by governmental action, and still less by action by local or state and local governments combined (that is, governments other than the federal government). But local governments do have a major responsibility to grapple with these problems and can make a major contribution toward their alleviation. In the American system of government, it is local governments that are responsible for providing educational services that over time will have a major bearing on the chances of the poor and racially disadvantaged to overcome their disadvantages. Local governments are also responsible for a wide range of health and welfare services, which are almost entirely oriented toward the poor in American cities. They have had, since the late forties, major responsibilities in connection with the housing of the poor. And, as far as the poor are concerned, local government recreational facilities are about the only recreational facilities available.

A second major set of problems confronting the older central cities lies in the fact that they have a huge legacy of obsolescence. Their stock of housing and other social capital—that is, public and quasi-public facilities of all kinds—is old, often physically deteriorated, and generally far from competitive with the newer parts of the same urban areas. It may be, as some have argued, that the best national policy would be to allow this obsolescence to continue and allow further deterioration of the older parts of the older cities. In this case, population would decline in these sections and, presumably at some stage, values would be so low that private renewal of such areas would become possible. Or, if desirable, public renewal could be undertaken, but on the basis of exceedingly low values.

Developments in recent years suggest that this obsolescence policy is hardly a likely course of action. For one thing, there is the plight of those who, because they are poor, or Negro, or both, have little chance to escape the deteriorating areas. Amelioration, for these hundreds of thousands of people, is both politically and morally necessary. Quite apart from moral issues, most cities and the federal government appear to have decided that it is necessary to replace obsolete social capital and to compete for residents and businesses in an atmosphere of rising expectations. That is, the cities feel they must offer an environment of public facilities services that, together with other attractions that the central locations may have, will offset the blandishments of the newer and presumably more modern sections of the metropolitan areas where standards of public services and amenity are high indeed.

In the newer sections of metropolitan areas—the new portions of central cities as well as the urbanizing fringes of the metropolitan area—the main governmental problem is the provision of the new social capital needed by a rising population, and a population that has peculiarly heavy demands for public services and facilities, notably schools.

In the aggregate, these urban problems have resulted in a diversion of resources from private to public uses via tax increases. But this relative expansion of the public sector is costly in another way. If local governments are to command resources, they must pay prices for these resources that are competitive with those prevailing in the economy, notably salaries of public employees. If they are to expand *more rapidly* than the private sector, they must bid away resources by paying even more, which largely explains the rapid increase in urban government salary levels, especially for occupational groups whose talents are in heavy demand in the private sector.

IDEAL SOLUTIONS

This catalog of governmental problems suggests something about the nature of the solutions. Assume for the moment that we are free to devise a structure of local government that is ideal from both an administrative and a financial standpoint.

First, consider the governmental fiscal problems associated with poverty and race. It seems clear that, in an ideal world, the financial burden of public services that exist primarily to cope with these problems would not rest on particular local governments with small geographic coverage. Poor people tend to be concentrated in the central cities of metropolitan areas for good reasons. The supply of housing that they can afford is in such places, the kinds of jobs to which their skills give them access tend also to be located in these sections, and the variety of social services they require tend to be available only in central cities. Indeed, it is probably in the national interest that the poor be concentrated in central cities, for it is rather unlikely that their needs would ever be sufficiently attended to were they not so conspicuous.

Another factor in the geographic location of the poor, and even more in the geographic location of those in racial minority groups, is national in character. This society is a very mobile one and over the years it has undergone rapid economic changes. There have been, in response to these economic changes, massive migrations of people from rural areas to urban areas, from central cities of urban areas to the suburbs, from the urban areas of the north and midwest to the southwest and west. No individual central city has been known to put up bill-boards advertising its attractions for the poor, trying to recruit them from other parts of the country. They have migrated to the cities in response to pressures in their older locations and attractions in the newer locations, but all these have been essentially national economic and social forces. Such being the case, it seems appropriate that the costs of attending to the needs of such people should be spread over a fairly wide geographic area. And because it is the economies or, rather, the economic prosperity of the larger metropolitan areas that have been the attraction for the poor and the disadvantaged, it could be argued that the metropolitan areas as a whole ought to finance the poverty-linked social services.

There is a good case for this argument because the great bulk of the wealth and income of the country is concentrated in metropolitan areas. But almost nowhere is there a governmental structure such that taxes can be levied throughout the metropolitan area on the economic base of the entire metropolitan area for the support of such services. In some places, in states that are overwhelmingly urban and metropolitan in character, the state government may be a reasonable substitute for metropolitan area government. But this is not true of all states, and, moreover, some metropolitan areas straddle state boundary lines. Also, the migration of the poor among the states has not been an even, proportional movement; some states, like New York, have been the recipients of very large numbers of poor immigrants because of accidents of geography (access to Puerto Rico) rather than economic strength. All this suggests that the national government is the proper source of support for the bulk of poverty-linked services provided in urban areas.

In addition, it could be argued that some of the poverty-linked services actually provided by urban local governments should be directly *provided* as well as *financed* by governments covering a wider area. One example of this is the suggested negative income tax, which would supplant state and local public assistance expenditures.

What about the rebuilding of the central cities and the provision of adequate amenities in the form of public services? In a broad sense, if a central city has sensible redevelopment policies and strategies, ones that actually provide a good pay off in social terms relative to the funds invested, the cities themselves should be able to finance the costs fairly readily. That is, the additional public expenditures in time will improve the environment of the city sufficiently so that its tax base—broadly defined—will be enhanced considerably.

There are some exceptions to this. First, there is need for outside help to offset some biases and imperfections in present arrangements. For example, recent heavy investment in urban highway facilities, based on outside financial support, may make it rather difficult to finance investment in public transportation facilities from local resources. A second qualification is that the particular local tax devices used to finance these socially self-liquidating investments have side effects. High central city taxes on business activity may make the central cities much less attractive locations for businesses capable of operating elsewhere. Equally important, high taxes based on the value of real property can discourage private investment which raises real property values. In old cities full of obsolete private structures, an ideal fiscal solution would avoid taxes that defer private rebuilding. Instead, such a solution would involve taxes that either encourage the needed rebuilding or are neutral in their effect. And the most nearly neutral kind of tax that is widely used and produces much revenue at any level of government is the tax on individual income.

The newer parts of metropolitan areas in general are characterized by relatively high levels of personal income and wealth. This suggests that they should be able to finance themselves with a minimum of outside help, provided they have boundaries that make some sense from the standpoint of the nature of the services provided and that do not fragment the potential tax base into wildly unequal portions. Also, because a good part of the problem in the newer areas is provision for new public investment, the outer areas would be able to finance themselves adequately only if they are free to meet the bunched-up (in time) needs they now face. That is, they should be able to borrow rather freely to meet current needs for capital outlays and repay this over the useful lives of the facilities. At a later stage, their capital needs will be much lower.

The poverty-linked services aside, many of the public services provided by local governments are in many ways like those provided by public utility companies. That is, they are not provided uniformly to the entire population, but rather in distinguishable quantities and qualities to individual families in the population, who consume them in accord with their personal preferences. For example, not all families use the same amount of water, not all use the same amount of highway transportation, and so on. There is a strong case for financing such services in the same way public utility services are financed—that is, via user charges, which are like prices, rather than through general taxes.

If the purpose of providing the public service is to offer different consumers the services they want, and place some value on, then they ought to pay for such services in proportion to the costs. Otherwise, governments will be called upon to provide a great deal more of the service than people would be willing to consume if they did have to pay for it—a wasteful use of resources; or the service will be in such short supply that a form of nonprice rationing will be employed to allocate the service among consumers. The outstanding example is street congestion in cities: users pay for highways in the aggregate but not for specific individual uses of the streets and therefore, not suprisingly, treat highways as a free good. The only deterrent to use of the streets at the most crowded times and in the most crowded places is the value one places on time; the rationing in effect then results in those who place a low value on time pre-empting the street space from those who place a high value on time. Ordinarily, in our society, rationing is on the basis of price. Somebody who values a service highly bids it away from someone who places a lower value on that service and would rather use his income for alternative kinds of consumption.

This has relevance for public services in both the newly developing parts of urban areas and the older cities themselves. To the extent that pricelike mechanisms are employed, there is likely to be a more sensible allocation of resources in urban areas. Moreover, prices are by definition neutral in their economic effects. People do not exchange money for services or goods unless they consider the value of the services or goods they receive at least equal to the money they surrender. Substituting neutral prices for unneutral taxes has much to commend it. Of course, there is a limit to the extent to which pricing devices can be used, but the general principle remains: where prices make sense at all, they should be utilized and not rejected simply because the services are organized under public rather than private auspices.

There is a further extension of the market analogy to urban government. People do differ in their preferences for various kinds of public and private goods and services. For some people, locally available recreational facilities—say, public parks and swimming pools—are exceedingly valuable services, but for others—those who prefer to travel long distances on vacation, for example—the value is much less. And such differences are not simply a matter of differences in income—people with similar incomes have different tastes.

Since tastes differ, it is entirely conceivable that one might find people of similar tastes—in this case similar preferences for public services—tending to move into particular sections of the metropolitan area. There are real advantages to such ordering of residential patterns based on differences in preferences for various kinds of public goods and services. Without this arrangement, some poeple would be taxed to provide services they do not desire, while others would find that there are services they desire and would be willing to pay more taxes for.

In an ideal urban governmental and fiscal structure, it would be desirable to try to provide some arrangements that foster this kind of expression of differences in tastes. One such arrangement would result in large numbers of small, separate service areas for kinds of public services that are likely to have this character, such as recreational services.

Neither user-charge financing (as a principal source of support) nor individual-preference-oriented service areas are appropriate for welfare and health services or any other poverty-linked services, and user-charge financing is inappropriate for schools as well. All of these are services provided to the poorer members of the urban community despite their inability to pay for the services, indeed *because of* their inability to pay. The consensus is that the rest of the community is better off if the poor are not destitute (hence public assistance) and have some medical care (hence clinics and free hospital care), and if their children are educated. Indeed, we feel so strongly about education that we *require* people to send their children to schools and levy the taxes necessary to provide the school places. Such "meritorious wants" as minimal health and educational levels contrast sharply with society's indifference as to whether individual families own more or fewer water-using appliances or own one, two, or three cars.

This description of ideal solutions has not mentioned a frequent source of controversy: suburban exploitation of the central city or central city exploitation of commuters. The poverty-linked services, as noted, do present a problem. Putting them to one side, it is entirely possible to develop a system in which there is no significant degree of exploitation of either set of residents and to do this without setting up any sort of a massive metropolitan governmental structure.

The truly needed metropolitan-area-wide governmental machinery is related to the nature of certain kinds of public services. Transportation, planning, water pollution, air pollution, and water supply are all services that, for the most part, cannot effectively be provided by small local governments and require fairly large geographic service areas. Although cost is one consideration, yet another is the provision of reasonably adequate standards of service. Where technology and geography dictate metropolitan governmental arrangements, they would exist in an ideal situation. Where technology does not dictate such arrangements, the real *metropolitan* governmental need is to ensure a wide area for financing the poverty-linked services.

THE REAL WORLD OF URBAN PUBLIC FINANCE

How do present arrangements for financing urban local governments compare with this ideal? First, there *is* a substantial local tax burden due to the financing of poverty-linked services, a burden that exists for many local governments but is especially important in the older central cities. Public assistance, for example, is the most obvious poverty-linked public service. The federal government provides substantial amounts of funds for this, roughly 55 percent of the total spent in 1964. In most states in the United States, the remaining funds are provided entirely from state government sources, and indeed the state government administers public assistance programs itself. However, there are urban states with large *local* public assistance expenditures. They include California, Ohio, Indiana, Minnesota, Wisconsin, New York, New Jersey, and Massachusetts. In fact, in all except six of the metropolitan areas with a population of over one million, there are significant locally financed outlays for public assistance. For the country as a whole, roughly one-sixth of the funds are provided from local financial resources.

Similarly, there are significant health expenditures (which in cities are primarily directed to the poor) and hospital expenditures financed from local tax funds. In 1964, the locally financed total of welfare expenditures, current expenditures for health purposes, and current expenditures for hospitals (net of charges received from hospital patients) was about $2 billion. Some idea of the relative importance of this amount can be seen by comparing it with the total of $20 billion that local governments received in that year from the local property tax. For the governments of the largest American cities (those with populations over three-hundred thousand), the ratio is much higher. Locally financed services that are fairly directly linked to poverty absorbed nearly one-fourth of the big-city property tax revenues in 1964, or one-sixth of their collection of taxes of all types. In a number of the larger metropolitan areas, if the local tax drain to central city financing of social services were equalized over the entire area, central city tax loads would be well below those elsewhere in the metropolitan areas, rather than well above, which is the more usual case.[3]

Another aspect of the poverty-linked services fiscal problem relates to the financing of schools in the older central cities. Most programs of state aid to the local school districts in a state ap-

3. Per capita property tax revenues are significantly higher in most large central cities than in their surrounding areas; see Dick Netzer, *Economics of the Property Tax* (Brookings, 1966), p. 118. Where they are not, it is usually because the central city relies heavily on local *nonproperty* taxes (New York, St. Louis, cities in Ohio, for example).

pear to be fair; typically, state aid programs are based on the numbers of children and the local property tax base per pupil. Big cities tend to have fewer school children per family in public schools than in other parts of a given state and also tend to have relatively high business property values. As a result, they receive relatively small amounts of state school aid.

But this apparent equity is misleading, because the assumption underlying almost all state aid programs is that the cost of providing a given quality of education is uniform throughout a state. There is much evidence that it is not—to provide an education equivalent in quality to that received in the better suburban schools would cost enormously more than in the slum schools in the big cities. One commentator, Christopher Jencks, recently estimated that this equivalent-quality education would cost approximately twice as much per pupil. The reason is obvious. The many disadvantages under which children in poverty and minority group families suffer at home and before they come to school mean that they require a great deal more in the way of special services, small classes, and the like to assure a performance in school equivalent to that of the suburban middle-class child. And state aid formulas generally do not recognize this.

There are serious problems with the existing arrangements for financing the rebuilding and improvement of central cities, aside from the poverty problem. The principal difficulty is the choice of tax instruments for local fiscal support. The main problem is the extremely heavy taxation of housing, which works at cross-purposes with the desire to rebuild and renew central cities. In the United States, local property taxes on housing equal roughly 20 percent of the rental value of housing. That is, they are equivalent to a 25 percent excise tax on housing expenditures. In the larger metropolitan areas, particularly in the northeastern part of the United States, the excise tax is more like 30 percent, and for some of the central cities well over 30 percent. There is no other type of consumer product, aside from liquor, tobacco, and gasoline, which is as heavily taxed in the United States today. The effect of this very heavy taxation, other things being equal, is to deter people from spending their incomes for better housing.

Note the "other things being equal" clause. In suburban communities, particularly bedroom suburbs, the public services that a family receives or has access to are very closely tied to the local taxes that the same family pays. Therefore, in a sense, the property tax in many suburbs is analogous to a general charge for the use of public services, or perhaps even to a local income tax. It is unlikely to be a deterrent to consumption of housing, that is, to the expenditure of consumer income for housing. For the central cities, this is not the case. Central cities provide a wide variety of services and tax a wide variety of property types. Individuals cannot reasonably assume that the prices of housing confronting them include an identifiable tax component that is in effect a charge for a preferred package of public services. What they do observe is that housing is expensive in the central city. It may not be any more expensive in the central city than in the suburbs. But an effective city-rebuilding strategy requires that the central cities encourage more private expenditure for housing, and this may in turn require that housing be much cheaper in the central city than in the suburbs.

It may be argued that any tax paid by individuals and families in a central city will have some discouraging effect on their choice of the central city as a residence. This is true, as is the argument that any tax that reduces incomes will have some bearing on housing expenditure. However, a tax specifically related to housing expenditure is much more a deterrent to the needed rebuilding of the central cities than a tax on income in general would be.

Another element in the choice of tax strategy for central city programs concerns the taxation of business by the central city. It is clear that many types of business activity have been decentralizing away from the central cities of the larger metropolitan areas. If, to all the other disadvantages of congestion and lack of adequate space, and so on, the central city adds business taxes higher than those elsewhere in the area, it may very well spur the further migration of businesses. No doubt this has *not* been a serious problem in many areas, although in a few cases property taxes on business may have had a discouraging effect on economic activity. More often, the over-all effect of taxation of business property in the cities at differentially heavier rates is to depress land values, which is not necessarily the worst thing in the world.

What about the newly developing parts of metropolitan areas? The major problem here is connected with boundary lines. The boundary lines of political subdivisions in the suburbs are those that have evolved over a long period. They have no necessary relationship to the natural areas for the performance of particular services or for grouping people of similar preferences, which is a less important consideration. Moreover, the tax base of the suburban areas tends to be so fragmented in some parts of the country that there are enormous disparities between needs and taxable resources, particularly in connection with financing the schools.

One consequence of this fragmentation has been what has been referred to as "fiscal zoning": controlling land use in newly developing areas in such a way as to minimize tax costs (have as few school children as possible) and maximize tax base (have nonresidential or very high value residential property rather than ordinary houses). It is easy to think of organizational arrangements that can offset this problem: governmental reorganization, additional state aid for particular functions such as schools, or some kind of second-tier local governmental structure—that is, some form of fiscal federation within metropolitan areas. The idea is to offer common access to the tax base of large parts of the metropolitan area and reduce the incentive to plan land use primarily from the standpoint of fiscal considerations, rather than from the standpoint of larger notions of the suitability of functional patterns in metropolitan areas.

Real world solutions also fall short of the ideal in connection with the application of user charges to finance particular public services. They are frequently not used at all in cases where they *can* be sensibly employed. They are also frequently used in a most inept fashion. Air and water pollution is an excellent example of failure to apply user charges where they clearly make sense. By and large, the construction and operation of sewerage systems and sewage treatment facilities is financed in the United States by local property taxes. Some places have sewer service charges of one kind or another, but they are by no means the majority. Yet here is a case where it is rather easy to identify the specific people who give rise to public costs. The benefits of water pollution control or air pollution control may be very broad, but the sources of the public costs are highly individual. Moreover, it is not impractical to apply charges that have some relationship to the costs occasioned. This has been done in the Ruhr basin in Germany for many years; there is an elaborate system of pollution charges designed to apportion the costs of treatment facilities among the industrial establishments that actually occasion these costs and also to deter firms from polluting.

DIRECTIONS FOR REFORM

This comparison of prevailing practice with one man's notions of what is ideal is, of course, not a practical program of reform. It suggests, for example, abolition of the property tax on housing in central cities, which is hardly an immediate possibility. But it does indicate one set of views as to the proper *directions* for reform—more outside aid for poverty-linked services (although 100 percent outside financing may be years off); refraining from increases in taxes on housing in the cities (although reduction may be even further off) and the substitution of other tax forms, preferably used on an area-wide basis; governmental structural improvements such as many have urged for years; and wider and more sophisticated applications of the price mechanism in local government.

What are the policy alternatives? One is to call for substantially increased federal (and in some cases, state) aid for a long list of urban, especially central city, activities. Federal assistance in the provision of urban services, either via aid to local and state governments or via direct federal performance (for example, expansion of social insurance, like Medicare), has increased sharply in the past few years. This assistance can be viewed as a belated recognition of the national interest in the resolution of certain urban problems, notably those related to poverty and those that leap geographic boundaries (for example, water pollution), with the increase in the federal role likely to level off at a new higher plateau, much as it did between the late 1930s and the late 1950s. Or it can be viewed as no more than the beginning of a continuously expanding federal role. The historical evidence suggests the former interpretation, but this is prophecy, not scholarship.

A second alternative is to reaffirm the received truth, discovered decades ago, that the property tax is inherently a good tax for local governments, which can be relied upon even more heavily, if only the abominations that characterize its administration are eliminated. This view has numerous proponents, but it is possible to entertain doubts as to whether a tax based on so ephemeral a standard as the "true value of property" can ever be equitably administered. Moreover, the persistence of bad administration over so many years makes one wonder whether good administration is publicly acceptable, even if attainable. It is worth noting that the advocates of a strengthened role for the property tax generally have little patience with those who propose to mitigate its effects on central city housing by special exemptions and abatements for administratively preferred types of housing investment.

The alternatives to the property tax are not easy ones. Proliferation of local nonproperty taxes imposed by existing local government units raises not only administrative problems but, more important, economic ones for central cities. If central cities are where the fiscal difficulties bind, they will be the heavy users of nonproperty taxes; differentially heavy taxation by central cities can surely affect their economic future, at the margin. The prospect of nonproperty taxes imposed on a metropolitan-area-wide basis, which would wash out competitive fears, is not promising, since there are few precedents in this country. But it remains an attractive concept. Finally, wider and more sophisticated applications of user charges demand local government imagination, administrative skill, and political courage. This course, more than any other, can run aground on the inherent conservatism of local government, a universal characteristic.

The Cost Disease of the Personal Services and the Quality of Life

WILLIAM J. BAUMOL AND WALLACE E. OATES

The authors of this selection are William Baumol, Professor of Economics at Princeton and New York Universities, and Wallace Oates, Associate Professor of Economics at Princeton. They trace urban fiscal problems, in large part, to the technology through which urban public services are produced. Baumol initially developed this thesis in an earlier paper, published in the American Economic Review, *entitled "Macroeconomics of Unbalanced Growth: The Anatomy of Urban Crisis."*

THERE ARE a number of economic activities which are widely thought to be fundamental to a high and improving quality of life. It is a diverse group encompassing such services as education and medicine, theatrical and musical performances, protection from crime, the operation of libraries and, perhaps, of fine restaurants. These activities also have another characteristic in common, one whose implications many will consider very unfortunate: they have all, at least in recent years, been exhibiting phenomenal rates of increases in their costs.

For example, in the United States during the period 1947–1967, the cost of elementary education per pupil has risen about 6½ per cent per year compounded. Similarly, for university libraries the cost per volume held has gone up over 6 per cent per year compounded. The figures for the other activities in the list all suggest similar patterns of increasing costs, and this has occurred during a period when costs in the remainder of the economy, as indicated by the standard price indices, have risen on the average less than 1½ per cent per year.

In the United States such rapidly increasing costs have in many cases led to significant decreases in the quality or the quantity of these outputs supplied. The streets grow increasingly dirty; libraries have curtailed the hours during which they are open; and hospitals become increasingly overcrowded. Many even believe that the quality of the elementary schools has been affected significantly. Any recent visitor to the United States must be all too aware of the dismal list.

Nor are other countries immune to these problems. Those capitals of Europe which are most noted for their cleanliness grow increasingly dirty, and visibly so. The costs of their theaters run ahead of their subsidies, and so on.

Yet this is so despite the fact that public expenditures on these services have not remained stationary. On the contrary, in the United States, expenditures of state and local governments, which are in considerable part devoted to such services, have risen from a total of $11 billion in 1946 to some $121 billion by 1969, a more than tenfold increase in less than twenty-five years, during a period in which GNP increased at less than half as rapid a rate. Surely, budgetary increases of this magnitude should have permitted not only the maintenance of the quantity and quality of these services, but significant increases in both. Their failure to do so certainly requires explanation.

We typically find these problems attributed to three basic causes: governmental inefficiency, growth in population served, and inflation. But on closer inspection, those do not appear to be the real villains. In the United States, for example, many universities, and much of medical and theatrical activity is not run by the government. Yet the costs of these activities go up just as rapidly as the others. Indeed, the cost of medicine has increased most quickly of all.

Nor can the explanation be the growth in the size of the population served. True, the postwar baby boom did increase the number of children to be educated and that, in turn, obviously added to the educational budget. However, the educational figures given before referred to cost per pupil; i.e., it had already been deflated to eliminate the effects of population growth. It was after elimination of these effects that we were able to report that cost of education (i.e., cost per pupil) had increased at 6½ per cent per annum. Obviously, the growth in student population does not explain this sensational rate of increase, except perhaps to the extent that the increased demand for teachers bids up their salaries somewhat more rapidly than they would have risen otherwise.

Finally, we cannot ascribe the problem to inflation. If inflation were the explanation. In an economy where prices rose at 1½ per cent per year we would expect cost per pupil also to rise at about 1½ per cent—not 6½ per cent—per year. Obviously, even after we take account of the effects of increasing price levels, we still have some 5 of the 6½ per cent growth in cost per pupil left over to be explained.

There is, of course, no single explanation for the paradox of the rapidly rising public budgets required to supply public services that seem to grow increasingly inadequate. Rural-urban-suburban migration patterns, the rising student population, the rather inflexible tax base in most cities, and a host of other problems have contributed to the financial plight of the public sector. Some of these may be problems peculiar to recent decades which may or may not persist in the future. However, in addition to these sources of rising costs, there exists a chronic cost disease that infects not only the public services but also a wide variety of services provided by private industry and by private nonprofit institutions. This cost disease threatens to price out of the market many of those services which we usually consider to be important contributors to the quality of life. Among the afflicted services, we find elementary and higher education; medical services; the handicrafts; the live performance of music, drama, and dance; libraries; and cuisine; in short, many of the things which we associate with a vital and attractive civilization.

We will contend that a substantial portion of the cost problems that beset these services must be ascribed to the nature of their technology, rather than to any of the villains that are usually conjured up—inflation or inefficiency, corruption (where the item in question is supplied by government) or greed and profiteering (where it is supplied by private industry). This cost problem has, in fact, beset the services for a long time and is likely to continue to do so for the foreseeable future.

It appears, moreover, that there is no painless cure for this disease. We can predict with confidence that the costs of these services will rise continually at a rate more rapid than costs for the economy as a whole. There is, however, one encouraging aspect of the problem. The very process which causes these compounding increases in the costs of services also generates the additional resources needed to meet those costs. The problem thus becomes that of society deciding which and in what quantity and quality particular services should be supplied. The real danger is that, unless the nature of the process is made clear, public misunderstanding or neglect may lead to the deterioration (or even the extinction) of certain services, some of which it may be in our interest to perpetuate.

LAGGING TECHNOLOGICAL PROGRESS IN THE
PRODUCTION OF SERVICES

A calculation based on several centuries of rather remarkable data suggests that the purchasing power of a day's wages (or what economists call real wages) are some twenty times as high in the United States today as they were in Elizabethan England. This rise in the value of a day's work reflects primarily the increased productivity of labor: with modern techniques of production, a man can produce many more goods and services per hour than he could three centuries ago. Continual improvements in methods of production have over time thus increased the productive capability of labor and thereby raised the real earnings of the typical worker.

It is not surprising to find that increasing output per man has been much more dramatic in some forms of productive activity than in others. However, these differences in rates of productivity increase have not assumed a random pattern with one set of activities experiencing rising output per man over one period, while another set realizes rapid increases in productivity at another time. Rather, there is a broad class of activities, which we will call (admittedly with some oversimplification) the personal services, that have shown themselves over the centuries to be relatively resistant to productivity-increasing innovation.

The personal services typically possess one or both of two closely related characteristics which make increases in output per man relatively difficult to come by. The first is that some of their outputs are inherently unstandardized so that techniques for their mass production are difficult to develop. Certain types of medical care are a good example. While, in some cases, standard patterns and treatment are available for particular ills, we know of too many cases of faulty diagnosis even in the finest medical laboratories to place great faith in routinized diagnostic procedures. Even where two patients are known to share a common ailment, the treatment appropriate for one may produce dangerously allergic reactions in the other. Consequently, most of us are extremely reluctant to forego the personal attention of the examining physician. It is not difficult to think of other activities for which standardization is virtually impossible, including such disparate services as painting, the teaching of children with special problems, and the repairing of watches.

The second obstacle to rapid and continued increases in productivity is the frequently intimate connection between the quantity of labor and the quality of the end product. It is not easy, for example, to imagine how we can mechanize the teacher's reading and criticism of students' papers, which appears so important for the development of writing skills. An increase in gross instructor productivity, in the sense of an increase in the number of students per teacher, would seem to have serious consequences for the quality of the "product." Once again, we can readily find further examples in widely different fields. The need for study and interpretation of certain legal problems requires the input of trained lawyers. On quite a different matter, the personal service and attention accompanying the serving of a good meal is frequently regarded as an integral part of the experience of dining out. In all these instances, reduced reliance on the use of labor is likely to have adverse effects on the quality of the service provided.

In some cases, product specifications seem effective to prevent any reductions in manpower below some point (which often has already been reached). The single bus driver who collects the fares, as well as driving the vehicle, in most cities represents the minimum number of persons possible for the job. In the New York subways in the 1920s there were six employees per train. This number was reduced one by one over the next two decades until, by the postwar period, there remained only the motorman and the conductor who operated the doors.

In the live performing arts, the obstacles limiting increases in productivity are perhaps the most clear-cut of all. A Schubert trio scored for a half-hour performance simply requires one and a half man-hours of labor in its public presentation, and that is all there is to the matter. As Alan Peacock has put it, "Removing Judge Bouck from the cast of *Hedda Gabler* would certainly reduce labor input to Ibsen's masterpiece, but it would also destroy the product. Nor could one increase the productivity of the cost by performing the play at twice the speed. Anyone who doubts this proposition should try playing modern long-playing disks at twenty-eight revolutions per minute."

We do not mean to say that in most of these activities increases in productivity are impossible. On the contrary, from time to time one can expect significant labor-saving innovations in their production. The use of programmed teaching materials has no doubt raised the teacher's productivity to some extent. The jet airliner has done the same for the live performing arts by permitting performers to travel from city to city much more quickly. If one is willing to accept modifications in the product, still greater reductions in the number of man-hours per unit of output become possible. The mass media, for example, have certainly yielded spectacular increases in the productivity of the actor and the musician.

Yet, while sporadic increases in labor output are possible and do occur in the personal services, it is nevertheless much more difficult to achieve regular and frequent increases in productivity than elsewhere in the economy. The techniques used today, for example, by the policeman in "pounding his beat," or those of the violinist or the master chef hardly differ from those employed by their counterparts a century ago. In how many lines of manufacturing can the same be said?

SLOW GROWTH IN PRODUCTIVITY AND THE COSTS OF SERVICES

Where real wages are low, the personal services are usually comparatively cheap. Anyone who travels to a less affluent country is impressed by the particularly low cost of servants and haircuts. Indeed, it has been suggested that the cost of a haircut relative to that of manufactured goods is a good rough and ready index of the state of development of an area. Similarly, the low cost of theater tickets in the unsubsidized theater in London relative to that in New York is no accident; it reflects, at least in part, the relative real wages in the two cities.

However, as productivity in the economy rises with the passage of time, the personal services find themselves at a growing cost disadvantage. The relationship is exhibited most clearly where wages follow the growth of productivity in manufacturing. In practice, where productivity in a firm or industry engaged in wage negotiations has been rising 5 per cent per year, it is hard to imagine a wage proposal by the union calling for less than a 5 per cent rate of increase. Moreover, as far as that industry is concerned, the cost effect of such a wage rise is exactly counterbalanced by the productivity gains. The hourly wage may rise 5 per cent, but so does the number of units of product per man, so that the labor cost per unit of output neither rises nor falls.

But for the economy as a whole that is not the end of the matter. The labor markets for the personal services and in manufacturing are not isolated from one another. If wages of policemen, teachers, or street cleaners fall significantly behind those in manufacturing, in a prosperous economy labor will simply move out of the former occupation and look for jobs in the latter. Scarcity of labor supply will force wages in the personal service upward, close behind those in the remainder of the economy. The evidence suggests that over longer periods wages in the personal services keep up with those paid elsewhere much more frequently than is sometimes believed.

Suppose then, to get back to our example, that because wages (and productivity) in manufacturing have been rising at an annual rate of 5 per cent, wages in the services are forced to increase at, say, 4 per cent per year. As was just observed, the wage rise in manufacturing will then not increase its labor costs. By contrast, if productivity in the services goes up, say, only 1 per cent, the more modest wage rise of 4 per cent will necessarily cause the costs of the services to increase some 3 per cent annually. Only one percentage point of the wage rise will have been absorbed by productivity increases. More generally, we see that, in a sector of the economy such as the personal services, where productivity does not grow as rapidly as wages rise, the cost per unit of output must rise persistently and cumulatively over time.

Of course, a 2 or 3 per cent differential in a given year does not amount to much. However, since the differential is continuing and cumulative, over a longer period it can become very substantial. In fact, with the passage of time, the arithmetic of compounding can produce spectacular results. It may prove helpful at this point if we follow through a hypothetical case to illustrate this whole process. Consider the history of two products: a personal service, say a haircut, and the other a manufactured good, say a fountain pen. Let us assume for simplicity that each is produced solely with labor and that in the initial year, it takes one man-hour to produce a haircut and one man-hour to produce a pen; so that a haircut and a pen have the same initial cost. If a man-hour of labor costs $1 in this first year, then the unit cost of each item will be $1. Let us suppose, however, that technical progress generates increases in the output of pens per man-hour at a rate of 3 per cent annually, while the annual rate of increase in haircuts per man-hour is only 1 per cent. Finally, we postulate as earlier, that wages rise at the same rate as productivity in the production of pens, namely at 3 per cent per annum. Since unit-cost is simply equal to the hourly wage divided by output per man-hour, we find that the cost per pen remains unchanged over time at $1: rising wages are at each step precisely offset by increased output per worker. In contrast, productivity increases in the provision of haircuts are insufficient to keep pace with the rising wages; as a result, the cost of a haircut increases steadily at 2 per cent annually (the difference between the rate of increase in wages and that of output per man-hour). While the cost of a pen remains at $1, the cost per haircut increases to $1.02 in year 2, to $1.22 by year 10, to $2.67 in year 20, and finally, after the passage of a century, a haircut will cost more than seven times as much as a pen.

The evidence in fact shows that such differentials between the rate of change of costs for many personal services and those in manufacturing have been with us for over a century, and that in recent decades they have in several important instances (such as the costs of education) been substantially larger than the differential in our preceding example. And this, we are convinced, has been a powerful force contributing to the growing fiscal distress of state and local governments throughout the United States and in other industrialized countries as well.

We should emphasize that while our illustration has assumed (fairly realistically) that wages constantly rise, increasing money wages really are not the source of the problem. So long as wages in the two sectors of the economy maintain approximate parity, whether they rise or fall, the *relative* cost of the personal services must increase in the manner described. Suppose money wages were to remain absolutely fixed over time. In that case in our example, the dollar cost of a haircut would actually decrease 1 per cent per year. But the cost of a pen would then fall 3 per cent per year, so that the annual 2 per cent differential rise in relative costs would remain.

In summary, in an economy in which one sector of the economy persistently lags behind the rest in terms of rate of productivity growth, the products of that sector must invariably rise in cost relative to cost levels in the rest of the economy, and that rise will be persistent and cumulative. This must be true so long as relative wages in the various sectors of the economy remain the same, and whether or not the overall level of wages is rising, falling or constant.

Thus, a slowing down of the rate of increase in money wages does not cure the cost problem of the personal services. Their difficulty, rather, is that with increasing productivity, an hour of labor becomes more valuable in terms of the manufactured goods that it can turn out. In these circumstances it becomes more and more expensive in terms of the potential output of its labor elsewhere (what economists call its "opportunity cost") to continue to supply the service. The service, in short, is the victim of technological progress in other sectors of the economy, and its problems grow worse with the increased efficiency achieved elsewhere by innovation. Faster technological progress is no blessing for the laggards!

RISING COSTS AND THE SUPPLY OF THE PERSONAL SERVICE

With costs that are likely to rise cumulatively over the foreseeable future, continued supply of the personal services will obviously run into a variety of difficulties. However, the market mechanism and governmental decision-making processes are most unlikely to treat all services similarly. Depending upon political pressure and consumer responses to rising prices and incomes, some services will fare better than others. Already we can see examples of at least four different developments. First, some services have virtually disappeared from the market, or at least their volume has fallen drastically. Handmade furniture, butlers and full-time maids are growing increasingly unusual. The doctor's house calls are also largely gone. No doubt certain other personal services will follow this pattern.

Second, some services will not disappear, but as an offset to their rising costs, their quality will be allowed to deteriorate progressively. Dirtier streets, subways with increasing accident rates, larger classes in some schools, and shorter rehearsal periods for plays are all examples of this phenomenon. The reader will have little difficulty in supplying others.

Third, certain other services will be transformed, in whole or in part, into unpaid amateur activities. Handmade pottery and furniture are now mostly produced as hobbies. Shaving is an interesting example of a successful takeover by the nonprofessional. In this case the change has inspired innovations which permit the amateur barber to provide a reasonably satisfactory substitute for the work of the professional.

Finally, there are services, notably medicine, and perhaps education, for which the public has at least so far generally resisted a curtailment in supply or in quality. For this we have had to pay the price: expenditures have simply had to keep pace with the cumulatively rising costs. Everyone who has recently purchased either of these services in the United States knows all too well how painful these rising costs can be.

EMPLOYMENT IN THE SERVICE INDUSTRIES

In fact, as incomes have risen people have demanded more education and better medical treatment. Obviously this has led to even greater outlays on these services than their rising costs alone can explain. This expansion in demand, along with the innovation-resistant technology of the personal services, has led to another important phenomenon: a significant shift in the allocation of the economy's labor resources. With the disappearance of personal servants and other types of service activities and the growth of amateurism in others, one might perhaps expect a decline of the proportion of the labor force employed in the services. The facts indicate that precisely the opposite has occurred. Since World War II the labor force in the United States has risen by almost 30 per cent from sixty-one million in 1947 to over eighty-four million by 1969. Yet the number of persons employed in manufacturing and agriculture is little larger today than it was in 1947. The great bulk of the increase in employment has occurred in the services. This phenomenon has led Victor Fuchs to describe the United States as the world's first "Service Economy," the first country in which more than one-half of the labor force is employed in the provision of services. Where the service sector accounted for 40 per cent of employment in 1929, this had risen by 1967 to 55 per cent.

This analysis can help to explain this striking pattern of development. Suppose that, as the economy's real income rises, the public desires to maintain constant the proportion of the personal services in the market basket of goods and services that it consumes: that is, when the consumption of manufactured goods goes up 20 per cent it wishes to increase its educational training by 20 per cent as well. Then, with the quantity of labor required per unit of manufactured goods declining at a rate significantly more rapid than that in the services, there must be continuous re-allocation of the labor force from manufacturing to the services. As it takes comparatively less and less time to produce the manufactures, to prevent a change in the relative outputs of the two types of products, more and more of the economy's labor force must go into the services. This appears to represent a reasonably accurate description of what has occurred in the United States in recent decades. After adjusting for the effects of price changes, Fuchs found that the share of total output in the economy originating in the service sector was about the same in 1965 as it was in 1929. But in spite of its relatively stable share of output, the service sector has, as noted earlier, absorbed a continually larger share of the labor-force. "The major explanation for the shift of employment," Fuchs concludes, "is that output per man grew much more slowly in the service sector than in the other sectors."

In particular, Fuchs's own estimates of the average annual

increase in output per man by sector over the period 1929-1965 are:

	Per cent
Agriculture	3.4
Industry	2.2
Service	1.1

This pattern of development in which the service sector accounts for a growing share of employment over time seems to characterize the experience of most other countries as well. Fuchs has found a similar expansion in service-sector employment over time among the western European countries; and, in a statistical study covering several countries at various points in time, discovered a strong positive correlation between the level of per capita income and the percentage of employment in the service sector. Similarly, Simon Kuznets, in a study of thirteen countries, finds for most a substantial increase over time in the share of the labor force employed in the production of services. Thus, the phenomenon we are considering by no means appears to be confined to the United States. Rather, it seems to be a typical characteristic of economic growth.

One word of caution is in order here. The service sector, as defined for accounting purposes, includes a highly diverse group of public and private activities, including everything from education and health services to laundries, insurance companies, and auto-repair shops. This "promiscuous ensemble of the service industries," as George Stigler has called it, makes generalization rather precarious. As one might expect, the experience among some service industries in terms of rates of productivity increase and changing levels of employment has been quite different from that of others. Nevertheless a number of studies of individual service industries do indicate quite clearly that many of the services normally associated closely with the quality of life do fit well the general description we have provided.

CHANGES IN THE QUALITY OF SERVICES

It is sometimes objected that the preceding analysis misses an essential element: the improvement in quality of many of the services that has occurred over the years. Productivity changes in the services, it is suggested, have taken the form of better output rather than increased quantity per unit of labor input. Although the direction of change in the quality of education or in the adequacy of repair services is sometimes questioned, there seems little reason to doubt, for example, that an appendectomy today is a much better product than the corresponding operation in 1900. While today's patient may pay more (directly or via taxes) for a piece of surgery, he certainly gets more for his money.

There is little question about the validity of this argument and the significance of such improvements in quality for the welfare of the community. But it is equally important to recognize that they are largely irrelevant for the central point of our present discussion—the rising quantity of money required to procure the service. The fact is that neither a 1900 appendectomy nor a 1900 education is available today no matter which of them the consumer prefers. He must be prepared to lay out today's higher prices if he is to obtain the service at all.

It may be comforting to the harassed mayor of a city to be assured that his constituents' children are getting a better education for the rapidly rising quantity of money he must budget for public schools. But this does not necessarily help him to raise the requisite funds. The basic point is that the relevant magnitude in the calculation of cost is the crude gross productivity figure, the number of persons served per hour of labor. Improved quality, with all of the difficulties involved in its estimation, need not affect the growth rate in the unit cost of the service, the issue with which we are primarily concerned here.

Yet, the point should not be overstated. Changes in product quality do affect the analysis in at least two ways. First, we noted before that rising costs tend to induce decreases in the quality of some services as a means to offset or conceal the effects on their prices. Obviously for those services for which improved techniques have managed to yield higher quality, the danger of quality deterioration is correspondingly smaller. Second, where quality rises sufficiently, society may actually be willing to reduce the quantity of a particular service that it acquires. If students were now able to learn in five years everything that they formerly absorbed in eight, then one might wish to consider a corresponding reduction in the number of years of schooling financed by the public sector. Yet such reductions in output have been proposed for few, if any, of those public services whose quality has patently been improved. As a result, their demands upon the public budget have continued to increase as rapidly as those of the public services whose product specifications seem not to have changed with the passage of time.

SOCIETY'S ABILITY TO FINANCE THE
RISING COSTS OF SERVICES

Our analysis seems to suggest that there is no real cure for the cost disease of the services; one can hope for palliatives, for means to ease the pain, but not for any permanent remedy. That is true, but the conclusion is not as gloomy as it may sound. If the preceding analysis is correct, the disease, by its very nature, provides the means with which it can be treated.

The analysis in essence shows that the rising relative cost of the personal services is part of the price of economic progress, for it results from the cumulative increases in productivity in manufacturing (and agriculture). Underlying the problem is the fact that manufactures are becoming progressively cheaper to produce (in terms of labor), while productivity in the personal services remains unchanged or rises relatively slowly. Since in this process productivity does not decline in any sector of the economy, it follows as a truism that society's command over goods and services must be increasing. It can afford some more of everything because its productive powers are rising generally.

The very process that generates the rising costs of the services automatically provides income sufficient to permit society to continue to purchase them. Should it so choose, the community can obtain ever-increasing quantities of the personal services despite the continuing increases in their prices. To do so, it only needs to shift each year some fraction of the labor force engaged in the manufacturing sector into the services. Taking an extreme example, suppose that output per man in manufacturing rises at 3 per cent per year while there is absolutely zero increase in productivity in the services. In this case, if 1 or 2 per cent of the manufacturing labor force were transferred annually to the production of services, then an ever-increasing supply of both manufactured goods and services would be the result. The output of services would rise, because more labor is continually being devoted to their production; at the same time, manufactures would also increase since the decline in workers in this sector would be more than offset by the continuing rise in output per man. As we noted earlier, a process of this general type seems in fact to have characterized the historical experience of the advanced, industrialized countries. Society therefore possesses the means to maintain or even increase the output of personal services over time should it desire to do so.

THE FUTURE OF THE PERSONAL SERVICES

We are certainly not entitled to conclude from all this that society should necessarily choose to increase the supply of each and every one of the personal services. After all, we will undoubtedly assign different degrees of importance to different services. Some may be judged essential despite their increasing price, while others may not be considered worth their higher opportunity cost (i.e., the increased quantity of manufacturing goods that one must give up for the service). We do not want to suggest that the maintenance of the quantity and quality of any particular service is a matter of public virtue or social obligation. That is a matter that the public must decide for itself.

We are concerned, however, that some services will deteriorate and disappear, not because it has been decided that their price is more than they are worth, but simply through negligence and lack of foresight. When a service runs into financial problems, it is rarely threatened by a cataclysmic collapse. Rather, it undergoes gradual reductions in quality which are disguised as artfully as its suppliers can manage; the supply itself dries up bit by bit, each loss often passing by unnoticed, until it is realized too late that the product has disappeared. Three years ago there were two professional chamber orchestras in the United States; today there are none. Many attended their concerts, but few were present at the funeral rites. Perhaps they did not justify their cost and so their demise may have been appropriate, but it is quite clear that their fate was determined more by happenstance than by deliberation. For many years, there was an annual decline in the number of new plays produced by the Broadway theaters, but hardly anyone may have been aware of the change from year to year.

Professor Alfred E. Kahn has described such a process as "the tyranny of the small decision." Each of the groups whose decisions affect the final outcome is concerned only with its immediate problems—the current tax rate or the rising price of theater tickets. In selecting its course of action, the individual or single group is in no position to give substantial weight to the consequences for the community as a whole. Yet the fate of a service that is important to the community can be determined inadvertently as the more or less haphazard consequence of a myriad of small, myopic decisions.

The character of the budgetary process contributes substantially to the problem. The services with their constantly rising costs are particularly vulnerable to unconsidered budgetary restrictions made without understanding of the cost behavior that their technology forces upon them. It is only natural, when the cost of some activity doubles or trebles in a decade when the quality of its product seems to be declining and other prices are relatively stable, to feel that somehow waste and inefficiency must be at the root of the problem. This is particularly true in the public sector where the connection between services received and taxes paid is often only vaguely understood by the individual citizen. He naturally abhors the significant increases from year to year in his tax bill; since these tax monies support a wide variety of public services, it is often difficult to establish the link between his tax liability and the quantity and quality of particular public services. Thus, we often find the same individual or group resisting forcefully proposed increases in taxation, while at the next moment, bemoaning the lack of adequate public service. Unfortunately, this pattern of behavior, while perfectly understandable, is likely to produce a cumulative deterioration in the level and quality of many of the personal services.

A difficult educational process will be required to convince both those who construct the public budgets and the taxpayer that the rising cost of the public services is not necessarily a manifestation of mismanagement. Once we understand the nature of their cost structure, we can begin to calculate how much money will be required to maintain a particular service over the long run, and only then can we decide rationally whether it is worth the price. If, all things considered, it is determined that the service in question should not be permitted to deteriorate, then the necessary resources must be provided. Whatever its form, the supply of the requisite resources will entail a long-term budgetary commitment which implicitly takes cognizance of the fact that, because of the nature of its technology, the amount that is sufficient to finance a personal service today will be inadequate tomorrow, and the amount that is adequate tomorrow will not be enough the day after that.

Failure to understand and to provide for these rising costs must condemn the service to decay and perhaps even to extinction. As we have seen, we can expect the wealth of our society to grow rapidly enough to permit it to meet these cost increases. There is, therefore, no excuse for the failure to provide sufficient financing for those of the services which rational deliberation determines to be worth their cost.

The City as a Distorted Price System

WILBUR THOMPSON

Wilbur Thompson, a pioneer in the field of urban economics, is Professor of Economics at Wayne State University. He is the author of A Preface to Urban Economics, *a well-known textbook in its area. This widely acclaimed essay, which first appeared in* Psychology Today *in August 1968, contains a perceptive critique of the system of prices implicit in the provision of urban facilities and urban public services.*

THE FAILURE to use price—as an *explicit* system—in the public sector of the metropolis is at the root of many, if not most, of our urban problems. Price, serving its historic functions, might be used to ration the use of existing facilities, to signal the desired directions of new public investment, to guide the distribution of income, to enlarge the range of public choice and to change tastes and behavior. Price performs such functions in the private market place, but it has been virtually eliminated from the public sector. We say "virtually eliminated" because it does exist but in an implicit, subtle, distorted sense that is rarely seen or acknowledged by even close students of the city, much less by public managers. Not surprisingly, this implicit price system results in bad economics.

We think of the property tax as a source of public revenue, but it can be reinterpreted as a price. Most often, the property tax is rationalized on "ability-to-pay" grounds with real property serving as a proxy for income. When the correlation between income and real property is challenged, the apologist for the property tax shifts ground and rationalizes it as a "benefit" tax. The tax then becomes a "price" which the property owner pays for the benefits received—fire protection, for example. But this implicit "price" for fire services is hardly a model of either efficiency or equity. Put in a new furnace and fireproof your building (reduce the likelihood of having a fire) and your property tax (fire service premium) goes up; let your property de-

teriorate and become a firetrap and your fire protection premium
goes down! One bright note is New York City's one-year tax
abatement on new pollution control equipment; a timid step but
in the right direction.

Often "urban sprawl" is little more than a color word which
reflects (betrays?) the speaker's bias in favor of high population density and heavy interpersonal interaction—his "urbanity."
Still, typically, the price of using urban fringe space has been
set too low—well below the full costs of running pipes, wires,
police cars and fire engines farther than would be necessary if
building lots were smaller. Residential developers are, moreover, seldom discouraged (penalized by price) from "leap frog-
ging" over the contiguous, expensive vacant land to build on the
remote, cheaper parcels. Ordinarily, a flat price is charged for
extending water or sewers to a new household regardless of
whether the house is placed near to or far from existing pump-
ing stations.

Again, the motorist is subject to the same license fees and
tolls, if any, for the extremely expensive system of streets,
bridges, tunnels, and traffic controls he enjoys, regardless of
whether he chooses to drive downtown at the rush hour and
thereby pushes against peak capacity or at off peak times when
it costs little or nothing to serve him. To compound this distortion of prices, we usually set the toll at zero. And when we do
charge tolls, we quite perversely cut the commuter (rush-hour)
rate below the off-peak rate.

It is not enough to point out that the motorist supports road-
building through the gasoline tax. The social costs of noise, air
pollution, traffic control and general loss of urban amenities are
borne by the general taxpayer. In addition, drivers during off-
peak hours overpay and subsidize rush-hour drivers. Four lanes
of expressway or bridge capacity are needed in the morning and
evening rush hours where two lanes would have served if movements had been random in time and direction: that is, near constant in average volume. The peak-hour motorists probably
should share the cost of the first two lanes and bear the full cost
of the other two that they alone require. It is best to begin by
carefully distinguishing where market tests are possible and
where they are not. Otherwise, the case for applying the prin-

ciples of price is misunderstood; either the too-ardent advocate overstates his case or the potential convert projects too much. In either case, a "disenchantment" sets in that is hard to reverse.

Much of the economics of the city is "public economics," and the pricing of urban public services poses some very difficult and even insurmountable problems. Economists have, in fact, erected a very elegant rationalization of the public economy almost wholly on the nonmarketability of public goods and services. While economists have perhaps oversold the inapplicability of price in the public sector, let us begin with what we are not talking about.

The public economy supplies "collectively consumed" goods, those produced and consumed in one big indivisible lump. Everyone has to be counted in the system, there is no choice of *in* or *out*. We cannot identify individual benefits, therefore we cannot exact a *quid pro quo*. We cannot exclude those who would not pay voluntarily; therefore we must turn to compulsory payments: taxes. Justice and air-pollution control are good examples of collectively consumed public services.

A second function of the public economy is to supply "merit goods." Sometimes the majority of us become a little paternalistic and decide that we know what is best for all of us. We believe some goods are especially meritorious, like education, and we fear that others might not fully appreciate this truth. Therefore, we produce these merit goods, at considerable cost, but offer them at a zero price. Unlike the first case of collectively consumed goods, we could sell these merit goods. A schoolroom's doors can be closed to those who do not pay, *quite unlike justice*. But we choose to open the doors wide to ensure that no one will turn away from the service because of its cost, and then we finance the service with compulsory payments. Merit goods are a case of the majority playing God, and "coercing" the minority by the use of bribes to change their behavior.

A third classic function of government is the redistribution of income. Here we wish to perform a service for one group and charge another group the cost of that service. Welfare payments are a clear case. Again, any kind of a private market or pricing mechanism is totally inappropriate; we obviously do not expect welfare recipients to return their payments. Again, we turn to compulsory payments: taxes. In sum, the private market may not be able to process certain goods and services (pure "public goods"), or it may give the "wrong" prices ("merit goods"), or we simply do not want the consumer to pay (income-redistributive services).

But the virtual elimination of price from the public sector is an extreme and highly simplistic response to the special requirements of the public sector. Merit goods may be subsidized without going all the way to zero prices. Few would argue for full-cost admission prices to museums, but a good case can be made for moderate prices that cover, say, their daily operating costs, (e.g., salaries of guards and janitors, heat and light).

Unfortunately, as we have given local government more to do, we have almost unthinkingly extended the tradition of "free" public services to every new undertaking, despite the clear trend in local government toward the assumption of more and more functions that do not fit the neat schema above. The provision of free public facilities for automobile movement in the crowded cores of our urban areas can hardly be defended on the grounds that: (a) motorists could not be excluded from the expressways if they refused to pay the toll, or (b) the privately operated motor vehicle is an especially meritorious way to move through densely populated areas, or (c) the motorists cannot afford to pay their own way and that the general (property) taxpayers should subsidize them. And all this applies with a vengeance to municipal marinas and golf courses.

PRICES TO RATION THE USE OF EXISTING FACILITIES

We need to understand better the rationing function of price as it manifests itself in the urban public sector: how the demand for a temporarily (or permanently) fixed stock of a public good or service can be adjusted to the supply. At any given time the supply of street, bridge, and parking space is fixed; "congestion" on the streets and a "shortage" of parking space express demand greater than supply at a zero price, a not too surprising phenomenon. Applying the market solution, the shortage of street space at peak hours ("congestion") could have been temporarily relieved (rationalized) by introducing a short-run rationing price to divert some motorists to other hours of movement, some to other modes of transportation, and some to other activities.

Public goods last a long time and therefore current additions to the stock are too small to relieve shortages quickly and easily. *The rationing function of price is probably more important in the public sector where it is customarily ignored than in the private sector where it is faithfully expressed.*

Rationing need not always be achieved with money, as when a motorist circles the block over and over looking for a place to park. The motorist who is not willing to "spend time" waiting and drives away forfeits the scarce space to one who will spend time (luck averaging out). The parking "problem" may be reinterpreted as an implicit decision to keep the money price artificially low (zero or a nickel an hour in a meter) and supplement it with a waiting cost or time price. The problem is that we did not clearly understand and explicitly agree to do just that.

The central role of price is to allocate—across the board— scarce resources among competing ends to the point where the value of another unit of any good or service is equal to the incremental cost of producing that unit. Expressed loosely, in the long run we turn from using prices to dampen demand to fit a fixed supply to adjusting the supply to fit the quantity demanded, at a price which reflect the production costs.

Prices which ration also serve to signal desired new directions in which to reallocate resources. If the rationing price exceeds those costs of production which the user is expected to bear directly, more resources should ordinarily be allocated to that activity. And symmetrically a rationing price below the relevant costs indicates an uneconomic provision of that service in the current amounts. Rationing prices reveal the intensity of the users' demands. How much is it really worth to drive into the heart of town at rush hour or launch a boat? In the long run, motorists and boaters should be free to choose, in rough measure, the amount of street and dock space they want and for which they are willing to pay. But, as in the private sector of our economy, free choice would carry with it full (financial) responsibility for that choice.

We need also to extend our price strategy to "factor prices"; we need a sophisticated wage policy for local public employees. Perhaps the key decision in urban development pertains to the recruiting and assignment of elementary- and secondary-school teachers. The more able and experienced teachers have the greater range of choice in post and quite naturally they choose the newer schools in the better neighborhoods, after serving the required apprenticeship in the older schools in the poorer neighborhoods. Such a pattern of migration certainly cannot implement a policy of equality of opportunity.

This author argued six years ago that

Egalitarianism in the public school system has been overdone; even the army recognizes the role of price when it awards extra "jump pay" to paratroopers, only a slightly more hazardous occupation than teaching behind the lines. Besides, it is male teachers whom we need to attract to slum schools, both to serve as father figures where there are few males at home and to serve quite literally as disciplinarians. It is bad economics to insist on equal pay for teachers everywhere throughout the urban area when males have a higher productivity in some areas and when males have better employment opportunities outside teaching—higher "opportunity costs" that raise their supply price. It is downright silly to argue that "equal pay for equal work" is achieved by paying the same money wage in the slums as in the suburbs.

About a year ago, on being offered premium salaries for service in ghetto schools, the teachers rejected, by name and with obvious distaste, any form of "jump pay." One facile argument offered was that they must protect the slum child from the stigma of being harder to teach, a nicety surely lost on the parents and outside observers. One suspects that the real reason for avoiding salary differentials between the "slums and suburbs" is that the teachers seek to escape the hard choice between the higher pay and the better working conditions. *But that is precisely what the price system is supposed to do: equalize sacrifice.*

PRICES TO GUIDE THE DISTRIBUTION OF INCOME

A much wider application of tolls, fees, fines, and other "prices" would also confer greater control over the distribution of income for two distinct reasons. First, the taxes currently used to finance a given public service create *implicit* and *unplanned* redistribution of income. Second, this drain on our limited supply of tax money prevents local government from undertaking other programs with more *explicit* and *planned* redistributional effects.

More specifically, if upper-middle- and upper-income motorists, golfers, and boaters use subsidized public streets, golf links, and marinas more than in proportion to their share of local tax payments from which the subsidy is paid, then these public activities redistribute income toward greater inequality. Even if these "semiproprietary" public activities were found to be neutral with respect to the distribution of income, public provision of these discretionary services comes at the expense of a roughly equivalent expenditure on the more classic public services: protection, education, public health, and welfare.

Self-supporting public golf courses are so common and marinas are such an easy extension of the same principle that it is much more instructive to test the faith by considering the much harder case of the public museum: "culture." Again, we must recall that it is the middle- and upper-income classes who typically visit museums, so that free admission becomes, in effect, redistribution toward greater inequality, to the extent that the lower-income nonusers pay local taxes (e.g., property taxes directly or indirectly through rent, local sales taxes). The low prices contemplated are not, moreover, likely to discourage attendance significantly and the resolution of special cases (e.g., student passes) seems well within our competence.

Unfortunately, it is not obvious that "free" public marinas and tennis courts pose foregone alternatives—"opportunity costs." If we had to discharge a teacher or policeman every time we built another boat dock or tennis court, we would see the real cost of these public services. But in a growing economy, we need only not hire another teacher or policeman and that is not so obvious. In general, then, given a binding local budget constraint—scarce tax money—to undertake a local public service that is unequalizing or even neutral in income redistribution is to deny funds to programs that have the desired distributional effect, and is to lose control over equity.

Typically, in oral presentations at question time, it is necessary to reinforce this point by rejoining, "No, I would not put turnstiles in the playgrounds in poor neighborhoods, rather it is only because we do put turnstiles at the entrance to the play-grounds for the middle- and upper-income-groups that we will be able to 'afford' playgrounds for the poor."

PRICES TO ENLARGE THE RANGE OF CHOICE

But there is more at stake in the contemporary chaos of hid-den and unplanned prices than "merely" efficiency and equity. *There is no urban goal on which consensus is more easily gained than the pursuit of great variety and choice—"pluralism."* The great rural to urban migration was prompted as much by the search for variety as by the decline of agriculture and rise of manufacturing. Wide choice is seen as the saving grace of big-ness by even the sharpest critics of the metropolis. Why, then, do we tolerate far less variety in our big cities than we could have? We have lapsed into a state of tyranny by the majority, in matters of both taste and choice.

In urban transportation the issue is not, in the final analysis, whether users of core-area street space at peak hours should or should not be required to pay their own way in full. The prob-lem is, rather, that by not forcing a direct *quid pro quo* in money, we implicitly substitute a new means of payment—time —in the transportation services "market." The peak-hour motor-ist does pay in full, through congestion and time delay. But *im-plicit choices* blur issues and confuse decision making.

Say we were carefully to establish how many more dollars would have to be paid in for the additional capac-ity needed to save a given number of hours spent commut-ing. The *majority* of urban motorists perhaps would still choose the present combination of "underinvestment" in highway, bridge and parking facilities, with a compensatory heavy invest-ment of time in slow movement over these crowded facilities. Even so, a substantial minority of motorists do prefer a different combination of money and time cost. A more affluent, long-dis-tance commuter could well see the current level of traffic con-gestion as a real problem and much prefer to spend more money to save time. If economies of scale are so substantial that only one motorway to town can be supported, or if some naturally scarce factor (e.g., bridge or tunnel sites) prevents parallel transportation facilities of different quality and price, then the preferences of the minority must be sacrificed to the majority interest and we do have a real "problem." But, ordinarily, in large urban areas there are a number of near-parallel routes to town, and an unsatisfied minority group large enough to justify significant differentiation of one or more of these streets and its diversion to their use. Greater choice through greater scale is, in fact, what bigness is all about.

The simple act of imposing a toll, at peak hours, on one of these routes would reduce its use, assuming that nearby routes are still available without user charges, thereby speeding movement of the motorists who remain and pay. The toll could be raised only to the point where some combination of moderately rapid movement and high physical output were jointly optimized. Otherwise the outcry might be raised that the public transportation authority was so elitist as to gratify the desire of a few very wealthy motorists for very rapid movement, heavily overloading the "free" routes. It is moreover, quite possible, even probable, that the newly converted, rapid-flow, toll-route would handle as many vehicles as it did previously as a congested street and not therefore spinoff any extra load on the free routes.

Our cities cater, at best, to the taste patterns of the middle-income class, as well they should, *but not so exclusively.* This group has chosen, indirectly through clumsy and insensitive tax-and-expenditure decisions and ambiguous political processes, to move about town flexibly and cheaply, but slowly, in private vehicles. Often, and almost invariably in the larger urban areas, we would not have to encroach much on this choice to accommodate also those who would prefer to spend more money and less time, in urban movement. In general, we should permit urban residents to pay in their most readily available "currency" —time or money.

Majority rule by the middle class in urban transportation has not only disenfranchised the affluent commuter, but more seriously it has debilitated the low-fare, mass transit system on which the poor depend. The effect of widespread automobile ownership and use on the mass transportation system is an oft-told tale: falling bus and rail patronage leads to less fre-quent service and higher overhead costs per trip and often higher fares which further reduce demand and service sched-ules. Perhaps two-thirds or more of the urban residents will tol-erate and may even prefer slow, cheap automobile movement. But the poor are left without access to many places of work—the suburbanizing factories in particular—and they face much re-duced opportunities for comparative shopping, and highly con-strained participation in the community life in general. A truly wide range of choice in urban transportation would allow the rich to pay for fast movement with money, the middle-income class to pay for the privacy and convenience of the automobile with time, and the poor to economize by giving up (paying with) privacy.

A more sophisticated price policy would expand choice in other directions. Opinions differ as to the gravity of the water-pollution problem near large urban areas. The minimum level of dissolved oxygen in the water that is needed to meet the standards of different users differs greatly, as does the incre-mental cost that must be incurred to bring the dissolved oxygen levels up to successively higher standards. The boater accepts a relatively low level of "cleanliness" acquired at relatively lit-tle cost. Swimmers have higher standards attained only at much higher cost. Fish and fisherman can thrive only with very high levels of dissolved oxygen acquired only at the highest cost. Fi-nally, one can imagine an elderly convalescent or an impover-ished slum dweller or a confirmed landlubber who is not at all interested in the nearby river. What, then, constitutes "clean"?

A majority rule decision, whether borne by the citi-zen directly in higher taxes or levied on the industrial polluters and then shifted on to the consumer in higher produce prices, is sure to create a "problem." If the pollution program is a com-promise—a halfway measure—the fisherman will be dis-appointed because the river is still not clean enough for his purposes and the landlubbers will be disgruntled because the program is for "special interests" and he can think of better uses for his limited income. Surely, we can assemble the managerial skills in the local public sector needed to devise and administer a structure of user charges that would extend choice in outdoor recreation, consistent with financial responsibility, with lower charges for boat licenses and higher charges for fishing licenses.

Perhaps the most fundamental error we have committed in the development of our large cities is that we have too often subjected the more affluent residents to petty irritations which serve no great social purpose, then turned right around and permitted this same group to avoid responsibilities which have the most critical and pervasive social ramifications. It is a travesty and a social tragedy that we have prevented the rich from buying their way out of annoying traffic congestion—or at least not helped those who are long on money and short on time arrange such an accommodation. Rather, we have permitted them, through political fragmentation and flight to tax havens, to evade their financial and leadership responsibilities for the poor of the central cities. That easily struck goal, "pluralism and choice," will require much more managerial sophistication in the local public sector than we have shown to date.

PRICING TO CHANGE TASTES AND BEHAVIOR

Urban managerial economics will probably also come to deal especially with "developmental pricing" analogous to "promotional pricing" in business. Prices below cost may be used for a limited period to create a market for a presumed "merit good." The hope would be that the artificially low price would stimulate consumption and that an altered *expenditure pattern* (practice) would lead in time to an altered *taste pattern* (preference), as experience with the new service led to a fuller appreciation of it. Ultimately, the subsidy would be withdrawn, whether or not tastes changed sufficiently to make the new service self-supporting—provided, of course, that no permanent redistribution of income was intended.

For example, our national parks had to be subsidized in the beginning and this subsidy could be continued indefinitely on the grounds that these are "merit goods" that serve a broad social interest. But long experience with outdoor recreation has so shifted tastes that a large part of the costs of these parks could now be paid for by a much higher set of park fees.

It is difficult, moreover, to argue that poor people show up at the gates of Yellowstone Park, or even the much more metropolitan area regional parks, in significant number, so that a subsidy is needed to continue provision of this service for the poor. A careful study of the users and the incidence of the taxes raised to finance our parks may even show a slight redistribution of income toward greater inequality.

Clearly, this is not the place for an economist to pontificate on the psychology of prices but a number of very interesting phenomena that seem to fall under this general heading deserve brief mention. A few simple examples of how charging a price changes behavior are offered, but left for others to classify.

In a recent study of depressed areas, the case was cited of a community-industrial-development commission that extended its fund-raising efforts from large business contributors to the general public in a supplementary "nickel and dime" campaign. They hoped to enlist the active support of the community at large, more for reasons of public policy than for finance. But even a trivial financial stake was seen as a means to create broad and strong public identification with the local industrial development programs and to gain their political support.

Again, social-work agencies have found that even a nominal charge for what was previously a free service enhances both the self-respect of the recipient and his respect for the usefulness of the service. Paradoxically, we might experiment with higher public assistance payments coupled to *nominal* prices for selected public health and family services, personal counseling, and surplus foods.

To bring a lot of this together now in a programmatic way, we can imagine a very sophisticated urban public management beginning with below-cost prices on, say, the new rapid mass transit facility during the promotional period of luring motorists from their automobiles and of "educating" them on the advantages of a carefree journey to work. Later, if and when the new facility becomes crowded during rush hours and after a taste of this new transportation mode has become well established, the "city economist" might devise a three-price structure of fares: the lowest fare for regular off-peak use, the middle fare for regular peak use (tickets for commuters), and the highest fare for the occasional peak-time user. Such a schedule would reflect each class's contribution to the cost of having to carry standby capacity.

If the venture more than covered its costs of operation, the construction of additional facilities would begin. Added social benefits in the form of a cleaner, quieter city or reduced social costs of traffic control and accidents could be included in the cost accounting ("cost-benefit analysis") underlying the fare structure. But below-cost fares, taking care to count social as well as private costs, would not be continued indefinitely except for merit goods or when a clear income-redistribution end is in mind. And, even then, not without careful comparison of the relative efficiency of using the subsidy money in alternative redistributive programs. We need, it would seem, not only a knowledge of the economy of the city, but some very knowledgeable city economists as well.

The Honest Citizen's Guide
to Revenue Sharing

HENRY AARON

Henry Aaron is a Senior Research Associate of the Brookings Institution, Washington, D.C., and Professor of Economics at the University of Maryland. Among his many contributions to the field of public finance, both in theory and in policy, are books on housing, social security, and welfare reform. He first presented this paper at the Annual Conference of the National Tax Association in 1971.

> And so these men of Indostan
> Disputed loud and long,
> Each in his own opinion
> Exceeding stiff and strong,
> Though each was partly in the right
> And all were in the wrong!

Moral:

> So oft in theologic wars,
> The disputants, I ween,
> Rail on in utter ignorance
> Of what each other mean
> And prate about an Elephant
> Not one of them has seen!

> from John Godfrey Saxe,
> "The Blind Men and the Elephant" *

Economic and political theory have made two major contributions to the debate on revenue sharing. The first contribution, made long ago in another context, is that differences in the *average* income among communities cause fiscal inequities. In order to purchase equal levels of public services, citizens in the poorer community may have to pay higher taxes than citizens

---

* *Illustrated Treasury of Poetry for Children*, David Ross, ed. (Grosset and Dunlap, 1970), p. 232.

with the same income in the richer community. This situation arises because a given tax rate yields more revenue when applied to a large than when applied to a small pool of income, retail sales, or property values. Furthermore, if people decide where to live partly on the basis of local tax rates, the lower tax rates in the wealthier community will tend to attract new residents, particularly high income families for whom taxes are important. These trends can be strengthened by zoning or other policies designed to repel the poor and attract the rich and by the presence in poor communities of more problems—crime, fires, trash, hard-to-educate children—which generate high public costs.

The foregoing propositions are simple but profoundly important:

1. Equal tax rates buy fewer services in poor communities than in rich communities;

2. If residential location is influenced by tax rates, the rich will tend to congregate in wealthy communities; and

3. These two effects are mutually reinforcing.

The corollary of this view is that, in the absence of such outside action as financial aid to governments of low income communities, fiscal forces will tend to increase economic disparities among communities. Those who deplore such disparities should favor aid to poor jurisdictions.

The second major theoretical contribution shows that under certain conditions revenue sharing will cause a reduction in local taxes to citizens in the aided community and that the reduction to each taxpayer will be proportional to his tax burden. In practice, of course, this effect might occur through a failure to enact tax increases which otherwise would have been imposed. In these circumstances, revenue sharing is the ideal instrument for correcting fiscal disparities *provided* that aid is so distributed that communities with relatively low incomes and bad problems receive most aid. In other words, the formula under which funds are distributed is absolutely crucial; a bad formula could increase rather than reduce fiscal disparities.

Unfortunately, the assumptions necessary to reach this rather

powerful conclusion are strong and unrealistic. Specifically, the
conclusions that must hold if there are "threshold effects." For example, if the community responds only when aid reaches a certain size, the size of this threshold may differ among otherwise
identical communities in unpredictable ways. Similarly, such
factors as whether a community is growing rapidly or stag-
nating or whether the community is proud or ashamed of its
political legacy may cause otherwise identical communities to
react differently to revenue sharing. When the impact of such
diverse influences is taken into account, the conclusion that revenue sharing is equivalent to a proportional cut in municipal
taxes no longer follows necessarily.

Given the typical inconclusiveness of theory in forecasting the
consequences of revenue sharing, one turns to empirical efforts
to measure the response of communities to outside fiscal aid. The
results of such efforts are similarly inconclusive, partly because
fiscal aids come with various kinds of conditions, political deals,
and arm twisting and partly because the studies have tended to
be somewhat mechanical statistical exercises rather than estimates of carefully designed models of government behavior.

The most recent and sophisticated effort to measure the impact of federal grants on state and local government expenditures finds that state and local governments return only 10 percent of any revenue sharing grant to citizens through
lower taxes. Although such work offers some hope that eventually we may be able to measure accurately state and local responses to federal aid, we cannot now predict with any confidence what the impact of unrestricted federal aid to state and
local governments will be on the tax and expenditure policies
of either the federal government or of state and local governments. The crippling effect of such ignorance on rational debate
has been made clear by Stephen Dresch who has shown that the
impact of revenue sharing on state and local governments depends acutely on which federal taxes must be increased or which
federal expenditures must be cut in order to create enough fiscal elbow room for revenue sharing, and that the impact of revenue sharing on individuals depends acutely on how state and
local governments respond to increased aid.

The inability to predict confidently the response of federal, state, or local governments expresses itself in implicity contradictory assumptions about these responses.

THE MANY MOTIVES FOR REVENUE SHARING

Among the more important objectives advocates have claimed revenue sharing will advance are:

1. the transfer of decision-making power concerning public expenditures from the federal government to state and local governments;

2. improvements in the ability of state and local governments to operate efficiently;

3. reduction in the degree to which state and local governments rely on regressive taxes—sales taxes and, particularly, property taxes;

4. removal of fiscal mismatch between overburdened state and local governments and the perennially overfinanced federal government;

5. equalization of the fiscal burden citizens in various states and localities must bear to provide equivalent services;

6. preservation of the size of the public sector by diverting excess federal revenues from possible tax cuts into expenditures by state and local governments.

This list is not exhaustive, but it is sufficient for purposes of illustration. The first objective of revenue sharing—to transfer decision-making power over public expenditures to state and local government will not be achieved if state and local governments allow revenue sharing to substitute significantly for local taxes. The theoretical model described above suggests that they will do so; the empirical study cited above suggests that they will not. If they cut taxes or delay tax increases, state and local governments will be unable to perform additional functions. In addition, this argument for revenue sharing suggests that at least some part of shared revenues should be diverted from categorical aids through which the federal government now induces state and local governments to act as the federal government's agent, since categorical aids vest some of the authority about how funds should be spent in the federal government. The goal of decentralizing political power will be partly frustrated if states reduce current assistance to local governments by all or part of the shared revenues they are required to "pass through" to local governments. In that case, power would be decentralized less than the intent of the administration's revenue sharing proposals.

The goal of enabling state and local governments to operate more efficiently is rather vague. For those who allege that the proliferation and complexity of present categorical grants cause inefficiency, the cure must lie in grant consolidation and simplification or in the replacement of present categorical grants by revenue sharing. For those who regard revenue sharing as an overhead grant which will help state and local governments to use categorical aid more efficiently, revenue sharing should not replace existing categorical aids. In either case, to the extent that shared revenues replace state or local tax effort, the efficiency enhancing power of revenue sharing is eroded. Similarly, if states elect to offset aid to localities by curtailing other general aid, cities, counties, and school districts will not experience the efficiency-enhancing effects revenue sharing is supposed to produce.

Those who hope revenue sharing will reduce reliance on regressive sales and property taxes must base their hopes on several assumptions. Unlike those who wish to help state and local governments make more decisions and to make them more efficiently, tax reform advocates must hope that shared revenues supplant state and local taxes. Moreover, they must be confident that the state and local governments will curtail growth in the relatively sluggish sales and property taxes rather than in the elastic and progressive income tax. Moreover, if a freeze or rollback in the property tax is the main goal, they must hope that states pass through to local governments not only the mandated share, but also the states' own share as well. They must feel confident that revenue sharing will not reduce other grant assistance, will not curtail other progressively distributed federal assistance, or substitute for progressively distributed federal expenditures. If these conditions are not met, revenue sharing may well reduce the overall progressivity of the tax system.

Most proponents of revenue sharing have alleged that a serious fiscal mismatch exists. By historical and political accident, the federal government has taxes that grow faster than the problems we wish to solve nationally, while the reverse is true at the state and local level. As the often repeated slogan goes, the federal government has the best taxes while the state and local governments face the worst problems. The vitality of this argument in the face of facts that flatly contradict it suggests that a nicely rounded phrase is indestructible. But even if this argument were supported by the facts, it presumes that shared revenues will flow to those jurisdictions most weighted down by problems. Since neither the state allocation nor the pass through formulas in the Nixon administration's proposal take need into account, this argument must presume that state governments will adjust other forms of aid so that shared revenues are concentrated on needy communities. Furthermore, this argument presumes that shared revenues will not replace other grants and that the federal government will not delegate to the states functions formerly fulfilled at the national level. If revenue sharing results in higher federal expenditures and taxation than would otherwise occur, then the greater federal tax effort will probably impair the ability of state and local governments to raise taxes. In any case, the alleged fiscal mismatch will not be reduced if state and local governments allow shared revenues to replace revenues from their own sources or if funds leak out to jurisdictions in comfortable financial circumstances.

Revenue sharing receives much support from those who see a fiscal imbalance among the states. Revenue sharing will reduce such imbalance, more or less, depending on the particular formula for allocating aid. This objective will be achieved regardless of state or local actions. Revenue sharing will tend to reduce the differences in tax effort citizens of different jurisdictions must make in order to buy equivalent public services. Whether they use shared revenues to cut taxes (or to defer increases) or to improve local public services is a matter of local choice. The point is that the costs of various levels of public services, in terms of tax rates will be equalized. Federal actions, however, could defeat or reinforce the power of revenue sharing. Should revenue sharing lead to cuts in other grants-in-aid which equalize fiscal burdens, the net equalizing effect would be reduced and perhaps erased

For equalization purposes, revenue sharing should be tied entirely to measures of disparity in fiscal capacity. Despite efforts to construct complex indices, measures of income, wealth, or the incidence of poverty remain the best guides to the presence of fiscal strengths and weaknesses. Even such formulas do not assure equalization of fiscal burdens among cities, since state legislatures might offset equalizing effects by altering other state aid formulas.

The argument that revenue sharing will help maintain the size of the public sector presumes that state and local governments will not reduce taxes or delay tax increases as a result of external aid. It presumes also that the federal government will not curtail other forms of assistance to make room for revenue sharing. In fact, it assumes that all other federal government expenditures taken together will be roughly as large with revenue sharing as they would have been without it.

CONCLUSION

The foregoing survey of the motives for revenue sharing indicates that advocates have made arguments that presume:

1. that state and local governments will and that they will not cut taxes (or postpone tax increases) as a result of revenue sharing,

2. that the federal government will and that it will not reduce categorical grants-in-aid if it provides revenue sharing,

3. that we have some idea of what federal taxes will be raised or expenditures will be cut to finance revenue sharing so that we can appraise the full effects of revenue sharing, and

4. that states will pass through to local governments exactly the legally stipulated portion of shared revenues, that share plus the state's share, or differing proportions according to the magnitude of the problems facing each jurisdiction.

The contradictory assumptions regarding the behavior of federal, state, and local officials in response to revenue sharing may explain the peculiar shallowness of the support for revenue sharing, and the extraordinary lack of persuasiveness of the passionate arguments advanced for and against untied fiscal aid. The contradictory responses to revenue sharing [which] advocates implicitly assume are like the many aspects of the elephant no one of them has seen.

None of the foregoing is meant to suggest that action to strengthen the federal system should wait until we know exactly how revenue sharing will affect political decisions at all levels. It does suggest that we should not base our attitudes about revenue sharing on vaguely stated objectives which upon close examination are inconsistent with one another because they depend on opposite responses by state and local governments. Support should be based rather on the one national objective that the federal government has exclusive power to achieve— fiscal equalization among states; fiscal equalization among cities cannot be imposed without much larger outlays or more arm twisting than presently contemplated if states wish to frustrate it.

Understanding Urban Government:
Metropolitan Reform Reconsidered*

ROBERT L. BISH AND VINCENT OSTROM

Robert Bish, Associate Professor of Economics and Urban Affairs at the University of Southern California, and Vincent Ostrom, Professor of Political Science at Indiana University, are pioneers in the application of public choice theory to issues of urban and metropolitan governance. This discussion is adapted from "Understanding Urban Government: Metropolitan Reform Reconsidered," a Domestic Affairs Study of the American Enterprise Institute for Public Policy Research, published in 1973.

THE OLD REFORM TRADITION: CONSOLIDATION

FROM EARLY in the twentieth century until the late 1960s, a single approach to diagnosing problems and prescribing improvements in government has dominated the thinking and recommendations of most analysts of urban government in the United States. That single approach has been called the efficiency and economy reform movement or the good government reform movement.[1]

In 1925 William Anderson succinctly summarized the principal recommendations of this reform tradition:

1. Each major urban area should be organized by only one unit of local government.

2. The voters in each major urban area should elect only the most important policy-making officials, and these should be few in number. Citizens will be confused by long ballots

---

* This presentation of "Alternative Systems of Government" is adapted from Chapters 2 and 3 in Robert L. Bish and Vincent Ostrom, *Understanding Urban Government: Metropolitan Reform Considered* (Washington, D.C.: American Enterprise Institute for Public Policy Research, 1973), pp 7–33.

1. For a good summary of the reform tradition for urban governance, see Robert Warren, *Government in Metropolitan Regions: A Reappraisal of Fractionated Political Organization* (Davis: Institute of Governmental Affairs, University of California at Davis, 1966), Chapters 1–3.

and be frustrated in their effort to choose among candidates for numerous public offices.

3. The traditional separation of powers should be eliminated from the internal structure of the single consolidated unit of local government.

4. The function of administration, on the other hand, should be separated from that of politics. The work of administration should be performed by specially trained public servants who are adequately compensated, and employed on a full-time basis.

5. Administration should be organized into an integrated command structure in accordance with the hierarchical principle, where authority tapers upward and culminates in a single chief executive. [2]

These principles had also been advanced by Woodrow Wilson during the last decades of the nineteenth century as being essential to good government. Wilson presumed that "the more power is divided the more irresponsible it becomes." [3] He was persuaded that the checks and balances inherent in the American system of government created major impediments to smooth, harmonious relationships in government, and that these checks and balances had "proved mischievous just to the extent to which they had succeeded in establishing themselves as realities." [4]

When considering problems of urban government, analysts in this reform tradition view small units of government as unprofessional and inefficient. The parochial commitment of small jurisdictions to local interests is seen as standing in the way of realizing the overall public interest of the larger metropolitan community. Fragmentation of authority and overlapping jurisdictions among numerous units of local government are diagnosed as the fundamental sources of institutional failure in the government of urban areas.

From this perspective, overlapping jurisdictions imply duplication of services. Duplication of services also implies waste and inefficiency in government. According to these analysts,

2. William Anderson, *American City Government* (New York: Henry Holt and Company, 1925), pp. 641–642.

3. Woodrow Wilson, *Congressional Government* (New York: Meridan Books, 1956; originally published in 1885), pp. 77, 187.

4. Ibid., p. 187.

efficiency is enhanced by eliminating the numerous small jurisdictions and by consolidating all authority in one jurisdiction
with general authority to govern each major urban area as a
whole. Such consolidations vest ostensibly enlightened leaders
and professional administrators with authority to coordinate all
aspects of metropolitan affairs through a single integrated structure of government.

Policy analysts in this tradition assume that consolidation of
all smaller jurisdictions into a single, overall unit of government
for each urban region or metropolitan area clearly fixes political
responsibility, making it possible for citizens to hold officials ac-
countable for their actions. Attention to numerous, overlapping
jurisdictions presumably overloads citizens, confuses responsibility and frustrates citizens in their efforts to control public policy.

The reform tradition proposing consolidation of all local governmental units into a single jurisdiction for each metropolitan
region has had a powerful appeal. The similarity between textbook ideas and the thoughts of practical men is evident when we
compare Anderson's formulation in 1925 with the recommendations made by the Committee for Economic Development on
how to modernize local government in the 1960s.[5] The CED
report included the following recommendations:

1. The number of local governments in the United States,
now about 80,000, should be reduced by at least 80 percent.
[In 1942 William Anderson recommended a reduction in the
units of government from 165,000 to 17,800.[6]]

2. The number of overlapping layers of local government
found in most states should be severely curtailed.

3. Popular elections should be confined to members of the
policy-making body, and to the chief executive in those governments where the "strong mayor" form is preferred to the
"council-manager" plan.

4. Each local unit should have a single chief executive, either elected by the people or appointed by the local legislative body, with all administrative agencies and personnel

5. Committee for Economic Development, *Modernizing Local Government*
(New York, 1966), pp. 11–12.
6. William Anderson, *The Units of Government in the United States: An
Enumeration and Analysis* (Chicago: Public Administration Service, 1942),
pp. 2, 46.

fully responsible to him; election of department heads should be halted.[7]

The theory of government inherent in this reform tradition suggests certain casual relationships among variables. Among these associations are the following: (1) Increasing the size of urban governmental units through consolidation will be associated with improved output of public services, increased efficiency, increased responsibility of local officials and increased confidence among citizens about their capacity to affect public policies. (2) Reducing the multiplicity of jurisdictions serving an urban area through consolidation will also be associated with improved output of public services, increased efficiency, increased responsibility of local officials and increased confidence among citizens about their capacity to affect public policies.

A critical issue in assessing this reform tradition is whether these relationships hold in the operation of urban governments. If these relationships always hold, then the bigger the unit of government and the less duplication the better. If the reverse holds, then the smaller the units of government and the more duplication the better. There may also be intermediate possibilities. For example, an increase in size for some functions might yield improvements to some magnitude and yield net disadvantages beyond that magnitude. In other circumstances a decrease in size might yield improvements to some magnitude but yield net disadvantages if reduced to a still smaller size. These relationships may vary with different types of public goods or services. It is these intermediate possibilities that deserve careful scrutiny.

THE NEW REFORM MOVEMENT: COMMUNITY CONTROL

Since the 1960s there has been a considerable tendency to question the performance of large-scale administrative agencies in the bigger cities of the United States.[8] Citizens' groups have

7. Committee for Economic Development, *Modernizing Local Government*, p. 17.
8. Representative statements of the new reform-community control positions include Milton Kotler, *Neighborhood Government: The Local Foundations of Political Life* (Indianapolis: Bobbs-Merrill, 1969), and Alan A.

complained about the inability of big city administrative agencies to provide desired police services, perform educational services, get garbage hauled away, resolve traffic problems and carry out other basic functions for which city governments are responsible. These critics do not attribute citizen alienation and rising costs to city government that is too small or to the existence of overlapping jurisdictions, but rather to its largeness, cumbersomeness and monopolistic position. Proponents of community control argue that public bureaucracies in major cities are so large and rigid as to be unmanageable no matter how well intentioned top officials and administrators may be. They also argue that voting for a mayor and few top officials for a large city is insufficient as a means of indicating the variety of citizen preferences.

Citizen preferences, life styles and problems vary from neighborhood to neighborhood. Community control advocates contend that highly centralized governmental units are often unable to respond to these variations among neighborhoods. They have proposed the creation of community councils and quasi-independent neighborhood governments to deal with this problem. They want greater control over government returned to the people so that they will be supplied with the services they prefer rather than an arbitrary level of service that fails to meet their needs. The new reformers have also noted that cost savings do not occur in cities over 100,000 for the most expensive functions such as education and police services, and thus, there is little reason for not organizing some services in relation to neighborhood conditions and assigning control over their provision to community councils or neighborhood governments.

These new reformers demand small enough political units so that (1) the different preferences of different groups of people within urban areas can be more adequately known to public officials, (2) public officials will be located close enough to practical problems so that those officials can be forced to respond to the conditions of life in different neighborhoods, and (3) bureaucracies can be kept small enough so that they are manage-

Altshuler, *Community Control: The Black Demand for Participation in Large American Cities* (New York: Pegasus, 1970).

able. The demands for community councils and neighborhood governments within major cities clearly entail a rejection of the basic presumptions inherent in the traditional consolidation approach.

It is not surprising then that proponents of each approach come to rather different conclusions about what is wrong in urban areas and what policies or changes may lead to improvement. The consolidation tradition sees large governmental bureaucracies as directed by enlightened leadership and professional administrators acting efficiently on the basis of a high level of knowledge about their environment. The new reformers see large government bureaucracies as unresponsive, unmanageable, and as lacking knowledge of the multitude of different conditions, neighborhoods, life styles and communities existing in large urban areas. Both are likely to be concerned with rapidly rising costs which exceed general inflationary tendencies. Traditional reformers attribute mushrooming costs to overlapping jurisdictions and duplication of services; the new reformers attribute those cost changes to the bureaucratic inefficiencies in the larger consolidated units of government.

The new reformers demanding community control over the provision of neighborhood public services within large urban areas clearly reject the propositions of the traditional reformers about the relationship of increased size and reduced numbers of jurisdictions to improved services, increased efficiency, increased responsibility of officials and increased confidence among citizens about their capacity to affect public policies. Instead they see increasing consolidation leading to a deterioration in public services, reduced efficiency, decreasing responsibility among officials, and a decreasing confidence among citizens about their capacity to affect public policies.

THE TWO-TIER SOLUTION

The challenge of the new reformers demanding community control has had a substantial practical appeal, which is reinforced by the observable deterioration of conditions of life in major cities. Officials in the largest cities often contend that urban problems are too great for them to cope with. A crisis exists! And the "crisis" is accompanied by new calls for reform.

One response has been to propose a two-tier solution: consolidation of all *major* units of local government into one general jurisdiction to have authority over all area-wide functions in a metropolitan region together with small local units to deal with community or neighborhood problems within the larger consolidated unit. The two-tier approach has its parallel in the relationship of states with the federal government in a federal system.

The most enthusiastic advocates of community control recognize that there is a role for larger governmental units to control air pollution, provide large regional water supply and sewer systems, create mass transportation facilities and redistribute income to improve the fiscal capabilities of lower income communities. There is less agreement on which specific functions are appropriate subjects for local community control. It also appears that traditional reformers are modifying their position with a recognition that different groups of people may prefer different mixes and levels of public goods and services and that bureaucracies organized on an area-wide basis for all public functions may not be the most efficient way to respond to the diversities within each metropolitan area.

The recognition that different citizens can legitimately have different preferences and tastes for public goods and services and wish to enjoy different life styles represents a major change from earlier reform arguments that a uniform level of public services, as decided upon by officials representing the community as a whole, should be provided to everyone. The recognition of a diversity in preferences is a major premise of the new reformers advocating community control. A compromise on this point by traditional reformers advocating consolidation is essential to agreement upon a two-tier structure of governments for metropolitan areas.

The compromise afforded by the two-tier solution, however, glosses over the basic challenge to the traditional reform movement made by the advocates of community control. The challenge implies that the logic inherent in the consolidation solution did not stand the test of experience. Where successful consolidation movements have created overall units of city government, as in the cases of New York (1898), Philadelphia (1854) and St. Louis

(1875) among many others, the logic of consolidation failed to cope with the problem of providing the means to deal with neighborhood problems. In fact, even the essentially two-tier structure of the New York City borough system has not been sufficient to deal with neighborhood problems.[9]

Academic discussion about a single unit of metropolitan government performing area-wide functions appears most reasonable until one confronts the practical problem of specifying boundaries for metropolitan regions. Just how inclusive is the overall tier to be? Are Washington and Baltimore, Philadelphia, Camden and Trenton, Newark and New York, and New Haven, Providence and Boston to be grouped in several urban regions or in a single region? In confronting the practical problem of drawing boundaries for the urban agglomerations of the Atlantic Seaboard, the Great Lakes, California or the Puget-Willamette Trough of the Pacific Northwest, the difficulties of devising a single unit of government capable of dealing with area-wide problems become overwhelming.

On the other hand, what size government is appropriate to deal with community problems as the lower tier of a federated urban government? The communities of interest and the scope of problems vary in size, and a single lower tier of governments for a large megalopolis may be insufficient to deal with them appropriately. What criteria can be applied to the design of a two-tier structure? The practical man may very well ask: Do we have any reason to believe that a two-tier approach will be sufficient to provide solutions to the range of problems confronting people in any major urban agglomeration?

THE PUBLIC CHOICE APPROACH

The diagnoses and prescriptions of traditional reformers and the new advocates of community control constitute two major approaches to problems of urban government. An alter-

---

9. It is interesting to note that the two-tier structure in New York City has been the subject of reform efforts directed at moving toward greater centralization by reducing the power and functions of boroughs and increasing the power of the city. Such reforms were undertaken as recently as the early 1960s. In the 1970s, demands for decentralization and community control have focused upon areas of much smaller size than the existing boroughs.

native way of thinking takes as its starting point the diversity of individual preferences and the diverse nature of goods and services rather than organization structure. This alternative approach is usually called the political economy or public choice approach. It has a long history, although it has often been obscured in the twentieth century. The best statements and examples of this way of thinking are contained in the essays by Alexander Hamilton and James Madison in *The Federalist*, Alexis de Tocqueville's *Democracy in America* and the contemporary writing of public choice economists and political scientists such as James Buchanan, Gordon Tullock, Charles Lindblom and Mancur Olson.[10]

Assumptions about Individuals · The public choice approach to the analysis of urban problems begins with a focus on individuals. Individuals are assumed to act on a knowledge of the alternatives that may be available to them. Such knowledge is assumed to be imperfect. As a consequence, individuals are expected to be fallible, and individuals will find information costly to acquire.[11] The conditions of fallibility and costliness of information applies to all decision makers, citizens, officials, professional experts, pub-

10. For an analysis of how the authors of *The Federalist* approached political analysis, see Vincent Ostrom, *The Political Theory of a Compound Republic: A Reconstruction of the Logical Foundations of American Democracy as Presented in "The Federalist"* (Blacksburg, Virginia: Virginia Polytechnic Institute, Center for the Study of Public Choice, 1971). The most explicit application of public choice theory to the analysis of urban governance is contained in Vincent Ostrom, Charles Tiebout and Robert Warren, "The Organization of Government in Metropolitan Areas," *American Political Science Review*, vol. 55 (December 1961), pp. 831–842, and Robert L. Bish, *The Public Economy of Metropolitan Areas* (Chicago: Markham, 1971). Other major writings utilizing a public choice approach include James M. Buchanan and Gordon Tullock, *The Calculus of Consent* (Ann Arbor: University of Michigan Press, 1962); Mancur Olson, *The Logic of Collective Action* (Cambridge: Harvard University Press, 1965), Gordon Tullock, *The Politics of Bureaucracy* (Washington, D.C.: Public Affairs Press, 1965); Charles Lindblom, *The Intelligence of Democracy* (New York: The Free Press, 1965). For a discussion of the development of the public choice approach and several hundred additional references see Vincent Ostrom and Elinor Ostrom, "Public Choice: A Different Approach to the Study of Public Administration," *Public Administration Review*, vol. 31 (March/April 1971), pp. 203–216.
11. For analysis of information problems see F. A. Hayek, "The Uses of Knowledge in Society," *American Economic Review*, vol. 35 (September 1945), pp. 519–530, and Gordon Tullock, *The Politics of Bureaucracy*.

lic employees, et cetera.

Individuals are also assumed to have diverse preferences and to weigh alternative possibilities in relation to their preferences. Individuals will choose those possibilities that they believe will gain them the greatest net advantage. All individuals are seen as self-interested, but self-interest may include a personal concern for the welfare of others.

Individuals are also assumed to exist in a society in which decision rules are used as a means for ordering relationships among individuals and in which some individuals occupying specialized positions are assigned governmental prerogatives to determine, enforce and alter legal relationships. For purposes of this analysis, we shall assume the existence of a constitutional order under which rules applicable to the conduct of government can be enforced against those who exercise governmental prerogatives at all levels of government. Thus, the exercise of local government authority contrary to the basic criteria of constitutional law and legislation consistent with constitutional authority is assumed to be unlawful. Persons are assumed correlatively to have access to judicial, legislative and constitutional remedies in seeking redress against officials and governments which violate constitutional rights or rights created under legislative authority of the state and federal governments. Relevant standards of state and national laws are assumed to be enforceable in relation to the conduct of local officials and local governments.

Assumptions about Goods and Services · Among the array of possibilities, individual citizens are assumed to have their own preferences for both public and private goods. The goods themselves possess diverse characteristics. Some, such as apples or bread, can be dealt with efficiently under private market arrangements, with public action required only to assure free market conditions, to maintain enforceability of contracts and to resolve disputes between individuals participating in market transactions. Private goods, like apples and bread, are highly divisible and packageable. Individuals can be excluded from consuming them unless they are willing to pay the price. Markets work reasonably well for most packageable goods where potential buyers can be excluded from the use of a good unless they are willing to pay the price to acquire it.

Other goods and services, such as national defense, police services, fire protection, control of contagious diseases, quality of the environment and income redistribution, are thought not to be susceptible to adequate handling in private markets. Men have formed governments to assist with the provision of these goods.

Public goods and services share the characteristic of being enjoyed or consumed by all members of a community in common. Individuals *cannot be excluded* from enjoying a public good once it is provided for someone else; and one individual's consumption or enjoyment will not subtract from its consumption or enjoyment by others. For example, once peace and security are provided in a community, they are available for anyone to enjoy. My enjoyment of that peace and security does not subtract from others enjoying that same peace and security. Yet peace and security do not just happen. They depend upon the organized activities of many people and require the expenditure of substantial time and effort.

Assumptions about Organizations • Public goods and services probably cannot be provided on a stable, long-term basis through purely voluntary efforts and financing. If payments were purely voluntary, each citizen would find it in his own interest to withhold payment so long as enough others paid to keep the benefits flowing. The result of many individuals withholding payment would be inadequate provision of public goods and services. Resolution of this dilemma is usually sought through some form of governmental organization. In this respect, government serves as a coercive means of seeing to it that each individual contributes his share, through the payment of taxes, for the provision of public goods and services.[12]

Governmental organizations also provide means for citizens to communicate their preferences for public goods and services through such mechanisms as elections. The provision of public

12. The logic of this issue is treated in Bish, *Public Economy*, Chapters 2 and 3.

reference to citizen preferences. From this perspective, government is not an end in itself but a means to provide for goods and services which are enjoyed in common by communities of individuals. Merely providing public goods and services without reference to citizen preferences makes no economic sense. Thus, the major question when diagnosing the performance of governments is how efficiently they provide citizens with the public goods and services that citizens prefer.

Different forms or structures of governmental organization create different incentives for public officials and public employees to "serve" the preferences of citizens or to ignore their preferences. The incentives created by different forms of organization will thus affect the efficiency with which producers of public goods and services respond to the preferences of citizens. This focus is different from that of the traditional reform movement—in which the focus is on strengthening the authority of knowledgeable, benevolent leaders to determine all subordinate interests.

The public choice approach, however, is often congruent with the analysis made by the advocates of community control who also recognize the diversity of citizen preferences for different public goods and services. The public choice approach is more inclusive than that of the community control approach since it provides criteria for determining which goods are most appropriately provided on a national or regional basis as well as which goods are best provided by relatively small political units.

When a good or service is used in common it is often possible to specify boundaries which encompass the community of people affected by the provision of that public good or service. A ground water basin, for example, may have quite precise boundaries, and the creation of a ground water replenishment district would need to take account of those who benefit from its use. An "air-shed" has less precise boundaries, but an air pollution control program would need to take account of the community of interests existing among polluters and users of the particular atmospheric conditions which might be thought of as an air-shed.

Some uses of roads, streets and highways, on the other hand, may be highly localized and the relevant community may be confined to a small enclave. Other streets may be principal thoroughfares that are used by a much larger community of people.

Still other highways may be used principally by interstate and national communities of users. If each different community is to be able to make optimal use of an interconnected system of neighborhood streets, urban thoroughfares and interstate highways, then different communities need to be organized. Their diverse preferences are taken into account only when the different communities participate in decisions about the uses which are of interest to them.[13]

We would expect the patterns of organization to influence the way that streets and highways are designed and used. In St. Louis, Missouri, for example, purely residential streets are sometimes organized as "private" streets where neighborhood associations assume responsibility for regulating their use and providing for their maintenance. Neighborhood interests are allowed to dominate, and those streets can be used by children on bicycles or rollerskates with minimal danger from automobiles. Without an appropriate organizational arrangement for neighbors to assume responsibility for neighborhood streets, every street is apt to become a thoroughfare dominated by automobile traffic as drivers seek out neighborhood streets to avoid other more congested thoroughfares. Without larger jurisdictions to provide major thoroughfares, however, local neighborhood associations would probably seek to avoid the problems of through traffic by diverting it elsewhere. Thus, both large and small jurisdictions of varying size seem to be necessary for the development, maintenance and use of a network of streets, thoroughfares and highways which serve diverse communities of interest.

Criteria for Evaluating Performance · The performance of governments, in the public choice approach, should be evaluated in terms of criteria which can be applied by citizens as well as officials. Criteria such as efficiency, responsiveness, and fairness or equity should apply to the performance of governments as well as to other activities.

The minimal condition for efficiency, for example, is that benefits exceed costs. The comparative efficiency of different organizations can be determined by which one provides the greatest

13. Robert Kanigel, "Improving City Streets to Death," *City,* vol. 6 (Winter 1972), pp. 45–47.

goods and services by governmental agencies is evaluated by surplus of benefits over costs. Because of measurement and budgetary problems in public sector activities, we may have to be content with determining which alternative provides a given level of service at least cost, or equivalently, which provides the best service for a given level of expenditure. Difficulties in finding appropriate measures of output usually require that proxy measures be used as indicators of output. A least-cost solution may then become a measure of producer efficiency in the absence of a measure of user or consumer satisfaction.

Difficulties in determining consumer satisfaction or demand in the absence of competitive pricing arrangements mean that responsiveness must also be taken into account in evaluating the performance of governmental agencies. Responsiveness can be defined as the capacity of a governmental organization to satisfy the preferences of citizens. The criterion of responsiveness is based upon the premise that individuals are the best judges of their own interests. Measures of responsiveness usually depend upon interviews conducted in a sample survey of a relevant population of citizens.

In the final analysis, benefits can be calculated only in relation to user preferences, and the criteria of efficiency and responsiveness are interdependent. The criteria of efficiency must include responsiveness as an essential component. However, the difficulty of measuring and evaluating public goods and services requires us to take account of both efficiency and responsiveness as separate but related criteria in evaluating the performance of public agencies.

The criterion of fairness or equity is difficult to formulate in a way that can be used to measure comparative performance. Still other criteria bearing upon organizational tendencies to amplify or correct errors might also be used. Our discussions will focus primarily upon efficiency and responsiveness as criteria for evaluating performance.

DEMAND

In the private sector, preferences are indicated when consumers shop around to purchase products from different suppliers.

Willingness to pay the price is an indication of consumer preference. Exchanges of this type seldom occur in the public sector. Instead, preferences for public goods and services are expressed through voting, lobbying, public opinion polls, petitions, public hearings, demonstrations, court proceedings, political party organizations and other indirect manners, including recourse to violence and civil disobedience when things are desperate. None of these institutional arrangements translate preferences into products in a perfectly responsive manner. What is more, incentive systems within such arrangements frequently lead citizens to "demand" public goods, not because they value the goods more than the cost of producing the goods but because taxing mechanisms disassociate costs from benefits and in some cases—perhaps many—put the costs on somebody else.

It is difficult, if not impossible, to identify "true" citizen preferences or demands for public goods. The incentives created by structures of institutional arrangements will affect the way that preferences are expressed in much the same way that light affects what we see. We can never see the "true" nature of reality. But we can become aware of how different spectacles and filters will affect our vision. We can also discover how different institutional mechanisms affect expressions of preferences.

Voting, either directly on issues or for representatives who in turn vote on issues, is one of the major ways in which demands for public goods and services are expressed.[14] Voting has several weaknesses as compared to market exchanges, however. A single vote usually has to serve as an expression of preference on many issues simultaneously, and it may not represent the voter's preferences on all the issues at hand. For example, a single vote for President entails "endorsement" of a candidate's positions on issues ranging from expansion of trade with China to the introduction of a negative income tax. Most often, however, a voter does not agree with a candidate on all issues, and thus, the vote he casts does not reflect all of his preferences.

14. Good analyses of voting problems are contained in James Buchanan, "Individual Choice in Voting and the Market," in *Fiscal Theory and Political Economy* (Chapel Hill: University of North Carolina Press, 1960), and in Anthony Downs, *An Economic Theory of Democracy* (New York: Harper and Row, 1958).

Even in single-issue voting, such as for school bonds, voters are limited to an all-or-nothing choice. No opportunity exists to select desired amounts. These problems of voting are sometimes referred to as the "all-or-nothing blue-plate menu problem," where à la carte purchasing is not permitted.

The problem of having only a single vote to express preferences on a wide variety of issues is diminished as governmental units become more numerous and specialized in their range of functions. Of course, the physical supply characteristics of many public goods may restrict the minimum size of an appropriate political unit. An air pollution control district, for example, with jurisdiction over an entire air-shed will be better able to provide the service of air pollution control. In addition, relations among some services may make it efficient to group them together—such as placing elementary and secondary education under the same school board. The specific organization of the public sector—which and what size political units are responsible for which public goods and services—can make considerable difference in a citizen's ability to voice his preferences accurately through the voting process.

Voting is not the only way in which citizens indicate their preferences to political officials. The opportunities to lobby, go to court, write letters or speak to officials, file petitions, testify at hearings or express feelings on individual issues in public opinion polls, all provide citizens with ways of expressing preferences more precisely on single issues. However, while preferences may be expressed more precisely, different citizens will have different opportunities for access. Further, given the costs of participation, citizens will not be motivated to indicate their preferences unless they feel that the benefits of such activity will exceed the costs.[15] Consequently, stronger incentives exist for citizens to express preferences for special programs of direct and measurable benefit to themselves than for policies which may provide small benefits to large numbers of citizens over a wide area.

15. Mark Sproule-Jones and Kenneth D. Hart, "A Public Choice Model of Political Participation," *Canadian Journal of Political Science*, vol. 6, 1973; and Mark Sproule-Jones, "Citizen Participation in a Canadian Municipality," *Public Choice*, vol. 16, 1974.

Citizen demands can be more precisely indicated in smaller rather than larger political units, and in political units undertaking fewer rather than more numerous public functions. This potential advantage must be compared with the costs of indicating preferences to many different political units. Citizens will be unlikely to find complete preference articulation easier with a single small unit for each public service. The optimal situation is more likely to be one in which each of several units performs multiple services.

Another factor which can affect the relative sensitivity or insentivity of a political system in responding to citizen preferences is the effect of size upon patterns of leadership recruitment and political entrepreneurship. The costs of becoming a candidate for public office with a reasonable probability of success are low in a small town where an individual is well-known by his neighbors and fellow townsmen. The cost of becoming a candidate for President of the United States is of radically larger proportions. Individuals in small jurisdictions may find it relatively easy to aspire to positions of local leadership.

So long as active political rivalry exists among competing organizations, professional politicians as political entrepreneurs will still be constrained by the necessity of appealing to a majority of the electorate. Citizen preferences will have a significant influence upon public policies. However, if any one entrepreneur becomes sufficiently dominant, he can use the police and other government organs to collect payoffs to finance the organization, and his men can coerce voters to turn out and vote for the organization slate. Such entrepreneurs can operate as political bosses, with "civic leaders" becoming their obedient servants.

Opportunities for political entrepreneurship will also be significantly affected by types of elections, forms of ballots and modes of representation as well as size of jurisdiction. However, the conditions favored by reformers proposing consolidation—short ballots and at-large elections—would appear to be those which are most conducive to the success of professional politicians seeking to pre-empt leadership recruitment through a permanent organization for slating candidates and canvassing voters. Advocates of consolidation do not necessarily object to such patterns of political organization, but are concerned that the organization winning control of the government be "responsible" to the electorate. How that might be done in the absence of benevolent organization men remains an unanswered problem.

Expression of demand in public organizations is plagued with persistent difficulties. Large organizations, in the sense that they encompass large populations and territory, can respond in relation to those problems which are uniformly experienced by everyone within their reach. The quality of the atmosphere and the conditions of major transportation networks, for example, have widespread and similar effects upon large numbers of people. Where neighborhood conditions and people's preferences vary substantially from one subarea to another, however, information about these variations is apt to be lost if people have recourse only to a single large unit of government. Both large and small units of government appear to be necessary if people are to be able to express their demands for different types of public goods and services.

SUPPLY

In addition to the expression of preference, supply and management considerations must be taken into account when analyzing the organization of public service agencies in metropolitan areas. As with preference articulation, the nature of public goods and services also creates difficulties on the supply side that are not encountered by a private firm producing a private good or service.[16]

First, it is very difficult to measure, let alone evaluate, most public services. For example, how does one effectively measure and value all the different outputs of a court system, a police system or an educational system? Not only are outputs difficult to measure and assign values but the same production inputs will result in different outputs depending on the characteristics of the area served. For example, sewers will require relatively more expenditures of resources to provide a given level of sani-

16. A good survey of supply problems is contained in Werner Hirsch, "The Supply of Urban Government Services," in Harvey S. Perloff and Lowden Wingo, Jr., eds., *Issues in Urban Economics* (Baltimore: The Johns Hopkins Press, 1968).

tation in hilly, low density areas, while fire services will require relatively more resources to provide a given level of protection in high density areas containing many adjacent multistory buildings. In addition, the same production process may provide different benefits and be valued differently by individuals with different opportunities to use the services provided. For example, we would expect students from Spanish-speaking homes to find it more difficult to benefit from the educational services provided in most schools than students from English-speaking homes.

Public services which are capital intensive in the sense that a large proportion of the cost involved is tied up in physical plant and public works are the most amenable to large-scale organization. Transportation facilities, water supply systems and sewerage works are examples of capital intensive services. These types of services usually emphasize physical effects, are more amenable to measurement and require proportionately smaller numbers of permanent employees in relation to the population served.

Many other public goods and services are highly labor intensive in their production. Payments to labor often account for 80 to 95 percent of the cost of a public service. The lack of physical output measurements in labor intensive services makes it extremely difficult to determine an employee's contribution to an organization's production, and the service nature of the public function makes the value of the output highly dependent on the quality of individual employee-citizen relationships. For example, patrolman-citizen relationships strongly affect citizen evaluation of police services and teacher-student relationships strongly affect citizen evaluation of educational services.

The administrator at the top of an organizational hierarchy simply has no easy check on the adequacy with which his subordinates discharge their public services in person-to-person relationships. He faces a real dilemma in how to direct his organization. The greater the uniformity of production processes, rules and quality of particular service activities, the easier it will be to monitor and control a large organization. However, the more uniform the output, the less likely that those citizens whose preferences and problems differ from the average will be satisfied with the service product. One must keep in mind that it is not the producers *as people* in public organizations that create the difficulty. The goods and services provided are not easily measurable and packageable. Thus public goods and services do not lend themselves to being produced by a firm that can rely heavily on measurements of sales compared with costs to determine efficiency.

The difficulty in measuring and evaluating the output of public service agencies leads to profound problems in organizing the public sector. Without an effective indicator of output it becomes difficult, if not impossible, to determine when the costs of production exceed the value of the service rendered. Top administrators depend upon management controls to direct the actions of employees who render a public service. However, there is no automatic way to determine when increased management costs associated with increases in organizational size exceed the benefit to be derived from adding extra employees.

These tendencies are exaggerated by the circumstance in which greater political prestige is associated with heading a large organization rather than a small organization. In addition, the greater number of steps in a career ladder for a large organization involve greater opportunities for advancement, and the most desirable positions in terms of high salaries and other perquisites are usually associated with management activities rather than service opportunities. Large expenditures for management create the most attractive career opportunities in most public organizations. All of these opportunities exist without reference to incentives for either improving the quality of public services or the net efficiency of public agencies. Public agencies with access to large fiscal resources have few if any incentives to economize.

The problems of measurement and evaluation of outputs necessary to determine production efficiency are not entirely unique to the public sector. For example, many of the service industries, such as advertising, interior decoration and law and medical practice, often face similar difficulties. However, in the private sector, failure to provide services comparable to those obtainable from competitors leads to a decline in business—and a very clear indication to the producer that something is wrong. Furthermore, if adaptability to meet competition is not achieved, inefficient producers are forced to accept less pay or move into some other area of economic activity. Competition among producers is much less present in the public sector.

In the economic analysis of private monopolies it is usually assumed that the monopoly firm will attempt to maximize profits although the quantity produced is less than would be produced by competitive firms. No simple assumption such as profit maximization is suitable for beginning an analysis of public agencies because the output is not generally priced and sold, and if it were, public officials probably would not be allowed to capture the profits for themselves.

A government is often conceived of as a natural monopoly which exercises exclusive control over the supply of a good or service in a given market area. A unit of government can occupy a monopoly position when that unit is the exclusive supplier of a good or service for local residents. Problems associated with monopoly organization have substantial implications for governmental performance.

Government organizations operating under monopoly conditions will have little incentive to innovate or reduce costs. Few employees will have an incentive to rock the boat because the costs of innovation will be relatively high in proportion to the benefit that the individual can derive. Most administrators and employees may prefer to settle into leisurely routines rather than fight the system in attempts to modify operations to meet citizen preferences. Small monopolies can be as lethargic as big monopolies. Needless to say, such behavior is not likely to lead to outputs efficiently produced to meet citizen preferences. The monopoly position of the public producer may protect him from individual citizens, even if he is inefficient and unresponsive in meeting their demands.[17]

Public monopolies pose even more difficult problems than private monopolies. With private monopolies we can assume that consumers will obtain net benefits from their purchases. Problems of unresponsive monopolistic behavior where outputs are not easily measured or evaluated and where political power can

17. Robert L. Bish and Robert Warren, "Scale and Monopoly Problems in Urban Government Services," *Urban Affairs Quarterly*, vol. 8 (September 1972), pp. 97–122.

be used by a public monopolist to collect taxes for maintaining his organization are potentially more serious than problems of private monopolistic behavior. Public monopolists without an appropriate structure of incentives can be even less responsive and less efficient than private monopolists.

The essential question regarding the organization of governments in metropolitan areas is this: Would we expect a fully integrated unit of government occupying a monopoly position over the production of all public goods and services to produce all goods and services equally well? On the basis of our analysis we have reason to believe that the answer is "no." We would not expect a fully integrated monopoly created by the consolidation of all public organizations in a metropolitan area to be equally effective in operating large-scale systems of physical works and in performing a variety of highly personalized public services in which person-to-person relationships critically affect the quality of service.

Instead we assume that the diverse nature of events in the world and the diverse preferences and life styles of people will make having recourse to multiple jurisdictions, both large and small, advantageous in the organization of urban governments. Rivalry and competition can alleviate some of the most adverse consequences of monopoly behavior in the public sector. If ample fragmentation of authority and overlapping jurisdictions exist, sufficient competition may be engendered to stimulate a more responsive and efficient public economy in metropolitan areas.

There are several ways that competition can constrain the monopolistic behavior of public officials. One is political competition, contests for elective office. If responsiveness and efficiency of the government drop below citizens' expectations, they can vote the incumbents out in the hope that their opponents will improve the government's outputs.

A second kind of competition can occur when people "vote with their feet." [18] If a citizen is dissatisfied with the benefits received from the local government where he resides he can sim-

18. The first explicit analysis of voting with one's feet to obtain preferred public goods is contained in Charles M. Tiebout, "A Pure Theory of Local Expenditures," *Journal of Political Economy*, vol. 64 (October 1956), pp. 416–424.

ply move to a governmental unit where the level and mix of services relative to the tax payments comes closer to meeting their preferences. Most metropolitan areas contain many different local government jurisdictions. Suburbanization in metropolitan areas may well reflect citizen dissatisfaction with the high costs and poor services rendered in central cities. If a person feels that good schools are important for his children and he cannot afford the tuition of private schools, the solution may be to move to a suburban school district where his family can secure the education he wants for it.

Still another kind of competition can occur when individuals seek out alternative producers of public goods without changing location. For example, firms, shopping centers and residents in wealthy neighborhoods often hire private police to patrol their areas when public police protection is considered inadequate. Private schools also offer an alternative to the public school system.

Competition can also occur among different public agencies if ample overlap exists. One unit of government may operate as a buyers' cooperative on behalf of local residents and firms rather than becoming a monopoly producer itself. In that case the local jurisdiction would have the power to tax and to use tax funds to arrange for some other agency to produce a public good or service. Such producers might be private enterprises as well as public agencies. So long as alternative producers are available, a local jurisdiction operating as a buyers' cooperative can press for the best deal. In such a situation producers will have incentives to improve the quality of services, increase efficiency and introduce viable innovations. The jurisdiction buying services might contract with a private vendor for street sweeping, with a public agency for police services and so on, thus using an array of different vendors to serve the community. Its chief administrative officer would operate as a purchasing agent demanding performance from vendors. Contracting for public goods provision permits smaller jurisdictions, which can best express the demands of local residents for varying mixes of public goods and services, to achieve efficient operation by purchasing their public goods from other agencies—private and public—which are the most efficient producers of those public goods and services.

PART THREE   The Economy of
the Central City

The Economy of the Central City:
An Appraisal

BENJAMIN CHINITZ

Benjamin Chinitz is on the faculty of the State University of New York at Binghamton, where he is Professor of Economics and Director of the Economic Growth Institute. Long active in urban economics, he is a past president of the Regional Science Association and served as Deputy Assistant Secretary for Economic Development in the U.S. Department of Commerce in the 1960s. Among his writings are City and Suburb: The Economics of Metropolitan Growth, *which he edited, and numerous articles drawing from his experiences in the now-classic studies of the New York and Pittsburgh metropolitan regions. This selection is from a book of essays in honor of Edgar M. Hoover, Professor Emeritus at the University of Pittsburgh, who, through his research on the economics of location, is one of the founding fathers of urban economics.*

INTRODUCTION

IT IS VIRTUALLY impossible to be original in describing the status of the central cities of our major metropolitan areas. The problems abound: congestion, pollution, slums, poverty, racial strife, crime, drug addiction, dirt, noise. People still argue about whether conditions are better or worse than they used to be and whether the people who now live in these cities are or are not better off than they used to be. This much is certain: not many are happy with conditions as they are.

What also seems to be beyond debate is that the fiscal condition of the local governments of these cities is as bad as or worse than it has ever been. The diagnosis is quite simple. The problems put pressure on the demand side· more money for welfare ██████ ███, █████ money for education; more money for police and fire protection, sanitation, and almost everything else on the list of locally provided goods and services.

Then there is the pressure for higher wages for city employees. That pressure stems, in part, from the general rise in earnings in the private sector of the economy, which makes it increasingly difficult to recruit people to the public sector at lower wages. But it also reflects the impact of the unionization of public employees and explicit pressure, via strikes and other devices, to increase wages and improve working conditions even for those who may not have the option of moving over to the private sector.

Finally, there is the faltering private sector of the central city that provides a weak base for local taxation. The big city mayors—Republican and Democrat and Independent—are all pleading for greater financial aid from their respective states but mainly from the federal government. Federal money and state money, one might suppose, are to be preferred over local money in all circumstances. But whether or not that is true, there can be no doubt that the urgency in the current plea for outside support reflects greater reluctance than ever to impose higher taxes on local business and households.

Such reluctance, in turn, can be attributed in part to the political consequences of proposing higher local taxes. Voters persist in an illusion which can be fatal to the incumbent, namely, that while the "old" man wants new taxes, the "new" man is likely to get by with the old taxes. But even a daring mayor has to contend with the competitive aspects of local taxation. Households and businesses can move to nearby suburbs where taxes are more favorable. Some people and some enterprises might even be induced to move to more distant areas.

This constraint, which was always there to some extent, is now deemed to be much more binding because it is assumed that the central city, taxes aside, is increasingly vulnerable to competition for the location of people and jobs. Nobody really knows with any precision how that competition is affected by increased local tax burdens. But when the city's hold on industry and people is assumed to be weakening, increased taxes are not likely to help matters.

In this paper, I will focus on the central city as a location for private sector activities. I want first to examine the assets and liabilities of the city as a location, much as we viewed them in the early days of urban economics, before the current sense of crisis set in. I then want to show how these assets and liabilities interact with exogenous forces to shape the changing competitive position and the growth of the city's economy. Third, I want to suggest that municipal policies can affect the local economy's competitive posture and that taxation is only one of many issues in this regard. Finally, I want to speculate about the future of the city as a place of employment.

THE CENTRAL CITY: A BALANCE SHEET

There is a vast literature on the subject of the city as a location for industry. But in the heat of the current preoccupation with the urban crisis, many of the simple points have been submerged if not forgotten.

By *assets*, I mean those characteristics of a city location that increase productivity and reduce costs. By *liabilities* I mean the converse: those characteristics of a city location that reduce productivity and increase costs. The latter are more readily identified and articulated; the former are more subtle and require greater elucidation. Let me take the easy side first.

The city's liabilities should perhaps more appropriately be termed "constraints" rather than liabilities. These are *rents* and *congestion.* The competition for space increases rents and acts as a deterrent to the location of some activities which might otherwise prefer to be located in the city. Outside the city, we assume the supply of land to be much more elastic.

The density of activity creates congestion. In simple terms, it takes more driver time and more gasoline to traverse a given distance. The same density that gives you congestion may also yield a lower cost per unit of business transacted, despite the higher operating costs but that's on the other side of the equation. Congestion gets translated into higher rents for space by increasing construction costs. Lately, particularly in New York, congestion

has assumed other dimensions: deterioration in telephone service
and power cutbacks on very hot days. Some of these manifesta-
tions of congestion are also experienced in the suburbs.

Rents and congestion are inherent in the logic of central city
growth. Their precise levels are of course not inherently determined. Elevators make a difference; size of cars makes a difference; relative use of private and public transport makes a
difference; street layout and building design make a difference.
We shall deal with some of these as "exogenous" influences in the
next section. But planning and clever design can only temper the
inelasticity of supply of space for activity and mobility; they cannot render supply completely elastic.

Do we capture all of the liabilities under the twin concepts of
rent and congestion? How about higher wages and higher taxes?
How about crime and insurance rates? On wages the evidence is
mixed. On taxes, congestion is again the root problem to the extent that public services are in greater demand and harder to
provide in conditions of high density. But the welfare burden
and such problems as crime insofar as they affect the cost of doing business directly or indirectly via taxation, would be hard to
subsume under the heading of congestion. These are more appropriately dealt with in the next section as "exogenous" developments.

The asset side is more complex. Face-to-face contact with a
wide variety of related individuals and activities is often defined
as the root or fundamental advantage of a city location. This is
the other side of the congestion coin. You can't walk too fast,
traffic is bumper-to-bumper, telephone service is unstable, restaurants are crowded; but you can achieve a great variety of
contacts in a day because of the sheer number and diversity of
people and activities concentrated in such a small area. What it
boils down to is that the unit cost of information is cheaper.

But the facilitation of face-to-face contact is only one of the assets of high density, and high density does not exhaust the asset
side of the balance sheet. More basically, the city derives its
strength from Adam Smith's famous dictum about specialization
and the extent of the market. Density permits a much higher
order of specialization because proximity of specialists, one to
the other, keeps down the costs of trade for a given scale of op-

eration. Thus each unit can concentrate on doing one thing very efficiently and on drawing its auxiliary needs at low cost from neighboring units. In short: the city is a mechanism for enlarging the market by containing transportation and communication costs, thus permitting a greater degree of specialization and hence higher productivity. Face-to-face communication and short-haul goods movements are the visual by-products of the process.

Another way to view the favorable impact of high density is in terms of capital saving. An enterprise in isolation must substitute capital for what might be current expenses for an enterprise in the city. It might take the form of higher inventories, more workers on the payroll, a computer, cars and trucks—all of which are designed to shield the firm against its isolation. In the city, the firm can augment its supplies on short notice and can purchase transport services, computing services, and the like from other firms which—to get us back where we were before—can afford to specialize in these services because there is a large market at close call.

All these considerations relate to concentration *per se*. They would be relevant if the city were lifted up bodily and put down in the middle of a desert. They might even apply with equal force if part of the city were lifted up and relocated. This is why the thought of relocating the whole garment center out of New York City, for example, is so tempting to some city planners. To the extent that the most vital interfirm linkages are contained within a given industrial complex, the dream has a certain appeal.

But there are at least two other forces making for concentration in the center that do not derive their fundamental logic from the economies of concentration *per se*. One has to do with the natural attributes of the areas where most cities are located, principally, their access to water. The other has to do with the "centrality" of the city in relation to the metropolitan area. These advantages motivate firms to seek city locations to minimize transport costs on freight and to maximize access, on average, to the region's labor supply. Each firm independently seeks a central location, and concentration is the *result*. By contrast, the gains which accrue from specialization, easy face-to-face contact, saving of capital, result *from* concentration. When you put the two sets of forces together in some kind of historical dynamic model, you have the essentials of the well-known concept of agglomeration.

Before we move on to consider those exogenous forces which erode the city's assets or aggravate its liabilities (and vice versa), a few further comments on the balance sheet may be helpful. First, the relevance of and the weights attached to each asset and liability will vary according to the needs and the objectives of the prospective locator. That's why we observe at any point in history that the city is relatively more attractive to some activities than to others.

Second, the flavor of my comments suggest a preoccupation with the Central Business District (CBD) of the central city rather than the whole central city. This is a correct inference, but it should not be overdrawn. Obviously, the asset-liability balance will come out differently for the same firm at a given point in time, for different locations in the city. But we want to keep the whole city in view, at least through the next section.

Finally, we should distinguish between *micro* dynamics and *macro* dynamics. The same firm over its own lifetime, even when the parameters of the larger system are constant, will strike a different balance for the city as a location because of its *own* changing needs and requirements. Furthermore, the city itself, as it grows and ages, even if the exogenous forces are unchanging—technology, tastes, etc.—will go through a revision of its balance sheet from the perspective of a given firm with fixed requirements.

In other words, there are a lot of dynamics—internal to the firm and internal to the city—that would prevent the city from taking on a very static image even if nothing were happening "outside" to shake things up. But in the sections that follow, we want to focus on the external dynamics.

Dynamics I: The Changing Industrial Mix · It is an elementary proposition in regional analysis that the relative growth of different areas will inevitably be affected by the changing industrial composition of the national economy. It is equally well established that the industrial composition of a nation's economy is roughly related to the state of development. At first, agriculture and other resource-oriented activities predominate. As productivity in these activities increases, labor is released for industrialization, and the manufacturing sector grows very rapidly as a share of the total. Finally, at very high levels of income, the service sectors—government, trade, finance and the like—move into first place. Currently in the United States, these service sectors account for 64 per cent of total employment, manufacturing [1] 31 per cent and extractive industries 5 per cent.

This transformation of the national economy, it is generally agreed, is responsible for, or at least is highly correlated with the relative decline of rural areas and the rapid growth of cities and metropolitan areas. Progress and urbanization go hand in hand. What is not so obvious is how these industrial trends have affected *intra*metropolitan patterns and the competition between city and suburb. The fact is that the city has been favored by these trends because precisely those sectors for which the city has a stronger attraction have grown most rapidly in the national economy. While the city continues to yield ground to the suburbs in almost all sectors, the overall performance of the city is sustained by the favorable industrial composition of national economic growth.

The impact of these trends is manifested in the very dramatic growth of "office" employment in the nation as a whole, and particularly in cities. By office employment, we mean employment that occurs in detached buildings that are entirely devoted to paper work. Office employment cuts across all sectors as traditionally defined, but as one might expect, it is far more important in the service sector than in the manufacturing sector. Corporate headquarters in the manufacturing sector do give the "office" component considerable status even in that sector. According to the only study of the office sector done so far, "jobs in detached office buildings account for about one-quarter of all white-collar jobs in the nation (or 12 per cent of total employment) and 40 per cent in the New York Region. These proportions have been rising in recent years, both here and abroad."

In the simplest terms therefore the central city, which always boasts a larger share of the metropolitan area's offices than of its

---

1. Manufacturing in this context includes Construction which, in a more detailed classification, is treated as a separate category.

factories, while losing ground in each, is benefiting from the fact
that the national trend favors offices over factories.

If nothing else had happened, central cities would have been
expected to grow even faster in response to *Dynamics I* than they
had before. So now, we must turn to the factors that have adversely affected the city in its competition with the suburbs.

Dynamics II: Transport Technology and Transport Policy • Economic theory suggests that reductions in transport costs extend
market areas and expand the opportunities for specialization and
trade. From this point of view, the city would be expected to
gain from the transport revolution of the twentieth century. In
some respects it has, but one would be hard put to argue that the
city has not lost out, on balance.

The gain occurs if, and only if, the city retains its advantage as
a production site; all that happens is that it can now serve a wider
market. For example, if the Metropolitan Opera remains in New
York City, as it apparently must, then New York City stands to
gain from the fact that more people can now reach the opera for
a given amount of travel time and cost than before automobiles
and highways were available. Similarly, if the Port of New York
retains its hold on international traffic, then the fact that a trailer-
truck can bring freight in from two hundred miles a lot faster
and cheaper expands the market area served by the Port.

Unfortunately for the city, however, the automobile and the
truck and even the airplane do more than simply reduce the cost
of transport relative to other things, which would favor greater
concentration. As alternatives to traditional modes—rail and
water—they alter the balance of advantages and disadvantages
at different locations and therefore undermine the very motive
for concentration at particular points, e.g., the central city, for
particular activities. The central city cannot accommodate highway and air facilities too well. The substitution of these new
modes for the old modes, therefore, favors other locations in the
metropolis as logical points at which to concentrate activities that
make heavy use of these new modes.

The substitution of automobiles for public transit further un-
dermines the special advantage of the center for labor supply.
True, the automobile makes it possible for the worker to com-

mute longer distances. The employer who sticks to the center for other reasons will benefit from the extension of the radius of the labor market. But now a large labor force can be conveniently assembled at almost any point served by the highway network; and the center is hardly the best place to assemble an auto-oriented work force.

The auto and the truck also modify the basic spatial character of specialization and concentration. Assume an employer who calculates that he must retain a presence in the center despite its liabilities—old and new. Under the old technology, that decision would entail a much greater commitment to the center than it does now because with improved mobility, there is greater opportunity to "fine-tune" one's commitment to the center. The front-office, the showroom, and those related activities that call for face-to-face contact can be located in the center while production and distribution activities can be located further out where space is cheaper, access to transport service is better, and access to labor as good or better. This spatial separation is facilitated by the new transport technology. In the extreme case, the production can go to Japan, to be linked to the home base by air freight.

Thus, every asset of the city is challenged by new transport technology, and some of its liabilities are aggravated. The substitution of automobile travel for mass transit to and from the center and within the center increases the desired space per capita, and in a very real sense, diminishes the overall capacity of the center to accommodate people and jobs. More space is taken up for parking. The greater speed and maneuverability of the truck compared to the horse-and-wagon by itself represents an improvement. But the potential gain from that source is frustrated by the high cost of rearranging the already developed center to accommodate the new vehicle. A city that is built with the new technology in mind can better compete with its suburbs.

On the whole, public policy has supported the thrust of the new technology. Nobody can tell us with certainty what would have happened if transport investments were entirely managed by the private sector and if the prices of all transport services reflected marginal social costs. The fact is that the public sector was relatively quick to supply the complementary capital investments in roads and terminals for the new modes and relatively slow in responding to the agonies of decline in the old modes. Since the center city had more to gain from the preservation of the old, it certainly was not favored by the dominant thrust of public policy.

Nevertheless, there is one aspect of *Dynamics II*, as suggested earlier, that has worked in the city's favor. *Dynamics I* has enlarged the national basket of activities, as symbolized by the growth of the office sector, in which the city retains a strong comparative advantage. The potential for the continued concentration of such activities in the center is enlarged by the revolution in air transport, which makes it easier for an activity of this type to serve an ever-wider market. In this respect, the classic theorem about the impact of transport costs on specialization and trade applies.

When you add it all up, you have to conclude that the center has been adversely affected competitively by technological progress in transport and the public policies which have embodied that progress in physical investments. The impact, however, is not only to hold back the city's growth but also to refine the character of the city's economy forcing it to specialize increasingly in those activities that gain most from the city's assets and suffer least from its liabilities.

Dynamics III: Technological Progress in Other Sectors • There are at least three other kinds of technological progress that have important implications for the competition between city and suburb. We will refer to them as *Dynamics III (A), III (B)*, and *III (C)*.

Dynamics III (A) is technological change in goods handling in plants and warehouses other than those occasioned by *Dynamics II*. The key here is the use of electric power, in combination with engineering design, to favor horizontal as against vertical layouts in such facilities. As a result, the twin pressures of high rents and congestion in the city act even more forcefully to favor outlying areas for the location of production and distribution facilities.

Dynamics III (B) is technological progress in communication and data processing, as symbolized by TV and the computer, which are well established but continuously evolving new forms and remote access. At first, these new gimmicks favor the center because their limited availability and high unit costs compel sharing of a kind that is more readily achieved in a dense market. But as unit costs go down and remote access is achieved, they tend on balance to reduce the disabilities of remote locations and alleviate the pressure to be in the center. They also contribute to the potential, as with *Dynamics II*, of achieving a finer spatial specialization by permitting the top decision-makers in the center to be in close contact with the information and other paper processing activities that can then be located at lower cost in outlying areas.

Many have speculated that further progress in communication will ultimately undermine entirely the "face-to-face" aspect of concentration which favors the center of the city. Even if that were true, it would not necessarily lead to the demise of the center, in terms of our balance sheet above. "Face-to-face" is the reflection of a complex pattern of specialization, the logic of which, rests essentially on a large dense market. Easy communication removes one motive for employers to want to be located in close proximity to each other. But they can substitute close-circuit TV for lunch at the club and retain their location in the center if there are other good reasons for doing so.

Dynamics III (*C*) takes us farther away from our subject but its relevance is soon obvious. I have in mind the technological revolution in agriculture which was alluded to above under *Dynamics I*. There we stressed the shifting industrial mix of the economy and the implications of such shifts for the city center, from the perspective of growth in employment. Here I want to stress the population migration effects.

Historically, the city, especially in the Northeast, was favored in its growth by a very elastic supply of labor. Hordes of immigrants came to these cities from abroad and from America's rural areas because they, like their contemporary counterparts, found the center city a more congenial atmosphere for launching their assimilation into the modern American economy. The happy coincidence of demand and supply worked in everybody's favor.

In recent decades, two factors have operated to create a very serious divergence of interests. On the demand side, the city's economy generates fewer opportunities for the uneducated, untrained, immigrant worker. On the supply side, these workers continue to favor the city voluntarily for the traditional reasons, or involuntarily because of suburban discrimination against racial minorities and poor whites. The city would prefer to make more living space available for workers who are in demand at the center. The immigrants frustrate this objective, in part by competing for scarce space, in part by adding to the tax burden because of their public service requirements, and in part by making the center generally less attractive to the middle- and upper-income groups. Obviously the movement of these groups to the suburbs has been motivated by "pull" factors as well, but the "push" factors cannot be denied.

Dynamics IV: Capital Accumulation and Higher Incomes • The city, as we said, is a capital-saving device. It is a device for sharing the costs of indivisible units of capital, thus reducing the unit cost per capita or per unit of output. In part, this saving is achieved at the expense of higher operating costs arising from congestion.

Dynamics I, II, and III all relate to various facets of progress. But if you can imagine achieving economic progress through capital accumulation alone, a process certainly theoretically possible, you would already have identified a reason for the relative decline of central cities. As wages rise relative to interest rates, there is increasingly less incentive to economize on labor. You go outward, where you can reduce operating costs, even if you have to incur higher capital costs in the process.

The same logic applies to the resident as to the employer. Living in relative isolation calls for a greater commitment of capital. You have to own your own home, provide for your own mobility and for a host of other services, available on a current account basis, albeit at higher prices, in the congested center. As your assets and borrowing power improve, you have less incentive to conserve capital and can give vent to your desire for easy, spacious living.

Thus, even with the state-of-the-art held constant, capital accumulation and rising incomes render the savings arising from density less relevant and the advantages of sparsely settled territory more relevant for both producers and consumers.

THE ROLE OF MUNICIPAL POLICY

In the previous section, we view the changing location of jobs and people as reflecting inexorable forces in the economy and society at large. Rural to urban migration is mainly attributed to the decline of job opportunities in agriculture and other resource-oriented industries and the concomitant growth of employment in service industries, which are city-oriented in their location. Technological change in transport—people and goods—accompanied by higher incomes are held to be responsible for the far more rapid rate of growth of the suburbs as compared to the central cities.

Typically, when we think of public policy as an influence on geographic patterns of development, we are more likely to consider aspects of federal government policy than local policy. We credit the Federal Interstate Highway Program and the Federal Housing Program with having accelerated the impact of the automobile on metropolitan growth patterns. We think of the geographic distribution of federal contracts as having significant effects on the distribution of economic activity and population. By contrast, we generally think of local policy as being restricted to a passive role. "How do we adjust to what is happening to us?" is the perspective we have on local policy.

In recent years, there has been a growing presumption that local policy can assume an active role in determining what happens, at least as far as employment is concerned. Local governments have increasingly adopted the view that they can influence the demand for labor in their jurisdictions by adopting and implementing policies that improve their competitive position. Some communities have offered subsidies in one form or another to prospective employers; other have attempted to ease local tax burdens. These measures directly affect the operating costs of the firm. Other measures operate indirectly by enhancing potential productivity. These include improved public services, better transport, and friendlier bankers.

Communities have, of course, also used local policy to discourage the location of certain industries inside their boundaries. The main instrument is zoning, which establishes the legal basis for saying "NO" to a prospective employer. Such communities also have the power to influence the composition of population within their borders. They do so not by inducing changes in the demand for labor but by defining the terms under which people can locate their residences within their borders.

Whether or not localities pursue explicit policies to influence employment and population inside their borders, programs and policies designed to serve other objectives are bound to have such side effects. Taxes are the prime example. The aggregate tax burden and the way that burden is distributed within the community both affect job and residential location even if they are largely decided on other grounds. But other policies are also relevant in this regard.

New York City, for example, is undergoing considerable change in the pattern of job and population growth. In the main, these changes reflect the workings of forces far beyond the control of city government. On the demand for labor side, the impact of these changes has been to retard the overall growth of jobs in the city but mainly to reduce absolutely the number of low-skill jobs. On the supply side, the reverse has occurred. On balance, the city as a place to live is increasingly less attractive to high-skill, high-income employees while low-skill, low-income populations are increasingly attracted there.

Insofar as city policy has been at all addressed explicitly to this problem, the focus has been on the supply side. Very simply, the city has attempted to arrest the decline of blue-collar low-wage employment by assisting employers who might otherwise leave the city to find suitable space for their operations. Although one cannot estimate with certainty the importance of space as a factor in relocation of production facilities, it is reasonable to assume that, in many instances, the proximate if not the ultimate factor motivating relocation is the lack of an adequate site at an acceptable price. Sometimes, the difficulty arises from plant expansion; at other times, from displacement caused by renewal or private pre-emption for higher value uses. In any case, it is felt that intervention by the city can augment the supply of space to those producers who would otherwise find it in their own best interests to locate outside the city.

The merits of this particular policy instrument will not be appraised here. Suffice it to say that it appears to have been of limited impact in dealing with the fundamental supply-demand imbalance. Moreover, there are other city policies motivated by noneconomic objectives of the city that have tended to exacerbate, not resolve the basic labor market imbalance. In this paper I will focus on two such policies which have received detailed treatment in research: housing and welfare.

The essential dilemma of the government has been clear for some years. To finance a very large and growing welfare burden along with conventional city services whose costs keep rising rapidly, it has had to extract revenue from a productive sector that is growing very slowly and is increasingly sensitive to comparative cost pressures. The dilemma seems difficult enough to resolve by itself; yet it is further aggravated by city policy. In other words, the city is actually making worse an already bad situation.

Let me suggest two criteria for judging such policies. The first is short run and static: it says that you should pursue those policies that do the least damage to your productive capacity while yielding the maximum effectiveness in combating poverty. The second criterion is longer run and dynamic: it says that you should prefer those policies which contribute to the automatic or natural resolution of the problem over policies which perpetuate or even exacerbate the problem. Generally, although not always, the two criteria reinforce each other to create a strong preference for one set of policies over another.

As applied to the case in hand, these criteria would argue for bringing relief to the needy in ways that do least damage to the local economy and provide maximum incentive to escape from poverty through gainful employment. A federally financed family-assistance plan which does not tax earnings at 100 per cent is readily seen as passing these criteria with the highest possible scores. In the absence of such an ideal resolution of the city's dilemma, it is unfortunately hard to argue that the second-best alternative is being pursued.

The sad fact is that the city is transferring *assets* to the poor, rather than just *income*. It is doing so by creating artificial incentives for the poor to occupy space that is either directly or indirectly in great demand for productive use. The full force of city policy can be made clear by imagining that the Pan-American Building were to be condemned by the city so it could be made available as housing for the poor. Nothing like this has happened to my knowledge; yet this is the logical limit of current city policy.

Which aspects of city policy give rise to this interpretation? First, there is the welfare practice of treating housings costs as an extra. Within reason, a household on welfare can compete for housing with no budget constraint; the city will simply pay whatever bill is incurred. Thus, space, which in its current condition or more likely through clearance or renovation would be attractive to firms or their employees wishing to locate in the city, is likely to be retained in the "poverty" market. Instead of deriving maximum value from the property and taxing that value to subsidize poor people to live elsewhere where the alternative uses are not so productive, the city, in effect, transfers assets to the poor, which they are not able to use anywhere nearly as productively. The net social loss is large and unambiguous.

The policy not only fails on the first criterion but its failure on the second is equally apparent. Paradoxically, the space which is most valuable to the potential producer, e.g., in Manhattan, is least relevant to the welfare recipient in terms of ultimately providing him with job opportunity and wages to displace welfare benefits. If the welfare recipient could be induced to seek cheaper space elsewhere, thus preserving a vital productive asset, he could, at the same time, increase the probability of locating closer to the relevant potential employer who is compelled by the nature of his business also to seek out cheaper space.

Again, to bring the point home, let us imagine the (politically) impossible: the city of New York derives revenue from its own industry to subsidize the co-location of low-skill jobs and workers in open tracts in the suburbs. But failing this, can we justify the indiscriminate use of space within the city for antipoverty purposes?

The illogic of this policy is reinforced by the city's housing policy, specifically, rent control. To begin with, rent control is a very inefficient antipoverty policy for the simple reason that 45 per cent of the occupants of rent-controlled housing are not poor. Viewed as a tax on the rich landlord, rent control is deficient in the sense that landlords can escape the tax through disinvestment. But what is most relevant to the issue at hand is the effect that rent control has on relative prices. Rent control confers a far greater bargain on the occupant in Manhattan than it does in other boroughs of the city. Median rents for controlled housing hardly vary from borough to borough ($21.80–$26.90 per room per month) whereas median rents for uncontrolled housing vary substantially ($30.00–over $50.00 per room per month), suggesting that rent control conceals the relative opportunity cost of space within the city.

The very high figure for Manhattan attests to the ongoing validity of a Manhattan location in the private sector despite all the heralded pressures to suburbanize. There is every reason to suspect that the city could enjoy greater private output and greater public welfare if its scarce resources—mainly space—were more strategically employed. At the same time, the resolution of the labor market imbalance might better be served in the long run by such policies.

NET IMPACT AND FUTURE PROSPECTS

Despite the widespread interest in the economic welfare of the central city, there are no standard data sources that permit easy calculation of comparative rates of growth of employment except for manufacturing, wholesale, retail, and a category called "Selected Services" in the U.S. Census. These four categories account for only slightly more than half of total employment. More comprehensive measures have been developed for a limited number of areas for selected time periods by painstaking research.

Both the standard sources and the special studies show a very mixed picture as between areas and as between time periods if we look only at the absolute growth of employment in the central city. When, however, we compare the central city to the rest of the metropolitan area and control for industrial mix,[2] the trend to

2. That is, we take into account the industrial structure of the city's economy and control for the influence of overall national rates of growth by industry.

the suburbs is rather persistent and pervasive. There are also some interesting surprises. For example, in a study of twelve metro areas over the period 1953–1965, Wilfred Lewis, Jr. found that New York City, which grew very slowly, experienced less suburban competition than places like Atlanta, Denver, and Washington, D.C., which grew much more rapidly in absolute terms.

The pattern of national growth was found to be favorable to the growth of central city employment in every case but one, as suggested above in *Dynamics I*. Also, while the suburbs grew faster than the central cities in all industrial categories, the suburban drift was more pronounced in manufacturing and retail trade than in the service sectors, as suggested in *Dynamics II*. When the national economy is growing rapidly, the favorable effect of national growth tends to outweigh the unfavorable impact of competition from the suburbs.

What will happen to employment in the central city in future decades? *Dynamics I* should continue to operate with considerable force in favor of the central city. The triple trend to white collar, service, and office employment shows no signs of abatement. *Dynamics II* offers considerable ground for speculation. Although the automobile is still chipping away at mass transit patronage and finances in many cities, there are significant counterdevelopments. New transit systems are being built, and there is some hope that rail-commuter travel will be put on a more solid basis by federal action. The revolution in differential access wrought by the automobile is irreversible, but we don't see in the cards another revolution with similar effects, and small incremental measures in favor of the city are definitely possible.

Dynamics III (A) is the great imponderable. We need more research on the extent to which sophisticated communication devices do, in fact, substitute for face-to-face contact before we can make any assessment of the locational implications of *Dynamics III (A)*. The relevance of *Dynamics III (B)* will wane as goods handling activities continue to shrink as a share of the total economy. The rural-to-urban shift that underlies *Dynamics III (C)*, the 1970 Census already tells us, is less of a factor in shaping the demographic characteristic of metropolitan areas. As for *Dynamics IV*, I see no reason why it should not continue to work in favor of lower densities.

What all this adds up to is that the city will most likely continue to lose competitively to the suburbs, but the aggregate demand for labor in the city will be sustained by overall national growth and the favorable "mix" aspects of that growth. To the extent that we continue to rely on local revenues to finance city needs, extreme caution is called for to protect the goose that lays the golden egg.

Comments on National Growth

JAY W. FORRESTER

Jay Forrester is Germeshausen Professor in the Sloan School of Management of the Massachusetts Institute of Technology. Renowned for his earlier work in electronics engineering, he has, in recent years, turned his talents to the development and application of computer simulation models which focus on fundamental issues of social policy. In Urban Dynamics, *his initial venture in the urban field (and in later efforts such as* World Dynamics), *Forrester has repeatedly cautioned against the effects of unbridled growth on human welfare. This essay, a nontechnical exposition of the public policy implications of* Urban Dynamics, *is adapted from an address that Forrester delivered to the American Public Works Association in 1972.*

FOR MORE THAN a hundred years, the improvement of technology has been the route to improvement in urban living. Public confidence in technology is deeply ingrained. When there is a problem, the country begins by seeking a technical solution. The reasons are twofold. First, technical approaches in the past seem to have succeeded. Second, technical programs are usually easier to visualize organize, and execute than are changes and improvements in the psychological, social, economic, and ethical aspects of our existence.

But the faith in technology is being clouded by doubt. Technology has been improving while at the same time social conditions have been worsening. Many people are beginning to wonder if there may not be a connection between the two. It is possible that the time is past when better technology automatically means better living?

The evidence of faltering confidence in technology is everywhere. People are objecting to more highways because our roads and turnpikes have not reduced the total time spent in travel. Sewer extensions are being questioned because they imply more houses marching across the remaining open area. Urban transit systems are being questioned because they go hand in hand with economic segregation of the population and the decline of the central city. Taxes are rising, but the technology purchased by taxes seems to be losing the battle.

Is it possible that our social system has changed since the days when improved technology did lead to improved living? Can a social system undergo changes in its apparent character so that yesterday's *solutions* to problems become the *causes* of tomorrow's problems? I suggest that indeed such changes in the behavior of our social system are possible, and that they are occurring.

A social system can change its behavior when the restraints under which it operates become different. In the past, the production of material goods was determined by and limited by the availability of capital and labor. To say that production is determined by capital and labor, implies that it is not determined by or limited by anything else. Our traditions and rules of thumb have been developed in a period when the inputs to production from nature were, for all practical purposes, unlimited. There was no significant shortage of agricultural land, water, natural resources, energy, or pollution dissipation capacity. But times have changed. In every direction production is now being limited by the maximum capacity of the natural environment. When the constraints shift from human effort, in the form of labor and the creation of capital, to a different set of limits, the entire character of the social system can seem to change. Our economic system is undergoing such a transition. Under the new conditions, remedies that worked in the past are apt to be disappointing.

The change to a new kind of behavior in our socioeconomic system is a consequence of population and economic growth. In the past, when land and natural endowments were unlimited compared to our needs, no pressures were reflected back from nature as a result of exponential growth. But as the natural limits are approached, reflected pressures develop ever more strongly. More and more effort is used in overcoming the limitations rather than, as earlier, producing effective human benefit. For a while, by expending enough energy and physical effort and capital, the barriers set up by nature can be pushed back.

But if we follow the route of fighting nature's limits we will exhaust ourselves. The limits can be pushed some, at ever increasing cost, but they cannot be eliminated.

The underlying cause of today's social pressures is growth. The changing attitude toward economic growth shows how completely our world is changing. Until ten years ago, everyone promoted growth. Boosterism was the central theme. States had development commissions to promote industry and to attract population. Towns and cities had chambers of commerce to promote growth. But times have changed.

In the present transition period the prevalent attitude is to accept growth with resignation as a burden to be borne. But that resignation is giving way to opposition. More and more there is active resistance to growth. Oregon, Vermont, Colorado, California, Florida, and Delaware have, in various ways, taken steps to limit the expansion of population and industry.

Not only is the national attitude faltering toward growth as the solution to social problems, but the country is also unclear on where to expect leadership in setting new social directions. Is the leadership for facing the fundamental issues of society to come from the national government or from local leadership? Can the national government set new directions, or is it limited to attempting minor improvements on the old patterns?

The Federal policy at the moment is, in effect, to attempt to relieve the pressures that result from growth while at the same time attempting to accelerate that growth. This is not said as a criticism of the national administration.

Our national political system does not permit a national administration to exercise effective leadership in new directions that break sharply with past traditions. Until new trends in thought are well established and widely recognized, there is no constituency to support a national government in a major reversal of past social beliefs. Leadership in small things can come from the national government. Leadership in big things must start with individuals and local governments.

The United States is now in one of those major periods of reorientation that occasionally face a society. Probably not since the founding of the country and the writing of the national Constitution has so much been at stake and so much unfettered and innovative thinking been necessary. The clichés, the folklore, and the Horatio Alger stories of the past must be shaken off as we face the fact that further growth, far from solving problems, is the primary generator of our growing social distress. But there is reason for hope and confidence.

The issues are being faced squarely by many individuals, groups, and even to some extent by cities and states. Many are beginning to see that the rising social and natural pressures will make it impossible to maintain the present quality of life if population and industrialization continue to grow. Instead of running ahead of the growth wave, it is becoming clear to many that ways must be found of facing the issue and controlling the expansionary forces that are coming to dominate society. The implications are staggering. The ramifications will extend into corporate and governmental organization, into the legal structure, and into values, goals, and ethical beliefs.

The detrimental consequences of continued growth are appearing not only as environmental damage. In fact, environmental damage from growth is probably one of the lesser threats to society. The greater threats may be psychological as frustration rises, as the individual perceives himself as powerless to affect his future, and as discord increases. Growth is bringing pressure on every facet of existence.

Imbedded in our folklore is a belief that larger size leads to greater economic efficiency. Up to a point, that probably has been true. But now in cities, even medium-sized ones, the economies of scale no longer favor additional growth. The cost per capita for the operation of a city rises steeply as the total population and the population density increases. At some point, and the largest cities have arrived at that point, the rising costs pull down the vitality of the entire socioeconomic process until further growth is impossible.

When costs from growth rise faster than benefits, we find ourselves in the position where "the faster we run, the behinder we get." Many people are beginning to recognize the futility of solving problems by further growth but, strangely enough, there is as yet little attention to the possibility of "catching up by stopping." If we could slow the growth of population and population density in a city while adopting policies to generate continual renewal and revitalization, it would be much easier to increase the standard of living and the quality of life. But under the existing circumstances, improving the services of a city leads, not to improvement in quality of life, but instead, to larger size with the additional services being swallowed up by more people who demand more of the municipal administration.

Why can public services not get ahead of demands? Why do the best of intentions for improving a city lead, instead, to greater social pressures, more commuting delays, increased drug addiction, higher crime rates, and greater welfare loads? The answer lies in what we have come to call the "attractiveness principle."

The "attractiveness principle" states that, to any particular population class, all geographical areas tend to become equally attractive. Or perhaps more realistically stated, all areas tend to become equally unattractive. Why do all areas tend toward equal attractiveness? It is because people move from unattractive areas to areas of greater attractiveness. I use "attractiveness" to encompass every aspect of a city that contributes to its desirability or undesirability. Population movement is an equalizing process. As people move toward a more attractive area, they drive up prices and overload the job opportunities, the environmental capacity, the available housing, and the governmental services. In other words, rising population drives down all of the characteristics of an area that made it initially attractive.

To illustrate the attractiveness principle, imagine for a moment the ideal city. Perhaps the ideal city would be one with readily available housing at low cost, a surplus of jobs at high wages, excellent schools, no smoke or pollution, housing located near one's pace of work, no crime, beautiful parks, cultural opportunities, and to this list the reader can add his own preferences. Suppose such a city existed. What would happen? It would be perceived as the ideal place to live. People from everywhere would move into the ideal city until the advantages had been so swamped by rising population that the city would offer no net attractiveness compared to other locations.

There is a necessary and fundamental compromise that must be accepted between growth and quality. To hope otherwise is to delude oneself. A White House report carried the title "Toward Balanced Growth, Quantity with Quality." The phrase "Quantity with Quality" is inherently a contradiction. It is a political transitional phrase that lies between the old concept of "growth is good" and the future realities in which growth is seen as the fundamental cause of rising social problems.

When there are no geographical or environmental limits, economic growth can run ahead of population growth to increase the public well-being. During the growth phase, the many goals of society tend to be independent of one another and can be separately pursued. In the past, if an individual wanted more personal freedom, he could move to the unsettled frontier, while at the same time improving his standard of living by farming rich and virgin agricultural land. But as space fills up, all of the social goals begin to interact more strongly with one another. More and more the system begins to offer only tradeoffs and compromises. If one wants a higher population, he must accept less personal freedom. If there is to be more industry, there will necessarily be more government regulation and more social groups to intervene in each step and action. If agriculture is to become more capital intensive, there will be more pollution and more long-term damage to the productivity of the land. As population rises against the environmental limits, there will necessarily be higher unemployment and more welfare with rising governmental costs that divert resources away from additional capital investment.

There is a fundamental conflict between quality and quantity, after quantity has grown beyond a certain point. It appears that the United States is now beyond that point. Further growth in population and industrialization means declining quality. How is the compromise between quality and quantity to be struck? Is it to be done uniformly for everyone, or is there to be a local choice between quality and quantity? "Balanced development" means the choice between quality and quantity.

A society has many goals. These impinge on one another more and more heavily as an economic system approaches the end of growth, enters the transition period, and eventually moves into some form of equilibrium. The multiple goals have the characteristic that no one of them can be maximized without unacceptable losses in one or more other goals. Some of the goals are material, others are social and psychological, but they all impinge on one another. We want freedom, but not at the expense of extreme hardship. We want to build more housing, but cannot forever at the expense of agricultural land. We want more capital investment to increase productivity and control pollution, but not to the detriment of government services.

Many people seem to assume that control of growth will circumscribe our freedoms but that continued growth will not. Nothing could be further from the truth.

But it is becoming more and more apparent that growth in population, industrialization, pollution, unemployment, welfare costs, inflation, and imbalanced trade is undermining local and state freedom. The symptoms resulting from growth are being attacked mostly from the national level with the result that national policies and the terms of national funding impose nationally determined values on all areas. National laws to cope with the results of uncontrolled growth restrict local choice. The higher the social stresses from growth become, the more governmental machinery will be assembled to fight the symptoms. On the other hand, control of growth can be done in many ways, some of which would also destroy freedom, but other ways can be devised to save freedom. However, the alternative of continued growth runs only in one direction—toward less individual and local freedom.

A whole set of pressures are now beginning to inhibit growth. The country faces an oil shortage. Pollution is no longer merely an industrial problem; to reduce pollution created by the individual, his automobile now has less performance, more maintenance, and higher gasoline consumption, and that in turn makes the oil shortage worse and our national dependence on other countries greater. Pollution has also become a major issue in agriculture as fertilizers and the wastes from animal feed lots pollute rivers and lakes. At the social level, rising crime, drug addiction, and mental stress, and community breakdown are all exerting pressure against further growth. Many pressures are developing to stop growth, some we can influence, others we cannot. A most important question is how we would like to have the growth-suppressing pressures distributed.

Pressures to slow the growth process will continue to rise. The pressures will tend to develop from every direction. Some of the pressures can be alleviated. But do we want to alleviate, where we can, the pressures arising from growth? Or, do these pressures serve a valuable purpose?

Unless ever-rising exponential growth can go on forever, and that is generally accepted as impossible, then some set of pressures will eventually stop growth. From whence should the growth-suppressing pressures come? Should the pressures be distributed throughout our society or should they be concentrated in only a few places within our socioeconomic system? This choice between concentration or distribution of pressures is of the greatest importance. The question arises because we have the power to alleviate pressures in some sectors of the society but not in others. If we alleviate pressures where we can do so, it will inevitably lead to a further rise in those pressures that we cannot control. The way we react to present pressures determines the nature of future pressures.

One set of pressures can be alleviated by technological means. We are very good at handling technology, and can eliminate those pressures if we wish. A second set of pressures can be alleviated by economic means, and those we know less about but can still influence. A third set of pressures are of a social nature —crime, civil disorder, declining mental health, war, drug addiction, and collapse of goals and values. These are the ultimate pressures with which we do not know how to cope.

If we alleviate the pressures that can now be overcome, those pressures make no contribution to slowing the growth process. Growth then continues until higher pressures are generated in other sectors. This process has been going on. The first pressures to arise were dealt with technologically by increasing building heights, improving transportation, bringing water from greater distances, developing new sources of energy, and improving medical treatment. As a result of such technological successes, growth continued until a variety of economic malfunctions began to appear—rising unemployment and welfare, worsening balance of trade, and inflation. To a small extent, the economic pressures have been alleviated and their consequences delayed. Growth has thereby continued until social deterioration has begun to manifest itself in serious ways.

In this sequence of technology solving one problem only to produce an insolvable problem later is buried the reasons for the antitechnology attitude that has begun to develop. In the past, technology appeared to be solving our problems. The technologists became self-confident. The public came to depend on them. The attitude took root that all problems could be solved by an ever-improving technology. But instead, the rising technology, with its consequent growth in population and industrialization, has carried the society to a complexity and a congestion that is producing rising symptoms of distress in the economic and the social sectors. The very fact that technology succeeds in meeting its narrow goals produces greater difficulties in other parts of our social system. The antitechnology feeling grows because of the repeated cycle in which pressures develop, technology produces an excellent solution within its narrow self-perceived goals, the social system becomes more compressed and frustrating, and the public perceives that the over-all quality of life has failed to respond to the technical solution. The failure to satisfy society results because meeting the subgoals of the technologist is less and less likely to truly enhance the combined composite value of all the social goals. For each technical goal that is improved, some social or economic goal is forced to decline.

Growth has continued past the point where suboptimizing is satisfactory. Suboptimizing means the meeting of a local goal without attention to consequences in other parts of the system. During the past period of our industrial growth, the various facets of the technical-socio-economic system were sufficiently uncoupled that suboptimizing was satisfactory procedure for decentralization. Suboptimizing allows different groups to pursue independently their own ends, with confidence that the total good would thereby improve. But as the system becomes more congested, the solution of one problem begins to create another. The blind pursuit of individually laudable goals can create a total system of degraded utility.

What does this discussion of technology and social goals mean? It means that in the past those who deal with the technological aspects of urban life have been free to suboptimize.

The public well-being was increased by the best possible job of drainage, waste disposal, transportation, water supply, and the construction of streets. But no longer is it true that improving each of these will improve a city. By solving each of these technical problems the technologist becomes a party to increasing the population of a city and the densities of population. He starts social processes that eventually reduce the quality of life. The public is recognizing that improved technology is not bringing an improved society. As a result, men who have sincerely dedicated their efforts to the public good, but perhaps have not foreseen the diversity of social consequences, have already begun to feel the backlash of public criticism.

So far I have developed several propositions. First, pressures are rising to inevitably stop growth. Second, the national commitment to growth is too strong for the national government to lead in a new direction until a broad constituency has already formed in the country. Third, if the nature of growth is to be recognized, and if experiments are going to be carried out to find a satisfactory way of moving from growth into equilibrium, leadership must come from the local and state levels. Fourth, technical accomplishments no longer offer a basic solution to social problems, instead, technology, as now being used, is often the cause of rising social difficulties. Fifth, all cities do at all times tend toward equal attractiveness. Given this set of propositions what freedom of action is left to a city?

A city can choose, to a substantial extent, the mix of pressures under which it wishes to exist. There are many components of urban attractiveness and if one of these is decreased, others can be improved. One cannot create the ideal city. But one can create certain ideal features if he is willing to compensate for these by intentionally allowing other features to worsen. In the past, we have improved the technological aspects of cities and have thereby unintentionally caused many of the economic and social characteristics to deteriorate. There are many facets to a city. There are many things that the public and an urban administration can do. One thing they cannot do is to produce the perfect city. They can, however, exercise a wide choice between imperfect cities.

I suggest that a valid goal for local urban leadership is to focus on improving the quality of life for the residents already in the city, while at the same time protecting against growth that would overwhelm the gains. In short, one might maintain the attractiveness for the present residents while decreasing the attractiveness to those who might inundate the system from the outside.

Such statements, I recognize, lead to ethical and legal controversy. I am saying that a city should look after itself first. Its own welfare should come ahead of concern for others who are taking no steps to solve the fundamental problems for themselves. If enough cities establish successful policies for themselves, there will be two results. First, a precedent will have been set for coping with the fundamental underlying source of difficulties. Second, the larger the number of areas that solve their problems for themselves, the greater will the remaining uncontrolled growth impinge on the other parts of the country, and the more quickly will the nation face the long-range issues of stress arising from excessive growth.

So what can a city do? It can influence its future by choosing between the components of attractiveness. The attractiveness components of a city fall into two categories according to whether they operate more forcefully on quality of life in the city or on inward migration and growth. These two categories are the "diffuse" and the "compartmentalized" characteristics of a city. The objective should be to maximize those diffuse characteristics of the city that improve quality of life while controlling the compartmentalized characteristics that can prevent expanded population and population density that would defeat the improvement for present residents.

The diffuse characteristics, such as public safety and clean air, are shared equally by all, their effect is not limited to particular individuals, and they apply alike to present residents and those who might move in. The compartmentalized characteristics of a city, like jobs and housing, are identified with particular individuals; they can be possessed by present residents but are not necessarily available to others from the outside.

Every diffuse characteristic of a city that makes it more attractive for the present residents will also make it more attractive for those who might move in and who would increase the population and density. Therefore, every improvement in the diffuse categories of attractiveness must be accompanied by some worsening in the compartmentalized categories of attractiveness to prevent self-defeating growth. The attractiveness characteristics of a city should be categorized in terms of whether they affect all residents or primarily potential newcomers. For example, the vitality of industry, a balanced socioeconomic mix of population, the quality of schools, the freedom from pollution, low crime rates, public parks, and cultural facilities are all desirable to present residents. If there is no counterbalance to restrain an expanding population, such attractive features tend to be self-defeating by causing inward migration. But the compartmentalized characteristics of a city primarily affect growth without necessarily reducing quality of life for present residents. The number of housing units and the number of jobs tend to be compartments in the sense that they have a one-to-one correspondence with individuals rather than each being shared by all. The absence of an unoccupied house and/or job can be a strong deterrent to in-migration, without necessarily driving down the internal quality of life.

I see no solution for urban problems until cities develop the courage to plan in terms of a maximum permissible building height, and a maximum number of jobs. A city must also choose the type of city it wants to be. To become and remain a city that is all things to all people is impossible. There can be many uniquely different kinds of cities, each with its special mix of advantages and disadvantages. However, the policies that create one type of city will destroy another type. A choice of city type must be made, and corresponding policies chosen to create the required combination of advantages *and disadvantages* that are characteristic of that type. One might have an industrial city, a commercial city, a resort city, a retirement city, or a city that attracts and traps without opportunity a disproportionate number of unemployed and welfare residents as some cities are now doing. But there are severe limits on how many types of cities can be created simultaneously in one place. When the choices have been made, and when effort is no longer dissipated in growth, there will be an opportunity to come to grips with social and economic decay.

The reader may be thinking that planning and controlling the size and composition of a city and the migration to it are un-democratic or immoral. It may even seem that I am suggesting control where there has not been control before. Neither is true. Every city has arrived at its present size, character, and composition because of the controls that have been exercised in the past. By adding to the water system, sewers, and streets, a city has, in effect, decided to increase its size. By building a rapid transit system a city is often, in effect, deciding to change the composition of its population by encouraging new construction in outlying areas, allowing inner areas to decay, and attracting low-income and unskilled persons to the inner ring at the same time that job opportunities decline. In other words, control on growth and migration has been exerted at all times. But the control has often been unintentional, with unexpected and undesirable results. The issue is not one of control or no control. The issue is the kind of control and toward what end.

The interurban control of population movement is the internal counterpart of international control of population movement. Except for the legal, coercive, psychological, and economic deterrents to human mobility, the standard of living and quality of life of all countries would fall to the level set by the population group that accepts the lowest standards. No group can be expected to exert the present self-discipline necessary to limit population and the environmental demands of industrialization unless there is a way to keep the future advantages of the present price from being swallowed up by inward migration. If the control of international movement of population is ethical then some intercity counterpart must also be ethical. Or, if the justification is only that of practical necessity, then the internal necessity arises in a country that is reaching its growth limit without having established a national means to implement a compromise between quantity and quality. Between nations, countries exert restrictions on population movement that are not allowed internally between urban areas. Even so, the policies of each city have a powerful effect on mobility and on the resulting character of the city. Because controls are implicit in every action taken and every urban policy adopted, a city should understand the future consequences of its present actions. A city affects its local choice between quantity and quality mostly by how it handles the diffuse versus the compartmentalized components of attractiveness.

The difference between diffuse and compartmentalized control of urban population can be illustrated by two extremes of policies that might govern the availability of water. Depending on how it is managed, the availability of water might be either a diffuse or compartmentalized control on growth. Consider a city with a limited water supply—more and more this will be the actual situation. To illustrate diffuse control, one could distribute water freely and equally to everyone, both present and future residents. New houses could be constructed, new industries could be encouraged, growth could be continued, and the water could be divided among all. If no other growth limits were encountered, growth would continue until the low water pressure, occasional shortages, and the threat of disaster from drought had risen to the point where out-migration equaled in-migration. Under these circumstances, net growth would have been stopped, but the equally distributed nature of the water shortage would have reduced the quality of life for all residents. The water shortage would be diffuse; it would be spread to all, former residents and newcomers alike. Alternatively, the opposite water policy illustrates compartmentalized control. Building permits and new water connections could be denied so that water demand is constrained to lie well within the water supply. Water would be available to present residents, but not to new. Under these circumstances, quality of life for the residents would be maintained, but growth would be controlled.

I believe that such choice between present and future residents is inherent to a practical solution of our urban problems. Unless control through such self-interest is acceptable, and ways are available to implement it, there is no incentive for any city or state to solve its own problems. Its efforts will be swamped from the outside. All will be pulled down while the nation continues to debate the issues endlessly and acts on symptoms rather than causes. There must be freedom for local action, and the consequent differences between areas, if social experiments are to lead to better futures and if there is to be diversity in the country rather than one gray homogenized sameness. Local areas must be able to control their destinies in different ways and toward different ends, if there is to be any meaning to President Nixon's hope of preserving "the ability of citizens to have a major voice in determining policies that most directly affect them."

If people are to influence the policies most affecting them, it follows that policies will be different in different places and the resulting tradeoffs between growth and quality of life will be different. If there is to be any substance to local choice, there must result differences between localities.

In the policies for a city that I am proposing, the ethical and legal issues are substantial. A city, in looking after its own well-being, will, no doubt, be accused of being selfish because it discriminates against nonresidents. But what are the alternatives? Must it discriminate against its present residents? Must it discriminate against its own long-term interests? Must it be forced to take only a short-range view of its future? Must it be a party to delaying the day when the nation faces the fundamental choice between quality and quantity? Our past policies have not been so successful that they should persuade us against new experiments.

If a sufficient number of cities find new ways of controlling their own destinies in spite of national policy and what other cities do, then pressures to work toward the long-term well-being of the country will be quickly generated. If some cities and states take effective steps to establish an equilibrium with their natural surroundings, and to maintain a viable and proper internal balance of population and industry, then the remaining growth in the country will quickly descend on those communities and states that have taken no such action. A national consensus to establish a viable balance with the capacity of the environment will quickly develop out of the contrasts that will be established between those who have and those who have not dealt with the basic issues of overcommitment.

A Computer Version of How a City Works

JOHN F. KAIN

This selection contains a critical review of Urban Dynamics *by John Kain, Professor of Economics at Harvard University. Kain's critique and Forrester's response (the following selection) appeared in* Fortune *magazine.*

THE INTENSE INTEREST in the problems of the cities in recent years has produced a great outpouring of books diagnosing and proposing remedies for the "urban crisis." The majority of these works are hardly noticed, being undistinguished and rather pallid imitations of one another. Jay W. Forrester's *Urban Dynamics* stands out in all this verbiage. The book has attracted attention because of the unorthodoxy of Forrester's recommendations, the self-assured manner in which he presents them, and his prominent use of the prestigious tools of systems analysis. With so many insistent voices saying that cities need more financial help from state and federal government, readers are likely to be impressed with Forrester's conclusion that help from the outside may "worsen conditions" in cities. Forrester, moreover, makes it difficult for readers to argue with him. With its appearance of rigor and scientism, its charts and diagrams, its arrays of numbers printed out by a computer, *Urban Dynamics* is rather intimidating.

Forrester relies on a computer model he developed to stimulate the growth, decline, and stagnation of a hypothetical city (or "urban area") from birth to old age (250 years). Such methods have a great deal of potential for the analysis of urban problems and have already demonstrated their value in a number of specific, though limited applications. However, the development of truly useful and trustworthy urban simulation models remains a distant objective and will require much greater resources than have yet been devoted to the task. Before adequate models become available, many inadequate ones will be put forward. Forrester's model is a conspicuous example. In his first chapter Forrester warns the reader that caution should be exercised in applying the model to actual situations. Subsequently, however, he expresses few reservations about the model's validity and freely uses it as a basis for prescribing public policy.

A GOAL OF MINIMUM TAXES

The hypothetical city in *Urban Dynamics* is, in Forrester's words, "a system of interacting industries, housing, and people." At the start of the simulations there is only new industry in the city, but as time passes enterprises mature and then decline. The speed of this aging process depends on conditions in the city. As businesses pass through these successive stages, they employ fewer workers and a smaller proportion of skilled workers.

There are similarly three kinds of people in the city: "managerial-professional," "labor" (skilled or high-income workers), and "underemployed" (including unemployed and unskilled workers). And there are three kinds of housing, corresponding to the three kinds of people: premium housing, worker housing, and underemployed housing.

The criteria used in evaluating the performance of the hypothetical city and the efficacy of alternative public policies are never explicitly set forth. However, minimization of taxes per capita would be a fair rendering of the underlying criteria. Forrester seems to think that the objective of the city is to produce the lowest possible tax rate.

The fiscal relationships in Forrester's urban system are intricate, but can be reduced to three fairly simple propositions: (1) Low-income households cost the city more in taxes than they pay, whereas the city makes a profit on high-income households. (2) Growing business enterprises are an unqualified good because they pay taxes and, by assumption, cost the city nothing in services. (3) Increases in local taxes and increases in local government expenditures produce "adverse" changes in the city's population and employment structure. It follows from these propositions that "urban-management policies" should be

designed to encourage new enterprises and managerial-professional people to locate in the city and discourage low-skilled
people from living there.

The influence of tax rates on employment and population structure in Forrester's city is powerful and pervasive. "Managerial-
professional" and "labor" families are assumed to be repelled by
high tax rates, whereas the "underemployed" are indifferent to
them. High tax rates, moreover, discourage the formation of new
enterprises and accelerate the aging of existing ones. There are
still other adverse effects. High taxes retard construction of both
premium and worker housing, which in turn discourages the
kinds of people who live in these kinds of housing from moving
to the city or remaining there.

Increases in public expenditures, the other half of the local
fiscal equation, also have disastrous effects on the system. It is
assumed that increases in expenditures per capita make the city
no more attractive to high-income people and new enterprises,
but make it substantially more attractive to low-income people.
There are some small offsets in the positive effects of higher expenditures per capita on upward mobility from the underemployed class into the labor class; but these are overwhelmed by
the direct and indirect effects on the size of the underemployed
population.

These examples are only a few of the "adverse" consequences
of higher taxes and increased public expenditures in Forrester's
model. Since the model is so constructed that a development
in one sector affects other sectors, these adverse effects cumu-
late throughout the system.

HELP FROM AN INDUCED SHORTAGE

Forrester uses his simulation model to evaluate several "urban-management programs" that have been tried or proposed,
and he concludes that they "may actually worsen the conditions
they are intended to improve." For example, he finds that "financial support from the outside"—presumably including revenue
sharing by the federal government—"may do nothing to improve
fundamental conditions within the city and may even worsen

conditions in the long run." But this conclusion is not at all surprising in view of what he does with the outside funds. Rather
than using them to reduce or hold down city taxes, as proponents of such intergovernment transfers envision, Forrester uses
them to increase city expenditures. Given the framework of his
model, the net effects are inevitably adverse. If instead Forrester had used the outside support to reduce city taxes, the net
effects would have been favorable to the hypothetical city. Virtually all of Forrester's evaluations of "conventional" policies are
similarly flawed; none is a faithful rendering of policies it sup-
posedly represents.

Considering the heavy emphasis Forrester puts on tax rates,
it is striking that he fails to consider the costs of his principal
recommendation: Each year demolish 5 percent of the low-income housing. The costs of acquiring and demolishing the prop-
erties would increase city taxes, and, within the framework of
the model, any increase in city taxes has adverse effects. But
Forrester considers only the favorable effects of the demolition
program. Given his model, these are considerable. The induced
shortage of low-income housing makes the city less attractive to
low-income people; fewer come and more leave. (Where they
go is a question the model is not designed to consider.) As before,
a decline in the ratio of "underemployed" to total population
makes the city more attractive to high-income people, encourages
formation of new enterprises and construction of premium and
worker housing, and impedes deterioration of dwelling units and
businesses. In addition, the land cleared by increased demolition
of low-income housing provides space for new enterprises and
for premium and worker housing.

The supply of vacant land is a critical variable in Forrester's
urban model. When more than half the land is still vacant, using
additional land produces increasingly favorable effects. But once
half the land in the city has been put to use—which in the simulations occurs at about one hundred years—further depletions
produce increasingly adverse effects. The city's growth is re-
tarded, and stagnation and decline begin. As more land is used
up, the scarcity of vacant land slows formation of new enterprises
and construction of premium and worker housing, and speeds

obsolescence of both enterprises and housing. Given the critical role of land availability in the model, it would appear that these adverse effects could be staved off if the city could simply extend its boundaries so as to absorb additional vacant land; but Forrester does not deal with this possibility.

WHERE THE SOLUTION LIES

Simplification is essential in computer simulation models, and neither Forrester's nor any other model can be criticized merely because it omits detail. But Forrester omits some basic behavioral relationships. The model's most serious weakness is that the suburbs never explicitly appear in it. For some simulation purposes, it might be permissible to disregard temporarily the interrelations between, say, the city and the rest of the nation beyond the metropolitan area. But what happens in a city strongly influences its suburbs, and vice versa. If the central city reduced its low-income population by one hundred thousand, the low-income population of the suburbs would have to increase by roughly the same amount. Although Forrester's model reflects no awareness of this aspect of metropolitan interdependence, suburban governments are all too aware of it. Indeed, much of the urban problem today is a result of suburban governments' successfully pursuing precisely the kind of beggar-thy-neighbor policies Forrester advocates for the central city.

Upon scrutiny, *Urban Dynamics* amounts to an intricate attempt to justify the responses of big-city mayors to a harsh fiscal environment. Existing intergovernmental arrangements saddled them with awesome responsibilities for the nation's social problems, but failed to provide them with commensurate financial resources. Much of the mayors' enthusiasm for now much-criticized urban-renewal programs is traceable to their desperate need for cash. In *Urban Dynamics,* pragmatic responses to an unbalanced allocation of responsibilities and tax resources are elevated to the status of rational and efficient policies for dealing with the complex web of problems popularly referred to as the "urban crisis."

The solution is not, as Forrester indicates, the pursuance of narrow self-interest by each local government. Instead we need to develop a more appropriate division of responsibilities and functions among governments, and thereby is minimum the undesirable incentives for local governments to follow policies that, while perhaps efficient from the viewpoint of narrow self-interest, are inefficient from the viewpoint of society as a whole.

Overlooked Reasons for Our Social Troubles

JAY W. FORRESTER

FROM THE CITY, the economy, and the environment come rising pressures on our social systems. Citizens, corporate executives, mayors, and national leaders strive to solve the problems, only to see matters worsen. Obviously, we do not understand how the structures and policies of our systems interact to *create* the troubles that surround us. In *Urban Dynamics,* using computer methods developed in my *Industrial Dynamics,* I undertook to show how the structures and policies of an urban area turn growth into decline. Several popular proposals for remedying urban troubles (job training, financial subsidity to a city, and low-cost-housing programs) proved to lie somewhere between neutral and detrimental in their effects on a declining urban area. But policies directed to rebalancing population categories and jobs can start an internal revival, with increased upward mobility for low-income groups. This approach to policy design is applicable to any of our social systems.

Many people recoil at the thought of anyone's designing social systems. But we have no choice. We already live in social systems that have been designed—by national and state constitutions, laws, tax regulations, and traditions. If we lament the decline of our cities, the pace of inflation, or the increases in environmental pollution, we are asserting a preference for a different design. Corporate executives and legislative bodies design our systems by establishing policies and laws, but with only intuition and experience to guide their choices. Intuition and experience are demonstrably unreliable in efforts to cope with the complex systems that surround us.

NEW POTENTIAL FOR ENLIGHTENED CHOICES

It is inhumane to go on trying to achieve humane objectives by means of policies that worsen the conditions they are meant to improve. In *Urban Dynamics*, I try to indicate ways of improving the functioning of social systems, which can and improving the living conditions of human beings and making it possible for them to realize their potentialities more fully. The point that a cold-blooded computer model can have humane uses has escaped some readers of my book, but not all. Erich Jantsch, a scientist who specializes in long-range forecasting and planning, wrote in the British journal *Futures:* "In reality, Urban Dynamics—or Social Dynamics, as the method might be called even more generally—enhances the role of human creativity and inventiveness in an unprecedented way. By studying the consequences of alternative courses of action for entire social systems, man acquires a new potential for making enlightened choices . . ."

As everyone sees, our present social systems exhibit disturbing trends and stresses. Grave doubts surround the management of corporations, the environment, and the economy. For example, we need better to interrelate taxation, government expenditure, fiscal and monetary policy, economic output, unemployment, and inflation. Past failures in economic analysis and economic policy recommendations have been blamed on inadequate data, but a much more likely explanation lies in the inappropriate structures of the models used, the timid and fragmentary approaches to analysis, and the willingness merely to explain the past rather than try to understand the future. Likewise, the possibilities for sudden and irreversible changes in the ecological relationships of man to nature can be effectively explored neither by discussion nor by analysis of historical data. We must use the more powerful approaches that are now becoming available for dealing with our complex systems. We must, and can, anticipate changes that will evolve from presently known structures and processes, but that have no historical precedents.

CONSEQUENCES BURST FORTH

The pressures on our society will continue to rise until the fundamental questions can no longer be ignored. Through all of recorded history, our traditions, laws, and aspirations have been based on the dynamics of growth—growth in geographical frontiers, scientific knowledge, standard of living, population, and pollution. Our social systems contain the positive-feedback processes that generate exponential growth. Exponential growth has the characteristic that in its early stages it seems unimportant, appears to be getting nowhere, and is largely ignored. But then, in the last two or three doublings in growth, the process passes from insignificance to domination. The consequences of a long history of exponential growth suddenly appear to be burst forth on an unprepared society.

Exponential growth cannot continue indefinitely, otherwise it would engulf the earth. *Urban Dynamics* shows the precipitous fall in standard of living and the changes in population mix that occur in the conventional urban area as it moves out of its growth stage into equilibrium. Similar prospects for major change and stress lie before our larger social systems. Growth will cease. Geographical frontiers have been exhausted. Natural resources are being used far faster than nature is recreating them. Ecological considerations probably exclude the possibility of even the present world population rising to the standard of living of the Western industrialized nations, so rising economic expectations will inevitably be frustrated, either in local stagnation or in a worldwide ecological disaster.

The present social malaise at all organizational levels is the first evidence of far greater pressures that will be generated by the world-wide suppression of growth processes. As with the urban area, there are many routes into the inevitable equilibrium. As we move toward that condition, we must, for our preservation, make wise choices about the kind of static earth we want, and adopt wise policies for attaining it.

THE DECEPTIVENESS OF SYSTEMS

Urban Dynamics described various characteristics of complex systems that lead us into self-defeating policies. These characteristics were first identified to explain, in management systems, the recurring choice of corporate policies that worsen the very troubles they are intended to correct. The same kinds of influences were rediscovered on the urban scene. They appear to be common to all our social systems.

· Complex systems are counterintuitive. They respond to policy changes in directions opposite to what most people expect. We develop experience and intuition almost entirely from contact with simple systems, where cause and effect are closely related in space and time. Complex systems behave very differently.

· Complex systems actively resist most policy changes. A new policy warps the entire system slightly, and so it presents a new ensemble of perceived information; the new information is processed through the new policy to produce nearly the old result.

· But influence points exist, often where least expected and often with a direction of influence opposite to that anticipated. These pressure points radiate new information streams that, when processed even through old attitudes and policies, produce new results.

· Complex systems tend to counteract programs that attempt to supplement and add to an action stream already in the system. For example, in *Urban Dynamics* a job-training program fails because the reactions within the system reduce the natural upward economic mobility, increase downward mobility, attract the unskilled, and in the end slightly enlarge the underemployed population.

· In a complex system the short-term response to a policy change is often opposite to the long-term effect. This treacherous behavior beguiles the executive and the politician into a series of steps, each appearing beneficial and each leading to deeper long-term difficulty.

· A system contains internal dynamic mechanisms that *produce* the undesirable behavior. If we ignore fundamental causes and simply try to overwhelm the symptoms, we pit great forces against one another, expending our energy to no avail.

· In a complex system, certain pressures go with each mode of behavior. To sustain a particular mode we must accept the corresponding pressures. The common tendency to alleviate one squeaky wheel after another constitutes incremental redesign that can move the system toward an undesirable and nearly irreversible mode of behavior.

In his review of *Urban Dynamics*, Professor Kain concentrates on another aspect of the book, its model, or theory, of system behavior in an urban area. Details of such a model change continuously as one addresses different questions or tests alternative assumptions. Although model details are of less long-term significance than method or the general character of systems, Kain worries details. If his doubts were justified, that might affect the particular conclusions of the book, but not the method.

Almost the only concrete, testable statement Kain offers has to do with his doubtful premise that outside financial subsidy to a city would be used to reduce taxes rather than increase expenditure. He says, "If instead Forrester had used the outside support to reduce city taxes, the net effects would have been favorable to the hypothetical city." Here he is speaking explicitly of what the model will do. Only minutes are needed to make the suggested change in the model and test his assertion. This was done. There is no significant improvement. So even this unlikely use of a subsidy—to reduce taxes—is a waste of resources in the hypothetical city.

REGRETTABLE PERHAPS, BUT INESCAPABLE

Even here where he has complete knowledge about the laboratory system and its governing policies, Kain should not be criticized by being unable, on the basis of intuition and judgment, to anticipate the effect of a policy change. But Kain and the social scientists he represents can be criticized for asserting with assurance the consequences of policy recommendations in our real-life systems when it has been repeatedly shown that intuition and judgment cannot yield such certainty even in the laboratory and with perfect information. Only after trying the policy change in a properly constructed, dynamic simulation model should one speak confidently about the consequences.

From his economist's viewpoint, Professor Kain primarily saw tax considerations in the book. As a test of his assertion that tax rates powerfully influence employment and population behavior in the model, the tax rate was changed to be constant and equal to the average outside tax rate. This change makes only a small improvement in the depressed condition of the city, an improvement not at all comparable to what results from the revival policies discussed in the book. Furthermore, the constant tax levy does not reduce the efficacy of the suggested revival policies, so no conclusions in the book would be altered

Again we see the danger of continuing to base political decisions on intuitive judgments and "conventional wisdom." As I noted above, complex systems are counterintuitive. This perhaps regrettable but nonetheless inescapable fact is a main source of our present discontents.

Urban Zero Population Growth

*William Alonso, Professor of Regional Planning at the University
of California at Berkeley, is best known for his classic development of a general theory of land rent. He has also written a number of incisive essays, critical of current fashion, on various policy
topics in the field of urban planning, including "The Mirage of
New Towns"* (The Public Interest, *Spring 1970*) *and the present
essay, which appeared in* Daedalus *in 1974.*

It is remarkable how rapidly the fashion for American states
and cities has shifted from the traditional boosterism to a questioning and even an abhorrence of growth. It is common to read
in the newspapers that states such as Oregon, California, Vermont, and Maryland want to stop or limit their growth, as do
cities such as San Francisco, Boulder, and countless suburbs.

Undoubtedly this has much to do with the new Malthusian
concern with the consequences of unlimited population growth
at national and world levels. Some seem to think that the place
to start controlling the nation's population growth is at the level
of their city, metropolis, or state. Others hope that, as the nation
moves toward zero population growth (ZPG), so will their communities. Both these views are misleading half-truths. Local policies to limit population are probably not very effective, and
when they are effective they are regressive and counterproductive in terms of social well-being. They are seldom aimed at reducing local birthrates (except among those on welfare in big
cities), but rather they are aimed at keeping outsiders out. Thus,
what is locally perceived as a growth or no-growth policy in reality merely affects the geographic distribution of people and
economic activity within some larger society such as the region
or the nation.

Neither is it credible that, when and if the national rate of
population growth moves toward zero, local populations will be-

come stable. In the first place, natural increase (the excess of births over deaths) varies enormously from one time to another, so that as the national rate approached zero, many areas would fail to reproduce themselves while others would continue to grow by natural increase. In the second place, continued structural change in the economy is inevitable, with or without economic growth. Indeed, my impressions is that such structural change would be deeper if conventionally defined economic growth were limited. Change in the economy would be mirrored in shifts in the location of economic activity and, accordingly, in population shifts. In short, a nationally stable population would be composed of many localities declining in population, many localities growing, and only some remaining stable.

Why should a city, a town, or a state prefer to stop its population growth? There are many conceivable reasons: growth might lower average income, or bring in poor people who do not mix comfortably with present residents; it might produce challenges to local social structure, or change life styles for the worse, or increase pollution and congestion, or overrun prized landscapes. These would be changes in the real city, which is composed of people and their relations to each other, to their institutions, and to their physical environment. But there is an unfortunate confusion which frequently overtakes the debate and which must be clarified at the outset. The word *city* is also used as the name of a municipal corporation which derives its income principally through taxation and, in exchange provides certain services to the population. This corporate entity is only one of the elements of the real city. Yet very often debate and evaluation of advantages and disadvantages are based on the limited viewpoint of the municipal corporation, and thus miss many of the most important consequences, good and bad, for the real city.

This confusion and some of its implications may be illustrated by a recent case in a wealthy metropolitan suburb where a substantial reserve of land was probably going to be placed on the market, and many thousands of new houses built. A consulting firm was retained, and it reported, after considerable analysis, that this would be very costly for the city. It remarked that it would be cheaper for the city to buy the land itself with money raised through the sale of municipal bonds. This report met an enthusiastic reception. It not only addressed the central preoccupation of local tax groups, it also confirmed the questioning of growth among local youth and cultivated older people, and it surprised and delighted environmentalists by showing that preserving the landscape made economic sense. So well did it match the concern of many people that its conclusions were widely quoted in the national press and are often cited as proving the case against growth.

But the case as presented confused the municipal corporation for the real city. The fiscal effects on the municipal corporation can be predicted very easily, and the consultant's diligence in gathering numbers was not really necessary. On the average, a new house has associated with it about two school-age children. The taxes it pays rarely cover even one child's school costs. It also imposes the costs of providing other municipal services, although these are small by comparison. Thus, in any such case, new houses are money losers for the municipal corporation. In this particular case it only made matters worse that, as a result of the current residents' wealth and love of learning, local schools were excellent and costs per child especially high. All of this was in spite of a market analysis which concluded that the average price of the new houses would be higher than the price of existing houses in that town. It is more common in similar cases for the new houses to be cheaper than the existing ones, and inhabited by people not as wealthy as the present inhabitants.

If we consider the real city of present residents, they would probably still be worse off, although the matter is not as clear. Some property values would rise; some merchants and other businessmen and their employees would profit; the small proportion of poor and minority in the city would have increased job opportunities and residential choices (and indeed they were the only ones to dissent from the nearly universal approval of the consultant's recommendations); the children of the upper middle class would meet a somewhat different group in school; some local businesses would more easily find certain types of labor; shopping and entertainment facilities might become more varied and extensive; and so forth. On the other hand, a lovely landscape would be largely filled up; congestion might increase; present residents would have to rub elbows with a slightly lower class and a broader ethnic group; there might be a slight increase in deviant behavior (on the part either of the newcomers or of present residents whose conduct might be redefined according to the more standard mores of the newcomers); and, of course, residents would pay higher taxes.

It is quite likely that a full consideration of these effects would result in the same conclusion: buy the insulation. But there is yet a further consideration, which to my mind is conclusive. What is the population of this city? Is it only those living there now, or does it include those who would move in if they could? If we are speaking of a future community of which there are two alternative versions, it makes as much sense to consider the interests of all the people who would make up the expanded version, as to consider those of the original version. After all, even if growth is prevented, given the mobility of Americans, only a fraction of the future residents will consist of those living there now. The future majority will consist of newcomers, although they will be socially and economically similar to present residents. Who is choosing for whom?

If this seems abstract, the matter can be put another way. Suppose that growth is restricted. What happens to the people who would have moved in but could not? Obviously neither they nor their children cease to exist. They will find second-choice homes; their children will go to more run-of-the-mill schools and impose their costly presence on people who are less able to afford this added burden than the wealthy residents of the suburb in question. It would appear that they will be worse off, and so perhaps will the present residents of wherever they end up. The rub is that what seems from the local viewpoint an issue of growth is, in a larger framework, an issue of distribution, both in the social and in the geographic sense—not whether these people and their children shall exist, but where and how. In the abstract, the distribution problem could be solved if residents of the excluding locality made compensatory payments (a form of rent) to those whom they would exclude. But no feasible way of arranging for this suggests itself.

The point of the example is that the current Balkanization of metropolitan areas into dozens and even hundreds of local governments encourages beggar-thy-neighbor strategies. Furthermore, confusing the municipal corporation for the real city leads to the meanest forms of municipal mercantilism, ones which ignore more important consequences for people. Perhaps the most hopeful recent development on this matter, in spite of setbacks, is the emergence of a number of court opinions, of which *Serrano* vs. *Priest* was the first, that, under the equal protection principle, rule it unconstitutional to rely on property taxes for financing schools. If these decisions stand, their logic points to their application to other services and broader geographic areas. Hopefully, too, they will lessen the influence of base motives on the formulation of local population policies.

I cannot abandon the subject of local fiscal impacts, however, without making clear the abysmal state of knowledge in this area. It is perfectly clear that an ordinary fertile family is a money loser for the local fisc. Similarly, the underprivileged create a fiscal drain through their children, their criminality, their sickliness, their morbidity, and their reliance on welfare payments. This was the basis of much of the urban renewal activity of the 1950s and 1960s, which tried to rid the central cities of such troublesome residents (where were they to go?), and bring back those who were then called "the people," the upper middle-class apartment and town-house dwellers without these problems. The fiscal consequences of factories, skyscrapers, commercial developments, apartment houses, and military bases are very poorly understood, even in the direct sense of the net balance between their direct contribution in taxes and the direct cost of the services they need. Their indirect effects are even less known. Such developments always affect property values and promote or retard other developments which are diffcult to predict and whose fiscal impact is also imperfectly understood, so that uncertainty is compounded in estimating their full fiscal effects. To my mind all of this makes the use of this basis for local population and development policy even worse, for it invites cruelty without certainty of advantage.

Our knowledge is no greater if we try to go beyond fiscal consequences to a more general evaluation of the impact of development upon the real city. Take the case of office buildings. They create jobs in construction, and later they provide white-collar jobs for the rising lower-middle classes and for a smaller number of professionals and administrators; they pay taxes, they increase congestion, they require new types of fire-fighting equipment, they alter the skyline and the look of the streets; they increase panoramic views for those who work in them while reducing those of residents in cities fortunate enough to have this problem, and so forth. Some of these are matters of fact which might be determined through investigation, some are matters of taste, and some are matters of conflict. Beyond these quite direct consequences, there are others, fairly closely linked, which can often be guessed at and even estimated. For instance, offices may generate nearby parking lots and eating places, which may then be used at night in association with entertainment activities; the new office space, by increasing supply, may affect rents, values, and usage of the older stock of offices; and so forth. Beyond this ring of effects there is another, vaguer but probably more significant in the long run. Offices are where information is received and processed, bargains are struck, and decisions are made. A city without offices is limited to hand functions subsidiary to another city's head functions, and its economic base will consist of branch plants and other dependencies. It will not generate the sorts of men and institutions that are in daily contact with the national and international web of information, ideas, and modes of decision. Compared to a city with offices, it will be out of touch, sluggish in its responses, and therefore fragile in the face of continuing technological and economic change.

On the whole, I think that office development is good on social, economic, and fiscal grounds, not too bad on ecological grounds, a matter of taste aesthetically, and often troublesome for traffic congestion. Yet, even with considerable familiarity with the professional and scholarly literature on the subject, I would be hard put to make an exhaustive list of the direct effects of office, manufacturing, or other types of development. Many of the effects that I can think of, I could not measure. Many that

I could measure, I could not evaluate. And many that I could evaluate hide within their total value sharp gains for some and losses for others.

It is an open question whether a community can effectively enforce a choice to grow or not to grow, however it arrives at this choice. Until recently virtually every city in America tried to encourage growth by a variety of local actions and by seeking state and federal preferential treatment. Although there have been some dramatic successes, there have been very few. Indeed, there is now in this country, as in many others, a national policy of establishing growth centers for depressed regions, which by a variety of federal, state, and local actions, tries to induce rapid growth in selected small cities, but these programs have had very limited success.

It might appear to be easier to limit growth than to promote it, but this is not the case according to a rich experience of national policies in Europe and the socialist countries. Moscow, Paris, London, and Warsaw are among the centers where vigorous policies have been followed to contain and even reverse growth. The means at hand have often appeared foolproof, including not only the tax incentives and disincentives, subsidies, land use regulations, and other devices familiar in American experience, but also direct command over the location of jobs and people through state control over many enterprises, location and expansion permits for industry, residence permits, and job and housing assignments for people. Even so, these centers have continued to grow, although perhaps less than without these measures. These powerful tools have failed in the face of more powerful social and economic currents. Even in totally controlled societies power is not controlled monolithically, but distributed among the agencies of the state. In setting priorities and bargaining over specific decisions, the agencies charged with territorial distribution have not been able to count as much as the sectoral ones.

A locality in America may similarly choose to discourage growth either by making it hard for people to establish residence, or by discouraging the creation of jobs which would attract people. While a small independent city might succeed in this, it appears that a metropolitan area cannot. An industry or person excluded from one municipality will find a place in another within the metropolis. Over-all metropolitan levels of population and employment are set largely by economic and demographic forces at national and international levels. Local policy affects primarily the intrametropolitan form and distribution of that development, and, if it is set by the selfish interests of the component municipalities, it does so inefficiently and unjustly. A suburb may be able to keep population or industry out, but it can do so only by directing it to other suburbs or by keeping it cooped up in the central city.

Examine the normal instruments by which a municipality keeps people out. It may restrict the use of space, either absolutely through land reserves such as parks which keep everyone out, or through zoning which keeps out those who cannot afford large lots. Other devices of varying subtlety are available. It may refuse to accept subsidized housing. Or it may set high standards through building and related codes which raise the cost of housing. Or it may set very high standards for public services, especially schools, creating high local taxes that will discourage those who cannot afford them. Or it may maintain very poor schools, so that it is unattractive to the suburbanizing lower-middle class looking for the advancement of their children through education, but acceptable to those who can send their children to private schools. Or it may refuse to provide utilities for large-scale developments, but permit low density development by allowing septic tanks and water wells. Or it may keep out the jobs that would bring in new people, primarily potential industrial workers, by zoning, or by strong regulation of pollution, or by not allowing necessary infrastructure such as highway access.

It is clear that all of these instruments aimed at keeping people out tend to keep out those of lower income. In short, local population control policies are regressive. Thus what we see today, in city after city, and often at the state level, is a three-cornered political fight among the advocates of business and development, the poor and working class and their liberal advocates, and the environmentalists in alliance with no-growth people who are usually middle-class young or upper-middle class. This situation brings about strange alliances between, for instance, business groups and minority people, or ecologists and tax leagues. These same conflicts and contradictions are mirrored within many people who, traditional liberals, find themselves unable to reconcile their environmental interests with their concern for social equity.

Unfortunately, little can be said about the consequences on a city of population growth, decline, or stability because the subject has been little studied. A rare recent study suggests that slow-growing areas show lower crime indices than comparable fast-growing areas. Possibly they have a different industrial structure. In addition, they tend to have a lower proportion of young adults because, under the rates of natural increase which have prevailed, slow growth is based on emigration, and it is the young who leave. For those who hope for greater tranquility with the passing of growth, it may be of interest to consider that this out-migration of the young may account for the low crime indices, since it is the young who are responsible for most crimes.

The absence of studies on the consequences of growth or no-growth cannot be blamed altogether on scholarly neglect. The difficulty is that the growth rates that have existed have included a substantial natural increase, so that a locality that has exhibited anything like zero population growth in the past decade has had a substantial net out-migration, of the order of 10 percent. An extreme case is McAllen-Pharr-Edinburg, Texas, which has held virtually stable in population through a natural increase of 25.8 percent and an out-migration of 25.4 percent. Since it is primarily the young who leave, this leads to a population with few young people and many old ones, and this, among other things, lowers the local birth rate and raises the death rate. Thus, Scranton, Pennsylvania, with a net out-migration of 20 percent for the past two decades, had a yearly rate of natural increase of only 0.16 percent in the 1960s.

Such large rates of net out-migration occur only in distressed local economies, for, given the high rates of natural increase in the last decade, no reasonably prosperous area failed to grow by about 10 percent. Thus we have no instances for study which combine local zero population growth with economic well-being.

But the relation of migration to natural increase is more complicated than this suggests, and makes local population growth a more complex matter than national population growth. The key point is that, demographically, the United States is quite self-contained while urban areas are highly open systems. On the surface this does not seem to be so. Currently the United States population is growing by 1.1 percent a year, and a fifth of this growth comes from abroad (much of it accounted for by returning Americans). Similarly, in the last decade, three-fourths of metropolitan growth was accounted for by natural increase and one-fourth by new arrivals.[1] But these figures for average net migration mask tremendous cross-movements of population. As a rule of thumb, it takes ten migratory moves in and out of a metropolis to leave or take away one net migrant.

The figures of the 1970 Census are not yet available, but figures for the 1955–1960 period serve to make the point. Net migration from nonmetropolitan to metropolitan areas was 1.2 million, but this was the trace of 10.2 million moves: 5.7 million into metropolitan areas and 4.5 million out of them.[2] There were 7.7 million moves from one metropolitan area to another. Thus, a metropolis like Philadelphia, with a net in-migration of 12,000 in the five-year period appears to have led a quiet life; but this net migration represents the trace of 668,000 moves in and out. A fast growing area, San Francisco, had a net in-migration of 56,000, but even so 361,000 people left it. Had arrivals been 15 percent lower, there would have been a slight out-migration. And, in Pittsburgh, the largest metropolis near zero-growth, we find that 180,000 left and 113,000 came, for a net out-migration of 67,000. Thus net migratory gains or losses are only surface ripples of powerful cross-currents, and even apparent migratory stability conceals vast exchanges of populations.

Recent studies of these flows have made surprising findings of consequence for local population policies. Rates of in-migra-

1. It is startling to most people to learn that three-fifths of this net migration into metropolitan areas came from abroad, and only two-fifths from nonmetropolitan areas. Thus, nonmetropolitan net migration accounted for only one-tenth of metropolitan growth in the decade.

2. The actual number of moves was higher. These figures report the numbers of those living in one area in 1955 and living in another in 1960. They do not count the very great numbers who went somewhere and returned home within this period, nor do they count intervening moves.

tion are higher for prosperous places, but rates of out-migration do not appear to vary, except perhaps marginally, with local economic conditions. Instead, they depend primarily on the local proportion of young people. It seems that the young leave home in about equal numbers whether their home district is prosperous or distressed.[3] Thus, a policy which increases pay levels and the number of jobs in poor areas in an effort to retain the young may shift net migration from negative to positive, but it will do so by attracting more newcomers rather than by slowing down the exodus.

Conversely, if prosperous areas want to slow down arrivals, they could do so by making themselves ugly in economic terms. Their young would continue to leave, while in-migration would slow down or disappear, resulting in net out-migration. This, in turn, would gradually lower their rate of natural increase because the diminishing proportion of young people in their populations would lower the birth rate while the increasing age of the population would raise the death rate. Eventually, there would be few babies to grow into youth and leave, and the out-migration rate would slow down. This is, no doubt, a fanciful scenario. It amounts to choosing poverty, unemployment, and old age. In brief, it amounts to choosing to be Scranton, and this is a choice that few will make. The alternative way of containing growth is by erecting barriers to migrants and this, as I have discussed, is likely to be ineffective; and if effective, it is regressive.

This example is based on the assumption that the local net reproduction rate would continue to be higher than a ZPG level.[4] To compensate for this, the age distribution for local ZPG would have to include far fewer young and far more older people than would a national ZPG situation. Even a metropolis which, through local family planning, achieved ZPG net repro-

3. I must note that this is a topic of considerable scholarly debate at the moment. It is quite clear, at any rate, that local economic well-being matters far less than had been thought in determining the rate of leaving.

4. This would be a net reproduction rate of one which would mean that each generation would just replace itself if current birth and death rates were continued indefinitely in the absence of migration. Strictly speaking, however, net reproduction rates would have to be somewhat below the ZPG rate to accommodate immigrants from abroad.

duction rates might eventually maintain a balance of in- and out-migrants only if it were slightly less prosperous than the average. Otherwise, although it would have fewer births, it would also have fewer out-migrants, and would show a positive net migration since the potential pool of migrants from other places would be proportionately bigger than its own.

There is yet another paradox. I have focused the discussion thus far on the consequences and possibilities of local policies of population limitation, since this is the usual frame of reference, and I have obviously been negative about them. But examination of current patterns and trends persuades me that, whatever the difficulties of induced zero growth, it is quite possible that we will be faced in the 1980s with about eighty metropoles (central cities and their suburbs) which have spontaneously arrived at something near zero population growth. Whether this is good or bad, we have little understanding and experience of what such metropoles will be like. They will certainly be different from anything in our present experience but we are ill-prepared to anticipate their problems and opportunities. The key difference will be that these will be reasonably prosperous places, whereas today only economically distressed ones show population stability.

This forecast is a chancy one, I realize, for two reasons. The first is that demographic forecasting has had an atrocious record. The second is that local forecasts are, of statistical necessity, much more prone to error than national forecasts. Nonetheless, I make this prognosis on the following basis.

In the past decade, the birth rate fell by about one-fourth and, in consequence, since the death rate held about constant, the rate of natural increase fell by about 40 percent. Should there be another one-fourth drop in birth rates in the coming decade, which seems perfectly possible in view of such social changes as the redefinition of female roles, the rate of natural increase will be cut approximately in half to about 4 percent. Of 243 metropolitan areas, nearly 60 percent had net out-migration during the 1960s and 10 percent, mostly small ones, had actual population losses. While net out-migration and population loss are more typical of the smaller metropoles, principally because of their economic fragility, four out of the ten largest metropoles had negative net migration, and an additional three had positive net migrations of less than 1 percent in the decade. At the same time, migration from nonmetropolitan areas is decreasing, and migration from abroad promises to stay stable by congressional decision.

Meanwhile, natural increase varies surprisingly widely. Localities that have large numbers of poor, of blacks, of Mexican-Americans, of Mormons, and of some other groups tend to have much higher birth rates. Localities that have experienced sustained net out-migration have lower birth rates. The interaction of these factors yields a range from virtually no natural increase for depressed areas in the Northeast to rates of 25 to 30 percent in the South and Southwest, rates comparable to those of underdeveloped countries. Even among the twenty largest metropoles the decennial rates varied from 7 to 25 percent.

This out-migration and variation in local rates of natural increase combined with a falling national rate point to the emergence of changes in quantity which amount to changes in quality. Whereas today any area that fails to grow or grows very little is poor and underemployed, should the birth rate continue to fall, we will have a new phenomenon: relatively prosperous areas which are stable in population, or which grow so little as not to matter.

What will such areas be like? They will have fewer young than today, and thus fewer children in school and a lighter fiscal burden. Economic evolution will be more by substitution than by adding new activities to existing ones, and may therefore involve more individual transitions. The burden of dependent aged will be greater. There will not be an appreciably greater continuity of population, since there will continue to be massive exchanges of the young with other areas. Two major sectors of the economy, construction and the education of children, will probably retrench.

Beyond this it is hard to see. It is possible that economic changes will be more of a shock because they will take the form of structural shifts rather than of adding on new activities. Possibly the young, being relatively scarce, will profit from accelerated social and economic mobility; but possibly the prepon-

derance of old people and the limits on expansion will create
a gerontocracy. Possibly minorities will be frustrated, since there
will not be new activities for them to move into and the old activities will be pre-empted. Possibly, however, they will benefit
from lessened competition for the older housing stock which will
permit them lesser per room densities together with lower rents.

There must be other questions about such circumstances that
are not yet conceived. It is to be expected that, when growth is
gone, there will be those who miss it, and that the current concern for bringing about ZPG may seem as quaint then as the
worries of the 1930s and 1940s about the economic implications
of the stable populations they erroneously forecast do now.

Local policies for zero population growth ultimately run into
the problem that ours is a highly interconnected society and
economy. No state or city is an island, entire unto itself. Local
policies may try to limit population by passing restrictive zoning, limiting housing permits, and the like. This is the I'm-all-
right-Jack-and-bar-the-door version, much favored by suburbs,
which forces out the young and is regressive. Local policies may
try to curtail economic growth, but effective policies lead to unacceptable social and economic consequences. And a local policy
of limiting births, which seems to me the most morally acceptable
of these policies, will do little to reduce growth because the young
from other places will inevitably arrive.

Because the nation is so interconnected, local population policies, whether for growth or no-growth, are usually an attempt at
a mercantilistic beggaring of neighbors; however, because larger
forces are operating in the system, they are likely to be ineffective. A hierarchy of levels is involved, so that what is viewed as
an issue of growth at a lower level is an issue of distribution at
the next higher level. Thus, growth decisions for each locality
within a metropolitan area should be bargained out among all
the components of the metropolis to insure that their effects on
the futures of the other localities will be considered. This is necessary both for fairness and efficiency. If the objectives, plans,
and actions of diverse localities are inconsistent, they cannot all
be right, and some will fail while others triumph. Only when
these various growth considerations are viewed together can it

be seen whether they add up, where joint action can be more effective than unilateral action for achieving complementary objectives, and where negotiation and compensation are needed to reconcile diverging purposes and interests.

For much the same reasons the growth decisions of the various metropolitan areas and other regions should be based on state and national considerations. The task is again one of coordination and mediation, and as yet we have very little operational knowledge of how to go about it, either technically or politically. Yet this is the issue which has attracted considerable, if confused, attention under the rather misleading name of "national growth policy."

In any case it is clear that, although questions of local growth should be treated as questions of distribution at a higher level, we should avoid what is often done, setting as policy goals arbitrary demographic rates (no growth or fast growth) or particular geographic patterns of distribution (dispersal or concentration). These rates and patterns are not proper goals, although they may be important instruments for advancing the real goals of material efficiency, of equity and fairness, of ecological integrity, and of a high quality of life. They are used as goals because they are easy to grasp and they avoid the real questions which are hard. They are also used, I suspect, because they substitute what appears to be a technical objective for what is really a political matter of deciding how to balance alternative and often conflicting goals, and how to deal with costs and benefits which are very unevenly distributed.

"National growth policy" should more properly be called "national territorial distribution policy," and local growth policies within metropolitan areas should be thought of as elements in shaping the distribution of metropolitan growth. In neither case am I suggesting that the ideal would have the higher level dictate to the lower one. The interests of each collectivity and each governmental unit must be represented in the making of the higher level policy. One of the urgent and unresolved issues of our times is the need to evolve processes to give a voice in the making of important decisions to the relevant collectivities, be they corporations such as local governments, or other collectivities such as ethnic and other interest groups. But this is a larger matter.

Something like national zero population growth seems to be desirable, and we appear to be moving rapidly in that direction. But it is quite clear that even in a situation of national demographic stability, some localities will grow, some will shrink, and some will stay at about the same population. Through all this, vast cross-movements of population will continue, as will structural changes in the society and the economy. Many of today's problems will continue to exist, and some new ones will arise. We will not arrive at an eternally tranquil late afternoon.

Transportation and Poverty

JOHN F. KAIN AND JOHN R. MEYER

This article, by two of our best-known urban economists, John Kain, Professor of Economics at Harvard, and John Meyer, Professor in the Harvard School of Business and President of the National Bureau of Economic Research, presents the findings of a conference on transportation and poverty that the authors organized and chaired in 1968. The American Academy of Arts and Sciences sponsored this conference, and it was financed by the Department of Housing and Urban Development and the Bureau of Public Roads of the Department of Transportation.

WIDESPREAD CONCERN about the problems of poverty and race has led to a proliferation of schemes for reducing the unemployment, increasing the incomes, and generally improving the well-being of disadvantaged groups in our society. Prominent among these are several that would use transportation to increase the employment opportunities of the poor. The concept that inadequate transportation must be numbered among the disadvantages of the poor and that improved mobility, particularly as it improves access to jobs, could increase their self-sufficiency was publicized widely in the aftermath of the Watts riots in 1965. The McCone Commission report on the causes of the riots concluded that "the most serious immediate problem [facing] the Negro in our community is employment. . . ." The commission suggested that, although a serious lack of skill and overt discrimination are major causes of high Negro unemployment, inadequate and costly public transportation also limit Negro employment opportunities.

The McCone Commission, therefore, recommended that public transit services in Los Angeles be expanded and subsidized. (Its report was strangely silent about the possibility of improving access to jobs by reducing segregation in the housing market.) This recommendation attracted considerable public attention, and the federal government, through the Department of Housing and Urban Development, has sponsored some demonstration projects designed to ascertain if better and more extensive transit services between ghettos and employment centers would yield additional jobs for ghetto residents. The entire subject is very fashionable. But it is astonishing how little knowledge lies behind the popular political opinions it provokes.

A NEW PROBLEM?

In light of the new public awareness of the relation between poverty and transportation, it is appropriate to ask whether the problem itself is new. Obviously, poverty is no new problem; nor is it a growing problem. But when the relation between transportation and poverty is examined, it becomes apparent that something *is* new. Postwar changes in urban ecology and transportation systems, while conferring significant improvements on the majority, have almost certainly caused a *relative* deterioration in the access to job opportunities enjoyed by a significant fraction of the poor.

To be sure, many, if not most, poor continue to live in centrally located residential areas; and these are reasonably well served by public transit to the central business district, where one usually finds the highest density of job opportunities. But in the past two decades, new job opportunities have grown more swiftly *outside* this central business district. It is estimated that there may be one hundred thousand fewer low-income jobs in New York City than there are low-income workers. A similar pattern has apparently emerged in several other American cities. Living in a neighborhood well served by public transit to the central business district is therefore less of an advantage for lower-income groups today than it once was.

THE AUTOMOBILE AND THE POOR

Reflecting these and other changes in the postwar pattern of American urban living, the total number of passenger trips by mass transit has declined in every year since World War II. Much of the early postwar decline must be viewed against the abnormal conditions of wartime, when transit use was artificially swollen by restrictions on automobile use; transit patronage in 1953 was almost the same as in 1940 or 1941. But the decline in transit use has continued well past 1953, and today transit patronage is about two-thirds of what it was in 1940 or 1953, in spite of a considerable growth in urban population during the past decade.

This can be explained by the fact that a growing proportion of the urban population chooses to travel by automobile. To a considerable extent this results from steadily expanding auto ownership. In 1950, six out of every ten United States households owned one or more private automobiles. By 1967, the figure was nearly eight out of every ten. But of family units with incomes between $2,000 and $2,999 before taxes, only 53 per cent owned an automobile in 1967. The percentage of those with autos in the below-$2,000 bracket is, of course, much lower still.

The low levels of auto ownership among the poor reflect the fact that the automobile, though a near necessity in much of urban America, is a very expensive one. The high initial capital outlay and operating costs of a private automobile are a heavy strain on the budgets of low-income households. In general, then, when adequate transit services are available, low-income households can and do obtain substantial savings by foregoing auto ownership.

The acquisition of an efficient private automobile (one without exorbitant maintenance costs) requires considerable financing, a chronic difficulty for the poor. Poor people, therefore, even when they own cars, generally own poor cars. Many of these are inadequate for long-distance commutation and expressway operation. Often they are also uninsured. Thus, statistics on car ownership among the poor, as adverse as they are, may paint a more favorable picture than is actually justified.

The dependence on public transit by the urban poor therefore continues to be very great. In the New York region, for example, less than 25 per cent of the households earning under $1,000 per year in 1963 used private automobiles to reach work; over 75 per cent used some form of transit. The proportions using automobiles were 57 per cent for those with incomes between $4,000 and $10,000, and 62 per cent for those with incomes over $10,000 per year.

Transit managements have made some effort to offset the steady decline in transit use by developing new markets. They have done this mainly by expanding route miles or services offered. The route miles of rapid and grade-separated rail transit service have increased about 2 per cent since 1945 and soon will increase further as new rail rapid transit systems under construction are completed. Route miles of all kinds of transit service, bus and rail, have risen nearly 20 per cent since 1955. In the same period, however, transit operators have curtailed the vehicle (revenue) miles of services offered by 20 per cent in response to decreases in ridership. To some extent this decline in vehicle miles of service has been offset by the use of larger vehicles with more seats. Nevertheless, the overall effect has been a reduction in the frequency and, therefore, the basic quality of the service rendered. In general, reductions in service offerings have been most severe on weekends and other off-peak periods (particularly evenings) and for commuter trains.

TRANSIT TO SUBURBAN JOBS

The effectiveness of the additional route miles, moreover, has been less than it might have been because modern bus transit tends to follow the same routes as the old streetcar lines. This means that a high percentage of services in most cities converge on the central business district. For an individual to make a trip from one point at the periphery of a city to another point at the periphery usually requires taking one radial line into the central business district then transferring to another line to make the trip out to his destination. This arrangement tends to be costly for both operators and users. Bus lines operating through a central business district encounter congestion, with all that entails for increasing operating costs. For the user wanting to make a trip from one peripheral urban location to another, the radial trip to and from the central business district means a much longer and more time-consuming journey than is geographically necessary. Commuters at all income levels, therefore, tend to use automobiles for such trips. Even the poor tend to do so whenever they can make the necessary arrangements, either by owning an inexpensive car or by joining a carpool.

In general, conventional transit is at a performance disadvantage compared to driving or carpooling when serving thinly traveled, long-distance routes between central city residences and suburban workplaces. Even when available, the transit service is often too little and too slow to compete with the automobile. Moreover, such transit service can impose dollars-and-cents handicaps that go beyond the direct costs in money and time of the commuter's trip itself. For example, conventional transit often adapts to limited demand by providing only peak-hour service between the suburban workplaces and centrally located residential areas. The worker must either catch the bus when it leaves exactly at closing time, or find some other mode of transportation, often at considerable additional expense. This means that the worker who depends on public transit cannot easily accept overtime employment. The unavailability of a worker for overtime work not only denies him a lucrative opportunity, but can involve costs to his employer as well. Limited public transit scheduling, for example, can make it difficult for the employer to stagger shifts or closing hours. (And staggered closing hours can be helpful in solving such other transportation problems as traffic congestion at peak commuter hours.)

It is therefore not surprising that transit operators serving suburban plants report that low-income workers frequently use transit only when obtaining their jobs and for the first few days or weeks of employment. Once the workers manage to save enough for the down payment on a car, or become acquainted with some fellow workers living near them, they drive to work or join a carpool. *If this is a common pattern, existing transit services may indeed be serving a critical function for low-income households, but one whose value is badly gauged by the fare box or by aggregate statistics on transit use.*

The basic problem, however, remains: Efficient transit requires that large numbers of persons travel between the same two points at approximately the same time. The growing dispersal of workplaces and residences means that this condition is satisfied less frequently than before. As jobs, and particularly blue-collar jobs, have shifted from areas that are relatively well served by public transit to areas that are poorly served, employment opportunities for low-income households dependent on public transit service have been reduced. Increasingly, low-income workers are forced to choose between a higher-paying job that is inaccessible by public transit, and thereby pay more for transportation (e.g., by buying and operating an automobile), or a lower-paying job that is served by transit. To put it in somewhat different terms, low-income households now have at their disposal at most only a bit more, and oftentimes less, transit service than they once did for reaching what is, in effect, a much larger metropolitan region.

THE PROBLEM OF RACE

The dispersal of the job market and the decline of transit systems have created particular difficulties for low-income Negroes. If the job of a low-income white worker shifts to the suburbs, he is usually able to follow it by moving to a new residence. If not, he may be able to relocate his residence to be near a transit line serving his new suburban workplace reasonably well. The low-income Negro worker, however, may not be so fortunate. Regardless of his income or family situation, if his job moves to the suburbs, he may find it difficult to move out of the ghetto. That is, his residence may not easily follow his job to the suburbs. For him, the service characteristics, coverage, and cost of the transportation system can therefore be especially critical.

Unfortunately, conventional transit systems usually do not provide adequate services between the ghetto and suburban workplaces. The black worker, confined to ghetto housing near but not directly at the urban core, cannot readily reach many new suburban job locations by simple reverse commuting on existing transit systems. Existing public transit tends to connect suburban *residential* locations with the very core of the central business district; it may not pass through, or even near, new suburban industrial or office parks, just as it may also fail to pass through the ghetto.

If the ghetto resident is able to reach a suburban workplace at all by public transit, the trip may be expensive. If he is lucky, he may be able to join a carpool with a fellow worker and share the considerable expense of a long-distance auto trip from the ghetto. Here, too, the limitations on his residential options and the remoteness of most suburban workplaces from the ghetto reduce the possibilities of him making an advantageous arrangement.

THE POLICY QUESTIONS

Despite the public discussion and federally financed experiments that followed publication of the McCone Commission report, virtually nothing has been done so far to establish a factual basis for evaluating the utility of improved transportation in reducing urban poverty and unemployment. In particular, answers must be found to a number of questions. What effects do existing transportation policies have on income distribution? Are they the ones that were anticipated? Can transportation policy be an effective tool for expanding the opportunities and increasing the welfare of the disadvantaged? Should transportation be used this way? If so, what specific policies and programs should be adopted for achieving these purposes?

Jobs and Transportation · Inferior access to new jobs is by no means the only disadvantage of the ghetto resident. Indeed, in terms of his participation in the labor market, it may be much less important than other factors. Thomas Floyd, who was deeply involved in the administration of demonstration projects in Watts and elsewhere, notes, "There is . . . reason to believe that some employers were using the transportation barrier as a convenient excuse for not hiring for other reasons. In additional to racial bias, there may be presumed or actual inadequate job skills or work habits." When the improved transportation services were provided, he observed, the jobs did not always materialize.

If transportation is but one of many factors influencing job opportunities, provision of more or cheaper transportation *by itself* is probably an inefficient method of reducing unemployment or increasing incomes. Effective measures to increase the opportunities, employment, and incomes of the long-term unemployed or underemployed must operate simultaneously on several fronts. Training, education, counseling, placement, and transportation programs complement one another. Most or all of these programs should have a role in any well-designed assault

on employment problems, and any one of these programs in isolation could well fail because it lacked other essential services.
On the other hand, simply putting all these programs into effect simultaneously would not guarantee results either. The different programs must be properly articulated and synthesized.

Income Redistribution and Transportation · Subsidies for urban transportation have long enjoyed wide support on the ground
that such subsidies help the poor. In spite of the fact that the poor
generally are more reliant on transit than the rich, the truth of
this proposition is less than self-evident.

Advocates of public transit subsidies need to be discriminat-
ing if the subsidies they support are actually to aid the poor.
Many proposed new systems, such as the BART system in San
Francisco and the transit extensions in Boston, will provide only
nominal benefits for the poor. In fact, it is probable that both
systems will have a highly regressive impact. They are to be subsidized out of the property tax, which is heavily regressive; and
virtually all of the benefits will accrue to high-income, long-distance commuters traveling between high-income suburbs and
central employment centers. They will do practically nothing to
improve accessibility between centrally located ghettos and suburban employment centers.

In general, users of high-speed, long-distance rail commuter
systems are among the wealthier classes of society. Local bus
systems, by contrast, frequently serve large numbers of low-income users. Paradoxically, these local bus services rarely require
large public subsidies. In fact, the available evidence suggests
that local bus systems serving low-income and dense central city
neighborhoods often make a profit, and often subsidize unprofitable long-distance commuter systems serving low-density, high-
income neighborhoods.

Another anomalous fact is that a disproportionate number of
taxi trips are made by poor persons. The explanation apparently
is that many locations are simply inaccessible to carless households except by taxi. For many of the poor, occasional use of
taxicabs as a supplement to transit and to walking is relatively
economical compared with automobile ownership.

New York provides contrasting figures that illustrate this point.

In New York, poor households do *not* make proportionately more taxi trips than middle-income families. The reason is that a smaller proportion of middle- and upper-income families own automobiles in New York than elsewhere. Moreover, the public transit system is much more extensive in New York than in most other cities and is thus a better substitute for taxicabs. In small cities and towns, however, taxicabs are sometimes the only form of public transit available to the poor. In these instances the poor and infirm may be almost the only users of taxicabs—because everyone else drives.

Thus, the apparently simple question of which income groups use which modes of transportation is a good deal more complex than is commonly imagined. Such hasty generalizations as "taxicabs are a luxury used only by the very rich"; "automobile ownership is limited to the well-to-do"; and "transit is used only by the poor" fail to hold up under scrutiny.

The mobility and transport choices of different income groups could be discussed more cogently if we had better measures of urban mobility. Unfortunately, the usual measure of "tripmaking" used in metropolitan transportation studies is poorly suited for defining mobility differences between different income classes. By definition, only vehicle trips (transit, truck, taxi, or automobile) and walk-to-work trips are counted as trips; walking trips other than those made to and from work are omitted. On average, such noncommuter walking trips are probably of far greater importance in low-income than in high-income neighborhoods. Poor people more often than higher-income people live in high-density neighborhoods where shopping, recreation, and employment are located close to home. Many trips that must be made by auto or transit in low density areas can conveniently be made by foot in high-density neighborhoods. Whether this means, as some believe, that the poor should be considered less mobile is not entirely clear.

In general, almost no data exist that describe how persons of different life styles, living at different urban densities and income levels, solve their personal transportation problems. Moreover, there is no hard information to demonstrate the existence of large and unfulfilled latent demands for alternative forms of transportation. Information on such matters is crucial for designing programs to improve the mobility of the poor and for evaluating the benefits of such programs as against their costs. Yet, to date, the information simply has not been gathered.

Indirect Costs · Most observers agree that the indirect and secondary costs of major transportation investment, such as urban expressways and rapid transit, have not been given adequate consideration when choosing locations and alignment, designing facilities, and deciding whether construction is justified at all. At least two major kinds of such costs can be identified.

First, there are uncompensated costs imposed on individuals —residents, property owners, and businessmen—who are forced to move. These uncompensated costs commonly include not only the direct money outlays for moving but also losses engendered by destruction of cherished friendships, familiar environments, business relationships, and other intangibles.

Second, there are collective costs. These consist of adverse changes in the neighborhood or environment and largely affect those who are *not* required to move. It is sometimes remarked that the owners whose property is taken by eminent domain are often the lucky ones. Those located nearby, but not within, the right-of-way frequently suffer disruption and loss of value for which they receive no compensation. There can be no doubt that the building of a major highway or transit line through a residential area causes fundamental changes to the neighborhood. These changes may be either beneficial or harmful—quite often, they are both.

There is some evidence that the disruption may be greater if the highway or transit line is put through a tightly knit working-class community as opposed to a middle-class area. Some observers have argued that the working-class family is more immobile than the middle-class family, and more tightly linked to an extended family that typically lives within walking distance. If true, when a decision is made to carry out construction in a working-class neighborhood, greater aid may be needed to compensate displaced residents and to assist the reconstruction of their environment.

Unfortunately, few operational tools are available for improving route selection decisions by taking such broader social considerations into account. To do so, several hard questions must be faced. How much community-wide benefit from construction of a road should be sacrificed for these neighborhood and individual values? Can cash payments of whatever amount compensate residents for the real character of their loss? If they cannot reconstruct their present environment, would adequate resources allow the displaced to construct a different but equally satisfactory or better environment? Is the problem in question essentially unique, or is it typical of all or most low-income communities? If it is typical, the road builders' options are, of course, limited. Almost any alignment would impose comparable costs on the affected communities. The range of choice is then narrowed to whether the road should be built, which remedial actions should be taken to limit the displacement or damage, and how generously the damaged population should be compensated.

Existing compensation formulas and mechanisms, unfortunately, fail to compensate many losers altogether and provide many others with grossly inadequate compensation. These inadequacies are responsible for much of the current resistance to urban transportation construction. A few individuals are often required to bear a disproportionately large share of the costs of urban transportation improvements in order to provide benefits for all. In these circumstances, spontaneous community action to oppose the new construction is hardly surprising.

Proposed Solutions · Perhaps the most ambitious proposal for improving urban transportation services for the poor is to make public transit free, thereby eliminating income as a determinant of transit use. Clearly, though, this is inefficient. A large proportion of transit users are not poor, and free transit would subsidize the affluent as well as the poor. Moreover, the major difficulty facing the poor, and particularly the ghetto poor, is not that transit is too expensive, but that it is all too frequently unavailable in forms and services that are needed. In general, transit use seems far more sensitive to service improvements than to fare reductions, even for the poor. Nor is "free" transit particularly cheap. It has been estimated that, nationwide, the costs of free transit would be approximately $2 billion a year, assuming no increase in service.

Boston can be used to illustrate the comparative costs of free transit and service improvements for the poor. Until very recently, access between Boston's Roxbury ghetto and rapidly expanding suburban employment centers has been nonexistent for all practical purposes. The costs of providing transit services between all Boston's poverty areas (i.e., census tracts with median family incomes below $5,500 per year) and low skill employment centers has been estimated at about $4.3 million annually. This is to be compared with an estimate of $75 million a year for free transit in Boston. The $4.3 million figure is, moreover, a total or gross cost; it would be less if any fare box revenues were realized. Furthermore, the $75 million subsidy for free transit would not provide any significant improvement in transit service between central city poverty areas and suburban employment centers.

An increasingly popular view is that public transit systems, as currently constituted, are incapable of increasing the mobility of the poor. The argument is that the transportation demands involved in serving outlying workplaces from central city residences are too complex to be met adequately by any kind of public transit services at costs that are competitive with private automobiles. At two persons per car, for example, the cost of private automobile operation often is comparable to or lower than bus transportation in serving dispersed workplaces.

If so, it may be cheaper and more effective to provide some form of personal transportation for the poor. One such proposal, which its originator terms "new Volks for poor folks," is to rent, lease, or otherwise finance new or relatively new cars for low-income households. Cheap used cars are seldom low-cost cars. If the cost of automobile use is to be reduced for low-income groups, their cars must be relatively new; if they are to have such new cars, the cost of credit must be lowered. A related proposal is to assist those workers who live in central ghettos and work in the suburbs to sell transportation services to fellow workers. Such sales would help pay the purchase and operating costs of an automobile. In many cities, however, this proposal would encounter a number of institutional and legal barriers.

Of course, new cars for poor people will not help nondrivers, who are now estimated to make up 20 per cent of the population over 17 years of age. In fact, any extension of automobile ownership among the able-bodied poor may only serve to further degrade public transit services for nondrivers. To provide mobility for nondrivers, some have advocated the development of so-called demand actuated systems. Different versions of this concept come under a variety of names or acronyms, including Taxi-bus, Dial-a-bus, DART, GENIE, and CARS. In all cases, however, the idea is to provide something approximating the point-to-point service of taxis, while achieving better utilization levels and load factors than transit vehicles can now achieve on fixed routes and schedules.

In these systems, vehicles intermediate in size between a taxicab and a conventional bus would be used to pick up and deliver passengers at specific origins and destinations. By use of electronic control and scheduling, it is claimed, loads could be assembled with a minimum of delay. Proponents believe these systems usually would have cost characteristics intermediate between the conventional bus and the taxicab. By providing more individualistic door-to-door service than public transit, these systems might be of particular use for the elderly and the infirm. Furthermore, if such systems have the advantages suggested, they might be a better and more politically acceptable solution to the problems of ghetto access than subsidies to extend ownership of private automobiles, particularly in older cities with high density central residential neighborhoods.

Indeed, were it not for franchise restrictions and prohibitions on group fares, taxicabs could improve their operating efficiency considerably without any technological improvements. Demand-activated systems are functionally identical with taxis, but have more sophisticated scheduling, control devices, and operating policies.

Indeed, many benefits would accrue to the poor if there were fewer restrictions on the provision of taxi and jitney services. A deregulated taxi industry would provide a considerable number of additional jobs for low-income workers. It has been calculated that removing entry barriers and other controls might expand the number of taxis by as much as two and a half times in most American cities. In Philadelphia, for example, this regulation could create an additional seventy-four hundred jobs for drivers alone; if these jobs went to the poorest 20 per cent of the population, unemployment among these poor would fall by about 3.2 percentage points.

Taxi operation can also be an imortant income supplement for low-income households even where it is not a full-time job. A significant number of Washington's taxi drivers own and operate their own cabs on a part-time basis as a supplement to a regular job. The off-duty cab often doubles as the family car, thus substantially reducing the cost of auto ownership and increasing the mobility of residents of low-income neighborhoods.

A much expanded taxi and jitney industry could also provide an appreciable increase in urban mobility, particularly for the poor. Except for restrictive legislation, jitneys and taxicabs might now be providing a significant fraction of passenger service in urban areas. The greater number of taxis per hundred persons in Washington, D.C., an essentially unregulated city, and the sizable capital value of medallions (franchises to operate a cab) in New York, Boston, and several other cities, attest to a substantial latent demand for these services.

In short, simply providing larger subsidies to transit systems is unlikely to be an effective way of increasing the mobility of the poor. New systems seem needed, and there is some agreement on their characteristics. Such systems would normally use a smaller vehicle than conventional transit, would be demand activated rather than on fixed routes and schedules, and would provide point-to-point service or some close approximation of it. Such systems would most likely have somewhat lower passenger mile costs than do taxicabs (even those operating in unrestricted markets like Washington), but unit costs probably would be somewhat above those of current transit systems. In some instances, such services, might merely supplement the more heavily used transit services; in others, they might replace such services altogether.

Ownership of these more ubiquitous systems might vary from place to place and from time to time. Where elaborate control and scheduling are required, a fleet might be necessary. In other instances, the services could be provided by large numbers of owner-operators working either independently or in a cooperative. Another possibility is nothing more complicated than organized carpooling, compensated or uncompensated.

Most such systems require very little long-lived investment. The most extensive capital requirements, of course, would be for the more elaborate, electronically controlled, demand activated systems. All would require major changes in institutions and regulatory frameworks. Fortunately, however, most also lend themselves to experimentation on a modest scale. Such experimentation could do much to improve our fund of information, which at this point is simply inadequate to support bolder policy initiatives.

PART FOUR   The Future of the Inner City

The Future of American Ghettos

ANTHONY DOWNS

*Though he has contributed widely to the primary field of his re-
search, urban studies, Anthony Downs is best known for his
seminal book,* An Economic Theory of Democracy, *one of the
most vital building blocks in the field of public choice. This essay,
taken from* Urban Processes, *published by the Urban Institute, is
adapted from a talk given at a National Academy of Sciences
symposium. Downs is president of the Real Estate Research Corporation, a consulting firm based in Chicago, Illinois.*

KEY BACKGROUND FACTS FOR THE FUTURE OF GHETTOS

SINCE THE WATTS riots in 1965, the conditions in, and future of,
what have come to be called "American ghettos" have become
key national issues of vital importance. Yet there is sufficient ignorance about the basic realities concerned so that any analysis
of this issue must begin with a clear statement of a few background facts. Then policies can be formulated and evaluated by
building on these facts.

What Does Ghetto *Mean?* · The first item to be addressed is
the meaning of the word *ghetto*. It usually denotes compulsory
living in some kind of an enclave by members of some identifiable group. However, it can be interpreted either economically
or racially. The economic interpretation refers to poor people
who are compelled to live together in ghettos because they cannot afford to move elsewhere. The racial interpretation refers to
people of a certain racial composition who are compelled to live
together in one district by outside pressures and discrimination
against them. This was the case in Europe in relation to Jewish

communities where the word *ghetto* was first used. I use the racial sense in talking about American ghettos.

Therefore, I define these ghettos as the entire nonwhite population of the central cities in our 224 metropolitan areas. Since 92 percent of all American nonwhites are Negroes, data about nonwhites are essentially the same as those about Negroes. This racial definition of American ghettos means that middle-income and upper-income Negroes, as well as poor ones, are included in what I have defined as ghettos.

In 1966, there were between twelve million and fourteen million persons in American ghettos defined in this way. We do not know the exact total because the Census Bureau is unable to find the great many people who live in ghettos. It admittedly under-counted the Negro population in 1960 by about 10 percent in the nation as a whole. In other words, the Census Bureau could not find about two million Negroes. In Chicago, we did a very careful study of school enrollment data to check up on the accuracy of the Census Bureau's population data. We discovered an undercount among Negroes of 16 percent, or a failure to count about 157,000 people in the city of Chicago in 1960.

But even allowing for an undercount, less than 7 percent of the total U.S. population lives in ghettos as I have defined them. This means that 93 percent of the population does *not* live in ghettos. I emphasize that obvious conclusion because the country as a whole is not likely to worry very much about what is happening to only 7 percent of its population—at least normal political processes may not pay much attention to this group. This apathy is particularly likely because the 7 percent concerned are among the lowest-income and least influential people in society.

Ghetto Population Dynamics · A second important background fact concerns the dynamics of ghetto population. We hear many people talk about how the United States must break up or disperse the ghettos, as though such actions were real possibilities. Actually, ghettos are not only failing to shrink, break up, or disperse—they are growing rapidly. From 1960 to 1966, all ghettos in the United States defined as noted above were growing in population at about 400,000 persons per year. In contrast, the

number of white persons in the same central cities dropped by
as much as 4.9 million from 1960 to 1966 because of massive out-
migration to suburban areas. These conditions created striking
disparities in the racial composition of population growth in central cities on the one hand, and suburbs on the other hand. From
1960 to 1966, over 100 percent of the net increase in the central
city population was Negro, since the white population was declining. In contrast, only about 2 percent of the population
growth in the suburbs was Negro, whereas 98 percent of suburban population growth was white. In fact, there was actually an
out-migration of Negroes from suburbs into central cities in that
period. This polarization of growth rates illustrates what the Kerner Commission meant by continued movement toward two separate societies.

Since 1966, the Census Bureau has issued new data which de-
pict trends very different from those described above. Those data
indicate a marked slowdown of Negro growth in central cities,
and a big increase of Negro growth in suburbs. Frankly, I do not
have much confidence in the accuracy of these figures. I believe
there has been a slowdown of ghetto growth, but I do not think
it has been as drastic as the Census Bureau shows. Rather, it appears to me that Negro growth in most large cities is continuing
except where the ghetto has spilled over into the suburbs. This
does not indicate any lessening of racial segregation in housing.
Rather, the segregated areas have passed over the central city
limits and spilled into suburban areas, as in St. Louis. Moreover,
even the Census Bureau's figures show that white out-migration
from central cities is occurring faster than ever.

It is undoubtedly true that fertility and birth rates among both
whites and Negroes have slowed down sharply in the past decade. Fertility rates—which indicate the number of live births per
thousand women between the ages of 15 and 44—reached their
peaks in both ethnic groups in 1957. Since then, these rates have
fallen by about 30 percent. Nevertheless, the Negro fertility rate
is still almost 45 percent higher than the white fertility rate.
This is mainly the result of educational differences between Negroes and whites. In fact, the fertility rate among college-edu-
cated Negro women is actually lower than among college-edu-
cated white women. Nevertheless, there is still a very high birth

rate in the Negro population as compared to the white population. And the main cause of ghetto growth now is natural increase within the existing ghetto population, rather than migration of more Negroes into big cities.

The "Law of Cultural Dominance" · The third background fact critical to this analysis is not really a single fact, but rather a theory of white residential behavior. This theory has been developed by my father and myself based upon our empirical observations over the years. It is admittedly not firmly grounded in statistical analysis, since adequate data are simply not available. Nevertheless, we believe the kind of behavior depicted by this theory plays a vital role in social change in large American cities. The imprecision of our theory is typical of the way practitioners must use imperfect raw materials in trying to develop concrete policies in the social sciences.

We refer to this theory as the "Law of Cultural Dominance." In our opinion, most white families do not object to living in the same neighborhood as Negroes. In fact, we believe a vast majority of whites of all income groups would be willing to send their children to integrated schools or live in integrated neighborhoods, as long as they were sure that the white group concerned would remain in the majority in those facilities or areas. The residential and educational objectives of these whites are not dependent upon their maintaining any kind of "ethnic purity" in their neighborhoods or schools. Rather, those objectives depend on their maintaining a certain degree of "cultural dominance" therein.

These whites—like most other middle-class citizens of any race —want to be sure that the social, cultural, and economic milieu and values of their group dominate their own residential environment and the educational environment of their children. This desire in turn springs from the typical middle-class belief of all racial groups that everyday life should be primarily a *value-reinforcing* experience for both adults and children, rather than primarily a *value-altering* one. The best way to insure that this will happen is to somewhat isolate oneself and one's children in an everyday environment dominated by—but not necessarily exclusively comprised of—other families and children whose social, economic, cultural, and even religious views and attitudes are approximately the same as one's own.

There is no intrinsic reason why race or color should be perceived as a value relevant to attaining such homogeneity. Clearly, race and color have no necessary linkage with the kinds of social, cultural, economic, or religious characteristics and values that can have a true functional impact upon adults and children. Yet I believe a majority of middle-class white Americans still perceive race and color as relevant factors in their assessment of the kind of homogeneity they seek to attain. Moreover, this false perception is reinforced by their lack of everyday experience and contact with Negroes who are, in fact, like them in all important respects. Therefore, in deciding whether a given neighborhood or a given school exhibits the kind of environment in which "their own" traits are and will remain dominant, they consider Negroes as members of "another" group.

It is true that some people want themselves and their children to be immersed in a wide variety of viewpoints, values, and types of people, rather than a relatively homogeneous group. This desire is particularly strong among the intellectuals who dominate the urban planning profession. They are also the strongest supporters of big-city life and the most vitriolic critics of suburbia. Yet I believe their viewpoint—though dominant in recent public discussions of urban problems—is actually shared by only a tiny minority of Americans of any racial group.

Almost everyone favors at least some exposure to a wide variety of viewpoints. But experience in our own society and most others shows that the overwhelming majority of middle-class families choose residential locations and schools precisely in order to provide the kind of value-reinforcing experience described above. This is why most Jews live in predominantly Jewish neighborhoods, even in the suburbs; why Catholic parents continue to support separate school systems; and partly why so few middle-class Negro families have been willing to risk moving to all-white suburbs even where there is almost no threat of any kind of harassment.

I am not trying to defend the behavior described by this "Law of Cultural Dominance." Yet however demeaning this phenomenon may be to Negroes, it must be recognized if we are to understand why residential segregation has persisted so strongly in the United States, and what conditions are necessary to create successful racial integration. The growth of nonwhite residential areas has led to "massive transition" from white to Negro occupancy mainly because there has been no mechanism that could assure the whites in any given area that they would remain in the majority after Negroes once began entering.

Normal population turnover causes about 20 percent of the residents of the average U.S. neighborhood to move out every year. Such moves occur because of income changes, job transfers, shifts in life-cycle position, or debts. In order for a neighborhood to retain any given character, the persons who move in to occupy the resulting vacancies must be similar to those who have departed.

But once Negroes begin entering an all-white neighborhood near the ghetto, most other white families become convinced that the area will eventually become all Negro, mainly because this has happened so often before. Hence it is difficult to persuade whites not now living there to move in and occupy vacancies. They are only willing to move into neighborhoods where whites are now the dominant majority and seem likely to remain so. So the whites who would otherwise have moved in from elsewhere stop doing so. This means that almost all vacancies are eventually occupied by Negroes, and the neighborhood inexorably shifts toward a heavy Negro majority. Once this happens, the remaining whites also seek to leave. They do not wish to remain in an area where they have lost their culturally dominant position. Yet the key mechanism in this transition is not any flight from the neighborhood by the whites that were there initially. Rather it is the failure of other whites to keep moving into the neighborhood.

Thus racial transition occurs, and stable integration is prevented, because there is no mechanism by which whites can simultaneously achieve two objectives. The first is living in an integrated neighborhood so that whites and Negroes can experience living together. The second objective is living in an area in which whites remain the dominant group.

For reasons beyond the control of each individual, whites must choose between complete segregation or living in an area heavily dominated by members of what they consider "another group." Given their values, they choose the former. Thus the "Law of Cultural Dominance is very important because it means that the growth of the Negro population in our big cities leads to more segregation and a constant expansion of the racial ghetto, rather than wider experience of racially integrated living. In my opinion, it would be highly desirable if race and color ultimately became insignificant factors in human interaction, similar to the color of one's eyes or hair. Yet it will be difficult to alter present attitudes, so that race and color really do become insignificant, if whites and Negroes do not ever have any experience in living together and discovering how similar they really are.

Thus, reducing the centrality of race and color as issues and barriers in human relations appears to require some means of allowing whites to live in integrated areas while remaining assured of dominance—at least as long as present white racial attitudes persist. One means of doing this would be the creation of integrated neighborhoods away from the ghetto, particularly in suburban areas distant from large all-Negro neighborhoods. In such areas, the appearance of a few Negro residents would not immediately herald the potential arrival of many more because of the pressure of nearby ghetto expansion. This possibility is directly relevant to one of the ghetto futures set forth later in this article.

I readily admit that this whole concept is extremely controversial and raises many difficult questions. For example, why should Negroes want to live in an integrated neighborhood if they must always be in the minority? After all, Negroes might also conceive of desirable integration as a mixture of racism in which *they* are the dominant group. However, if both whites and Negroes insist on local dominance in order to achieve integration, we will never have any integration.

The Fiscal Squeeze on City Governments · The fourth significant background fact concerns the fiscal squeeze on local and state governments. This squeeze is especially acute in older central cities where the concentration of low-income population is much greater than in newer suburbs. Some aims of city governments tend to drive wealthy people out of the central city. In addition, certain factors and practices in American urban areas tend to attract the poor into central cities. Those cities contain the oldest housing in metropolitan areas, since they were built first.

In the United States, the oldest housing is typically in the worst physical condition, and is, therefore, the least expensive and the most available to poor people. This is not necessarily true in many parts of the rest of the world. Particularly in relatively underdeveloped countries, the poorest people in society live in brand new housing. They build such housing themselves in the form of shacks created on the edge of each major city. However, in the United States we have such high moral principles that we impose middle-class standards on the construction of all new housing—even housing designed for lower-income occupancy. Therefore, we do not allow anyone to build a new substandard quality unit—that is, a shack. Yet many poor people can afford to live only in extremely low-quality housing. Since we prevent them from building new low-quality housing, they must make older housing low-quality enough so they can afford it. This means they must go and live in the center of our large cities where the oldest housing stock is concentrated. As a result, we have a high concentration of low-income populations, particularly recent in-migrants, in the middle of our central cities and in some older suburbs. In relatively underdeveloped countries, low-income in-migrants are concentrated on the outskirts of the cities, or scattered through them.

Moreover, our rigid political boundaries mean the central cities are fiscally isolated from the remainder of the metropolitan area. So the rising concentration of low-income residents within their boundaries creates a growing need for expenditures by those cities to serve the costly needs of poor people. At the same time, property values stagnate or even decline because those poor people cannot afford to maintain their homes in good condition, or to spend enough money to keep local stores prosperous. The resulting squeeze on central city finances is worsened by inflation and rising wages. So central city governments —and even suburban governments—find themselves in an increasingly desperate financial position. This is extremely important in part because it reduces the willingness of middle-income citizens to engage in income redistribution, since their local property taxes are skyrocketing anyway.

Keeping in mind all the background facts described above, let us now consider alternative possible futures of American ghettos. In theory, we could conceive of hundreds of various futures containing different conditions. However, I believe it is useful to arbitrarily conceive of three basic alternatives in order to focus on the key choices facing society.

The Present-Policies Alternative · The first of these futures is the *present-policies alternative*. It would involve continued segregation in housing and schools, continued concentration of Negro population growth primarily in central cities instead of elsewhere, and continued failure of society to transfer any really large economic aid to the most deprived portions of central cities. Under these circumstances, many older central cities will gradually become fiscally bankrupt. They will have rising expenditure needs for their own poor populations on the one hand, and on the other a relatively declining or stagnant tax base, since many well-off residents and businesses will move to the suburbs. Already some major cities are drastically curtailing their basic services because of such a "fiscal squeeze." Youngstown, Ohio, shortened its school year; Chicago has threatened to fire thousands of teachers if it does not get major state aid for its schools; and Newark has closed its public libraries. Many other cities are letting their physical plants deteriorate and their services decline in quality.

Moreover, several larger U.S. cities will become predominantly Negro in population if the trends existing from 1960 to 1966 continue. About half of the ten largest cities in the U.S. already have more than a majority of Negro students in their public elementary schools. This is a harbinger of changes yet to come, when many of these cities will become like Washington. Its total population is 65 percent Negro, and it has a public school enrollment that is 95 percent Negro. Under these circumstances, at the same time that Negro mayors rightfully assume power in these cities, the cities themselves will be in ever more desperate financial condition. Many are already destitute; but their situation will become even worse. Hence those Negro mayors will have to appeal to Congress for federal aid. But by that time Congress will be far more dominated by legislators elected from suburban districts. Under the present-policies alternative, those districts will be almost entirely white. By 1985, the suburbs will represent about 41 percent of the nation's population, as opposed to 33 percent in 1960. Central cities will decline from 31 percent to 27 percent. So the suburbs will be the dominant force in Congress, and if the present-policies alternative prevails, they will still be over 95 percent white.

Congress is already refusing to give any large amounts of money to white central city mayors. So what will happen when Negro mayors ask Congress for even greater assistance? The result could conceivably involve major frustrations, disorders in central cities, and severe retaliation by the white community. This might in turn lead to a serious loss of individual freedom in the United States for all blacks and many whites. I am not saying that such a drastic outcome is a certainty, or even that the probability of its happening under a present-policies alternative is over 50 percent. On the contrary, I believe that probability is somewhere in the 10 to 25 percent range. But even that range represents a rather frightening prospect, considering the kind of risk I am talking about, and its relation to the fundamental privileges of our free society.

The Enrichment-Only Alternative · The second basic future that our society could choose is what I call the *enrichment-only alternative*. It would involve continued segregation and continued concentration of Negro growth in central cities and a few older suburbs, just as in the present-policies alternative. However, the enrichment-only alternative would also include a massive economic transfer of income to the depressed areas in ghettos and other parts of central cities. This would occur through various federally supported programs in housing, income maintenance, crime prevention, education, health, job-creation and training, and so forth.

In order to be effective, this alternative would have to possess several important characteristics. First, it would be quite expensive in terms of public funds. My very rough estimate is that it would require from $10 billion to $30 billion per year more than we are now spending on these kinds of activities. These numbers emphasize a crucial conclusion we all hate to face: there are no cheap solutions to basic urban or ghetto problems. Second, the enrichment-only alternative should involve private-sector action to a maximum degree. This is necessary both to enlist the imagination and energy of free enterprise, and to prevent ghettos from becoming "public reservations" completely dependent upon government activity.

However, maximum private-sector involvement would *not* reduce the need for large public expenditures. Many Americans now have an image of the private sector "rescuing" the ghetto like the white knight on TV, whose lance magically removes all deficiencies at the merest touch without any real effort. Nothing could be farther from the truth. Private firms will not attack ghetto problems without being paid large subsidies to do so. This is essential because poor ghetto residents cannot afford to pay for better living conditions themselves. We do not expect private firms to build the equipment that is taking us to the moon through their charitable contributions. Nor do we create expressways by mustering the voluntary efforts of junior executives who donate their lunch hours to progress. Rather, we pay private firms billions of dollars in public funds to achieve such objectives. A similar expenditure will be necessary in combating ghetto problems.

A third key characteristic of the enrichment-only alternative is that it must involve far more Negro control over programs and activities in Negro areas than now exists. Fourth, it must be based upon a widespread concern about ghetto problems among all American citizens, especially members of the white suburban middle class. Their political support is critical in financing the necessary programs.

This alternative is now verbally favored by many whites as a means of "bribing" Negroes to stop agitating while remaining separated from them. It is also favored by many Negroes who want to build up Black Power, but recognize they cannot do so

without white money. Yet the Kerner Commission rejected this
alternative because it encourages continued development of two
separate societies in America: one black and one white. The
Commission believed that two separate societies cannot be made
equal in nature or in opportunities for their residents. They felt
that the enrichment-only alternative essentially postpones America's basic commitment to providing true equality to black citizens.
Moreover, it will be much harder to realize this commitment when
black ghettos are even bigger than they are today.

The Enrichment-Plus-Dispersal Alternative · The third alternative future involves what I call *enrichment-plus-dispersal*. It
combines large-scale federal aid to deprived ghetto areas with
policies aimed at encouraging Negroes to move into white suburban areas and whites there to accept them peacefully. There
are several reasons why dispersal of at least future *increases* in
Negro population throughout major metropolitan areas would
be desirable. Most of the new jobs being created in society are
appearing in suburban areas. So helping combat ghetto unemployment requires somehow linking up those jobs and the people in ghettos who need them. Also, if the nation really wants to
expand its supply of decent low-rent housing, it must build many
units of such housing on vacant land because clearance and redevelopment take too long. But where is the vacant land in our
major metropolitan areas? Most of it is in the suburbs.

Even making existing suburban housing easily accessible to
Negro families would greatly expand the choice of environments
available to them—at least for middle-income and upper-income
Negro families. Furthermore, such families could gain better access to high-quality schools if they became dispersed throughout
existing suburbs. Finally, and most important, only some form of
dispersal ultimately avoids the continuance of two separate and
unequal societies in the United States.

It is important to realize that *dispersal* is not the same as *integration*. Dispersal of Negroes into suburban areas might result
in the creation of many scattered "mini-ghettos" or "ghettolettes"
or even predominantly Negro suburbs. Yet even this development would certainly expand the choice of residential environments available to Negro families. It would also provide at least

some experience for members of both races in living or going to school together—vastly more such experience than the current massing of huge numbers of Negroes in solidly black ghettos. Thus, dispersal is one way to cope with the difficulties posed by the "Law of Cultural Dominance" I described earlier. After all, it is reasonable to suppose that if American Negroes had com pletely free choice of where to live, they would probably distribute themselves spatially the same way that the American Jewish population has distributed itself.

Most American Jews live in clusters located in predominantly Jewish neighborhoods or suburbs. But hundreds of thousands of individual Jewish families have scattered themselves throughout predominantly gentile neighborhoods. A similar combination of clustering and scattering is what we might ultimately expect of the Negro population if dispersal continued over a long period of time.

There are not now many political forces supporting the enrichment-plus-dispersal alternative. Suburban industrialists who need workers, and white, central city politicians who fear imminent unemployment, are about the only two groups favoring dispersal. Opposition to it has been increased by ghetto rioting and by the rise of Black Power and Black Nationalist sentiments.

Nevertheless, a start toward dispersal could be made by industrial firms working with local communities to build integrated housing and open up local real estate practices. Even if most Negroes are moved by the commendable pride of Black Nationalism to remain in central city ghettos, it seems incredible to me that *none* of the nearly fourteen million Negro residents of American ghettos will want to move to the suburbs. So a start toward dispersal is not inconsistent with rising Black Nationalism.

SOCIETY'S EXISTING CHOICE AND ITS IMPLICATIONS

What choice is American society now making among these alternatives, and what are its implications for future events and policies? It seems clear to me that society has for the moment chosen the present-policies alternative. That is, we are now doing nothing more to stop deterioration or counteract deprivation in central city ghettos, or to encourage dispersal, than we have done in the past. Social inaction on policies aimed at attacking the fundamental conditions in ghettos means that Negroes and other poor people in urban slums still suffer from all the ill effects of both poverty and discrimination. This is true even though middle-class Negroes are definitely benefiting from wider opportunities for employment and power than ever before.

A second consequence of society's choice of the present-policies alternative—and of other forces that would exist anyway —will be rising Black Nationalism among Negroes. Insofar as Black Nationalism means great pride in being black and in the virtues and historical contributions of Negroes in America and the world, we should all commend and encourage it. But the success of Black Nationalism in really solving ghetto problems will be frustrated by the lack of money and other resources in black communities. The inherent poverty of the ghetto community means Black Nationalism cannot cope with that community's deficiencies without massive funding from whites.

A third consequence of the present-policies alternative is that many major urban subsidies will continue to benefit middle-income and upper-income households rather than the poor. Unfortunately, most Americans—especially the households who benefit —fail to recognize these subsidies for what they really are. For example, every American homeowner who deducts his local property taxes and the interest on his mortgage from his federally taxable income is receiving a housing subsidy. The higher his income, the greater the tax saving from these deductions. Consequently, this subsidy primarily benefits the wealthy and many poor people do not gain anything from it. Either they are not homeowners, or their incomes are not high enough so that deductions provide significant tax savings.

Today we hear a great deal of discussion about a federally subsidized family allowance for the poor. In fact, another deduction from federally taxable income—the $750 per person exemption—already constitutes a kind of family allowance. Again, the biggest dollar benefit in tax savings from this allowance goes to the well-off because they are in the higher tax brackets. Still another hidden subsidy arises from our construction of urban expressways. These expensive roads mainly benefit relatively well-off suburban commuters and downtown property owners. At the same time, they impose high moving and other displacement costs on poor slum residents whose houses are destroyed by roadway construction.

Thus, contrary to popular conceptions, our society does not oppose subsidizing individual households. We only oppose subsidizing those who need it most, in contrast to those who are relatively well-off! As one wit has said, we believe in socialism for the rich, and free enterprise for the poor. This policy extends to many other areas, such as farm subsidies (which go mainly to very large and wealthy farmers), research and testing subsidies to drug firms (which have extremely high profit ratios) and oil depletion allowances. I realize that we also provide many direct transfer payments to low-income families, such as social security and welfare. Nevertheless, our present policies support a network of subsidies which have far different effects from those normally associated with the word *subsidy* by the average citizen.

There is another consequence of the present-policies choice: the substitution of rhetorical change for real change. True progress concerning any major urban problem requires both serious institutional change and large expenditures. Real progress is thus very expensive in terms of both money and power. Our leaders—supported by the majority of the people—do not at present want to pay these real costs. As a result, they are unable to tackle basic urban problems effectively. But they are unwilling to admit this; so they substitute the instantaneous mythical change of rhetoric for the costly institutional changes involved in real progress. Consequently, in urban affairs, leaders in both political parties and in the private sector continually rely on words instead of deeds, and make rhetorical promises as though they were carrying out actual solutions. So we hear many stirring but essentially empty slogans like "Black Capitalism," the "intervention of the private sector," and "the importance of voluntary effort."

As a social scientist, I am bound to point out that this rhetorical approach to change has a doubly deceitful effect. On the one hand, it falsely assuages the well-off. They are eager to believe that these serious problems are being adequately treated without major costs to themselves. Therefore, they are happy if they hear supposed solutions discussed so often it appears that they must actually be occurring, since this enables them to evade paying the serious costs of real progress. On the other hand, purely rhetorical change eventually disillusions the disadvantaged even more than they are now. At first, their aspirations become stimulated by public promises. But the ultimate failure of the government to deliver in accordance with its promises further reduces their faith and the credibility of the government—and the credibility of society and authority in general. The resulting sense of cynicism and rejection of basic social institutions is of critical importance to the future of our society. This corrosive attitude is not only affecting the poor, but also our own children and young people, who feel their idealism is being betrayed by false rhetoric. The result is a serious decline in the basic trust and feeling of governmental legitimacy required to hold any society together.

True, actually carrying out major institutional changes also creates problems, tensions, and stress. In fact, that is why we have avoided trying to make many key social changes. So I am not suggesting that futures other than the present-policies alternative represent easy solutions either. But at least they do not suffer from the corrosive hypocrisy of such policies as the 1968 Housing Act. It promised to build twenty-six million new units in the next decade, and yet provided grossly inadequate funds for fulfillment of that promise. And it is only one of the many recent cases of the social disease of simultaneous overcommitment and underdelivery.

Alternatives to the Gilded Ghetto

JOHN F. KAIN AND JOSEPH J. PERSKY

Joseph Persky, co-author of this essay with John Kain, is a member of the Department of Economics of the University of Illinois at Chicago Circle. The paper is taken from a symposium in The Public Interest *on "The Future of the Ghetto."*

WE ARE FACED today with a spate of proposals and programs for improving the ghetto through economic development, renewal, and reconstruction. The intellectual basis of many of these proposals stems from a false analogy of the ghetto to an underdeveloped country in need of economic development. This oversimplified and misleading view ignores the strong linkages that tie the ghetto to the remainder of the metropolis and to the nation. When the nature of these linkages and the complex relationship between the ghetto and metropolitan development is understood, the potential destructiveness of these proposals becomes apparent. In this article we attempt to describe these interrelationships and the ghetto's consequent culpability for an expanded list of urban problems

THE GHETTO AND THE METROPOLIS

If we begin with the usual list of "ghetto problems"—unemployment, low income, poor schools, and poor housing—it is easy to see the appeal of proposals aimed at making the ghetto livable. Moreover, casual observation of the slow pace of school desegregation, residential integration, and fair-employment practices would indicate that the promise of integration and the gains achievable from the process are to be made only at an obscure point in the future. Thus, in the short run, the argument for ghetto improvement would have us view the ghetto as something of a community unto itself, a community that could substantially benefit from economic development and especially heavy investments of physical capital.

The weakness of this argument, however, is attested to by a growing body of evidence that indicates that (1) the above list of ghetto problems is much too short, because it ignores the serious implications of the growing ghetto for the metropolis as a whole and that (2) the ghetto itself is responsible for, or seriously aggravates, many of the most visible problems of urban Negroes.

The central Negro ghetto has produced a significant distortion of metropolitan development, which has added substantially to problems in central city finance, metropolitan transportation, housing, and urban renewal. The decline of central cities has been hastened by a conviction in the white community, both individual and corporate, that the ghetto would continue its rapid expansion, carrying along its associated problems of concentrated poverty and social disorganization.

Although historically lower income groups have tended to live in central cities, this residential pattern was the result of a highly centralized employment structure. Low-income households, constrained by limited housing and transportation budgets, clustered tightly around the workplaces in the densest accommodations available. High-income households, by contrast, with more disposable income and preferences for less congested living conditions, found it expedient to commute to suburban areas where land costs were lower. These lower housing costs in suburban locations more than compensated them for the time, inconvenience, and out-of-pocket costs of commuting. Today, it still remains true that low-income households cluster more closely around their workplaces than do high-income households. However, with the accelerating pace of suburbanization of industry and jobs—itself no doubt due partly to the ghetto's expansion —these jobs are found less frequently in cities. Thus the poor are found less frequently in the central city; it is mainly the Negro poor who are found there. The inference is inescapable; *central cities are poor largely because they are black, and not the converse.*

The residential locations of whites in similar income groups support this contention. This is clearly shown in Table 1, which gives the proportion of low-income whites and Negroes living in the suburban rings of the ten largest metropolitan areas (Table 1 also includes data for all whites and Negroes). For example, 45 per cent of Detroit's poor white families live in suburbs, but only 11 per cent of its poor Negro families do so. These figures belie the argument that Negroes are concentrated in central cities because they are poor. This finding is consistent with the work of numerous researchers who have concluded that little of the existing pattern of Negro residential segregation can be explained by income or other socioeconomic characteristics. One of the authors of this article has elsewhere estimated that, on the basis of Negro employment locations and of low-income white residential choice patterns, as many as 40,000 Detroit Negro workers and 112,000 Chicago Negro workers would move out of central ghettos in the absence of racial segregation.

This residential pattern imposed on the Negro has led to an unduly large proportion of poverty-linked services being demanded of central cities. At the same time, the expansion of the ghetto has encouraged the exodus of middle-income whites. The

TABLE 1.   *Per cent of White and Negro Families (total and poor) Living in the Suburban Ring of the Ten Largest Urbanization Areas* *

		White		Negro	
		All families	Families with incomes $3,000	All families	Families with incomes $3,000
1	New York	27.8%	16.3%	9.4%	8.2%
2	Los Angeles	65.2	61.6	27.3	23.3
3	Chicago	47.6	37.2	7.7	5.9
4	Philadelphia	50.8	37.4	15.7	14.2
5	Detroit	58.9	44.9	12.1	11.3
6	San Francisco-Oakland	57.8	48.8	29.2	25.8
7	Boston	74.3	64.0	19.2	13.9
8	Washington	75.7	59.6	9.8	10.4
9	Pittsburgh	70.5	63.3	29.4	27.1
10	Cleveland	59.2	39.3	3.1	2.4

* For New York and Chicago the suburban ring is the difference between the SMSA and central city. For all other cities it is the difference between the urbanized area and central city. Both San Francisco and Oakland are counted as central cities.

result has been rapid increases in local government expenditures and a severe constraint on the ability of central cities to raise revenues. Hence, the current crisis in city finances. Although the problem can be handled in the short run by various schemes of redistributing governmental revenues, a preferable long-run solution would involve a major dispersal of the low-income population, in particular the Negro. Central cities will continue to have a high proportion of the poor as long as they contain a large proportion of metropolitan jobs. However, there is no rationale for exaggerating this tendency with artificial restraints.

HOUSING, TRANSPORTATION, SCHOOLS

Housing segregation has also frustrated efforts to renew the city. At first sight the logic of renewal is strong. By offering federal subsidies to higher income whites locating within their boundaries, central cities have hoped to improve their tax base. The same logic underlies community efforts to woo industry. However, to the extent that these groups consider the city an inferior location, because of the existence of the ghetto, such subsidies will continue to fail. As long as the ghetto exists, most of white America will write off the central city. Spot renewal, even on the scale envisioned in the Model Cities program, cannot alter this basic fact.

In this context, even the small victories of central cities are often of a pyrrhic nature. So long as the central business district (CBD) manages to remain a major employment location, the city is faced with serious transportation problems, problems that would be substantially reduced if more of the centrally employed whites were willing to reside in the city. To a great extent, the CBD stakes its existence on an ability to transport people rapidly over long distances. Pressures for more expressways and high-speed rail transit are understandable—and yet both encourage the migration to the suburbs. The city must lose either way, so long as the ghetto is a growing mass that dominates the environment of its core and the development of its metropolitan area.

From the above argument, it is clear that the impact of the ghetto on the processes of metropolitan development has created or aggravated many of our most critical urban problems. These costs are borne by Negroes and whites alike. However, the same interaction between the ghetto and metropolis has produced other important distortions whose costs fall almost exclusively on the Negro community. The ghetto has isolated the Negro economically as well as socially. In the first place, the Negro has inadequate access to the job market. For him, informal methods of job search, common to low-skilled employment, are largely limited to the ghetto. Jobs may be plentiful outside of the ghetto, yet he will know little or nothing of these opportunities. Moreover, the time and cost necessary to reach many suburban jobs, frequently compounded by the radial character of public transit services, often will discourage Negroes from taking or even seeking such jobs. Granted that the ghetto generates a limited number of service jobs, this effect is more than offset by the discriminatory practices of nonghetto employers. Research on the distribution of Negro employment in Northern metropolitan areas indicates the importance of these factors, by demonstrating that the proportion of Negroes in an area's work force is dependent on that area's distance from the ghetto and the racial composition of the surrounding residential neighborhoods. These distributional characteristics also affect the level of Negro employment. Estimates indicate that as many as twenty-four thousand jobs in Chicago and nine thousand in Detroit may be lost to the Negro community because of housing segregation. These figures are based on 1956 and 1952 data and may well underestimate the current situation. The continuing trend of job decentralization also may have aggravated the situation.

De facto school segregation is another widely recognized limitation of Negro opportunities resulting from housing market segregation. A large body of evidence indicates that students in ghetto schools receive an education much inferior to that offered elsewhere. Low levels of student achievement are the result of a complex of factors including poorly trained, overworked, and undermotivated teachers, low levels of per student expenditures, inadequate capital plants, and the generally low level of students' motivation and aspiration. This last factor is, of course, related to the ghetto's poverty and social disorganization.

The continued rapid growth of central city ghettos has seriously expanded the realm of *de facto* segregation and limited the range of possible corrective actions. For example, in 1952, 57 per cent of Cleveland's Negro students went to schools with more than 90 per cent Negro enrollment. In 1962, 82 per cent went to such schools. By 1965, Chicago, Detroit, and Philadelphia all had more than 70 per cent of their Negro students in these completely segregated schools.

In addition to sharply curtailing Negro economic and educational opportunity, the ghetto is an important disorganizing force. It represents the power of the outside community and the frustration of the Negro. The sources of nourishment for many of the psychological and sociological problems too common to Negro Americans can be found here. Drug addiction, violent crime, and family disorganization all gain a high degree of acceptance, creating a set of norms that often brings the individual into conflict with the larger society. Kenneth Clark puts the case well: "The dark ghetto is institutionalized pathology; it is chronic, self-perpetuating pathology . . ." Although this pathology is difficult to quantify, it may well be the ghetto's most serious consequence.

In reviewing our expanded list of problems, it may seem that we have made the ghetto too much the villain. Physical segregation may have only been the not-so-subtle way to avoid discriminatory practices that might otherwise be rampant. Many ghetto problems might still exist in some other guise. Nevertheless, the problems as structured *now* must continue as long as the metropolis harbors this "peculiar institution."

Nothing less than a complete change in the structure of the metropolis will solve the problem of the ghetto. It is therefore ironic that current programs which ostensibly are concerned with the welfare of urban Negroes are willing to accept, and are even based on, the permanence of central ghettos. Thus, under every heading of social welfare legislation—education, income transfer, employment, and housing—we find programs that can only serve to strengthen the ghetto and the serious problems that it generates. In particular, these programs concentrate on beautifying the fundamentally ugly structure of the current metropolis and not on providing individuals with the tools necessary to break out of that structure. The shame of the situation is that viable alternatives *do* exist.

Thus, in approaching the problems of Negro employment, first steps could be an improved information system at the disposal of Negro job seekers, strong training programs linked to job placement in industry, and improved transit access between central ghettos and outlying employment areas. Besides the direct effects of such programs on unemployment and incomes, they have the added advantage of encouraging the dispersion of the ghetto and not its further concentration. For example, Negroes employed in suburban areas distant from the ghetto have strong incentives to reduce the time and cost of commuting by seeking out residences near their workplaces. Frequent, informal contact with white coworkers will both increase their information about housing in predominantly white residential areas and help to break down the mutual distrust that is usually associated with the process of integration.

Prospects of housing desegregation would be much enhanced by major changes in urban renewal and housing programs. Current schemes accept and reinforce some of the worst aspects of the housing market. Thus, even the best urban renewal projects involve the government in drastically reducing the supply (and thereby increasing the cost) of low-income housing—all this at great expense to the taxpayer. At best there is an implicit acceptance of the alleged desire of the poor to remain in central city slums. At worst, current programs could be viewed as a concerted effort to maintain the ghetto. The same observation can be made about public housing programs. The Commission on Civil Rights in its report on school segregation concluded that government policies for low-cost housing were "further reinforcing the trend toward racial and economic separation in metropolitan areas."

An alternative approach would aim at drastically expanding the supply of low-income housing *outside* the ghetto. Given the high costs of reclaiming land in central areas, subsidies equivalent to existing urban renewal expenditures for use anywhere in the metropolitan area would lead to the construction of many more units. The new mix by type and location would be likely to favor small, single-family homes and garden apartments on the urban periphery. Some overbuilding would be desirable, the object being the creation of a glut in the low-income suburban housing market. It is hard to imagine a situation that would make developers and renters less sensitive to skin color.

These measures would be greatly reinforced by programs that increase the effective demand of Negroes for housing. Rent subsidies to individuals are highly desirable, because they represent the transfer of purchasing power that can be used anywhere in the metropolitan area. Other income transfer programs not specifically tied to housing would have similar advantages in improving the prospects of ghetto dispersal. Vigorous enforcement of open housing statutes would aid the performance of the "impersonal" market, perhaps most importantly by providing developers, lenders, and realtors with an excuse to act in their own self interest.

SUBURBANIZATION OF THE NEGRO

Even in the face of continuing practices of residential segregation, the suburbanization of the Negro can still continue apace. It is important to realize that the presence of Negroes in the suburbs does not necessarily imply Negro integration into white residential neighborhoods. Suburbanization of the Negro and housing integration are not synonymous. Many of the disadvantages of massive, central ghettos would be overcome if they were replaced or even augmented by smaller, dispersed Negro *communities*. Such a pattern would remove the limitations on Negro employment opportunities attributable to the geography of the ghetto. Similarly, the reduced pressure on central city housing markets would improve the prospects for the renewal of middle-income neighborhoods through the operations of the private market. Once the peripheral growth of central city ghettos is checked, the demands for costly investment in specialized, long-distance transport facilities serving central employment areas would be reduced. In addition, programs designed to reduce *de facto* school segregation by means of redistributing, bussing, and similar measures would be much more feasible.

Although such a segregated pattern does not represent the author's idea of a more open society, it could still prove a valuable first step toward that goal. Most groups attempting to integrate suburban neighborhoods have placed great stress on achieving and maintaining some preconceived interracial balance. Because integration is the goal, they feel the need to proceed slowly and make elaborate precautions to avoid "tipping" the neighborhood. The result has been a small, black trickle into all-white suburbs. But if the immediate goal is seen as destroying the ghetto, different strategies should be employed. "Tipping," rather than something to be carefully avoided, might be viewed as a tactic for opening large amounts of suburban housing. If enough suburban neighborhoods are "tipped," the danger of any one of them becoming a massive ghetto would be small.

Education is still another tool that can be used to weaken the ties of the ghetto. Formal schooling plays a particularly important role in preparing individuals to participate in the complex urban society of today. It greatly enhances their ability to compete in the job market with the promise of higher incomes. As a result, large-scale programs of compensatory education can make important contributions to a strategy of weakening and eventually abolishing the Negro ghetto. Nevertheless, the important gains of such compensatory programs must be continually weighed against the more general advantages of school desegregation. Where real alternatives exist in the short run, programs consistent with this latter objective should always be chosen. It is important to note that truly effective programs of compensatory education are likely to be extremely expensive and that strategies involving significant amounts of desegregation may achieve the same educational objectives at much lower costs.

Bussing of Negro students may be such a program. Like better access to suburban employment for ghetto job seekers, bussing would weaken the geographic dominance of the ghetto. Just as the informal experience of integration on the job is an important element in changing racial attitudes, integration in the classroom is a powerful learning experience. Insofar as the resistance of suburban communities to accepting low-income residents and students is the result of a narrow cost-minimization calculus that attempts to avoid providing public services and in particular education, substantial state and federal subsidies for the education

of low-income students can prove an effective carrot. Title I programs of the Elementary and Secondary Education Act of 1965
and grants to areas containing large federal installations
are precedents. Subsidies should be large enough to cover more
than the marginal cost of educating students from low-income
families, and should make it *profitable* for communities and
school districts to accept such students. The experience of the
METCO program in Boston strongly suggests that suburban
communities can be induced to accept ghetto school children if
external sources of financing are available.

Because the above proposals would still leave unanswered
some immediate needs of ghetto residents, a strong argument
can be made for direct income transfers. Although certain constraints on the use of funds, for example rent supplements, might
be maintained, the emphasis should be on providing resources
to individuals and not on freezing them into geographic areas.
The extent to which welfare schemes are currently tied to particular neighborhoods or communities should be determined,
and these programs should be altered so as to remove such limitations on mobility. Keeping in mind the crucial links between
the ghetto and the rural South, it is essential that the Southern
Negro share in these income transfers.

THE GHETTO AND THE NATION

Although there are major benefits to be gained by both the
Negro community and the metropolis at large through a dispersal of the central ghetto, these benefits cannot be realized
and are likely to be hindered by programs aimed at making
the ghetto a more livable place. In addition to the important ob-
jections discussed so far, there is the very real possibility that
such programs will run afoul of major migration links with the
Negro population of the South. A striking example of this problem can be seen in the issue of ghetto job creation, one of the
most popular proposals to improve the ghetto.

Although ghetto job creation, like other "gilding" programs,
might initially reduce Negro unemployment, it must eventually
affect the system that binds the Northern ghetto to the rural and
urban areas of the South. This system will react to any sudden

changes in employment and income opportunities in Northern ghettos. If there are no offsetting improvements in the South, the result will be increased rates of migration into still restricted ghetto areas. While we need to know much more than we now do about the elasticity of migration to various economic improvements, the direction of the effect is clear. Indeed it is possible that more than one migrant would appear in the ghetto for every job created. Even at lower levels of sensitivity, a strong wave of in-migration could prove extremely harmful to many other programs

The major result of the massive migrations of the 1940s and 1950s was to make the metropolitan areas of the North and West great centers of Negro population. In 1940 these areas accounted for only 20 per cent of all Negroes in the country, whereas in 1960 37 per cent of all Negroes lived in these same areas. Moreover, statistics on the migration of Negroes born in Southern states indicate a definite preference for the largest metropolitan areas of the country over smaller cities.

DEVELOPING THE SOUTH

Some appreciation for migration's contribution to the growth of Northern ghettos is provided by a comparison of the components of Negro population increase. Fifty-four per cent of the 2.7 million increase in Northern Negro populations from 1950 to 1960 was accounted for by net in-migration of Southern Negroes. Although the data on more recent population changes are scanty, the best estimates suggest that Negro net migration from the South has been averaging about one hundred thousand per year for the period 1960 to 1966. It therefore appears that the contribution of Southern migration to the growth of Northern ghettos, even though it may now be on the decline, remains substantial.

The pattern of Negro migration is in sharp contrast with the pattern of white out-migration from the same areas of the South. Thus, there are about 2.5 million Southern-born whites and 2.5 million Southern-born Negroes in non-Southern metropolitan areas greater than a million, but 1.42 million whites and 4.2 million Negroes in non-Southern cities of 250,000 to a million. Cities greater than 250,000 account for 89 per cent of Negroes who have left the South, but only 60 per cent of whites. The framework of opportunities presented to the individual Negro migrant is such as to increase the desirability of a move out of the South and to stress the comparative desirability of large cities as against rural areas and medium-sized cities.

Belated recognition of the problems created for Northern metropolitan areas by these large-scale streams of rural migration have led in recent months to a large number of proposals to encourage development in rural areas. Not surprisingly the Department of Agriculture has been quick to seize the opportunities provided. A "rural renaissance" has been its response. Full-page advertisements headed, "To save our cities, We must have rural-urban balance," have appeared in a large number of magazines under the aegis of the National Rural Electric Cooperative Association. These proposals invariably fail to recognize that Negro migration from the rural South differs in important respects from rural-urban migration and has different consequences. Failing as they do to distinguish between beneficial and potentially disruptive migration, these proposals for large-scale programs to keep people on the farms, everywhere, are likely to lead to great waste and inefficiency, while failing to come to grips with the problem that motivated the original concern.

IMPROVING SKILLS

A second important approach to easing the pressure on the ghetto is to improve the educational and skill level of incoming migrants. An investment in the underutilized human resource represented by the Southern white and Negro will pay off in either an expanded Southern economy or a Northern metropolitan job market. Indeed, it is just this flexibility that makes programs oriented to individuals so attractive in comparision to programs oriented to geography. To the extent that a potential migrant can gain skills in demand, his integration into the metropolis. North or South, is that much eased. In light of these benefits, progress in Southern schools has been pitifully slow. Southern Negro achievement levels are the lowest for any group in the country. Southern states with small tax bases and high fertility rates have found it expedient in the past to spend as little as possible on Negro education. Much of the rationalization for this policy is based on the fact that a large proportion of Southern Negroes will migrate and thus deprive the area of whatever educational investment is made in them. This fact undoubtedly has led to some underinvestment in the education of Southern whites as well, but the brunt has been borne by the Negro community.

Clearly it is to the advantage of those areas that are likely to receive these migrants to guarantee their ability to cope with an urban environment. This would be in sharp contrast to migrants who move to the ghetto dependent on the social services of the community and unable to venture into the larger world of the metropolis. Nor are the impacts of inadequate Southern education limited to the first generation of Negro migrants. Parents ill-equipped to adjust to complex urban patterns are unlikely to provide the support necessary for preparing children to cope with a hostile environment. The pattern can be clearly seen in the second generation's reaction to life in the ghetto. It is the children of migrants and not the migrants themselves who seem most prone to riot in the city.

Thus, education of potential migrants is of great importance to both the North and South. The value of the investment is compounded by the extent to which the over-all level of Negro opportunity is expanded. In the North, this is dependent on a weakening of the constricting ties of the ghetto. In the South it depends on economic development *per se*.

CONCLUDING THOUGHTS

This article has considered alternative strategies for the urban ghetto in light of the strong economic and social link of that community to the metropolis in which it is imbedded and to the nation as a whole. In particular the analysis has centered on the likely repercussions of "gilding programs."

Included prominently among these programs are a variety of proposals designed to attract industry to metropolitan ghettos. There have also been numerous proposals for massive expenditures on compensatory education, housing, welfare, and the like.

Model Cities programs must be included under this rubric. All such proposals aim at raising the employment. incomes, and well-being of ghetto residents, *within* the existing framework of racial discrimination.

Much of the political appeal of these programs lies in their ability to attract support from a wide spectrum ranging from white separatists, to liberals, to advocates of black power. However, there is an overriding objection to this approach. "Gilding" programs must accept as given a continued growth of Negro ghettos, ghettos which are directly or indirectly responsible for the failure of urban renewal, the crisis in central city finance, urban transportation problems, Negro unemployment, and the inadequacy of metropolitan school systems. Ghetto-gilding programs, apart from being objectionable on moral grounds, accept a very large cost in terms of economic inefficiency, while making the solution of many social problems inordinately difficult.

A final objection is that such programs may not work at all, if pursued in isolation. The ultimate result of efforts to increase Negro incomes or reduce Negro unemployment in central city ghettos may be simply to induce a much higher rate of migration of Negroes from Southern rural areas. This will accelerate the already rapid growth of black ghettos, complicating the already impressive list of urban problems.

Recognition of the migration link between Northern ghettos and Southern rural areas has led in recent months to proposals to subsidize economic development, educational opportunities, and living standards in rural areas. It is important to clarify the valuable, but limited, contributions well-designed programs of this kind can make to the problems of the metropolitan ghetto. Antimigration and migrant improvement programs cannot in themselves improve conditions in Northern ghettos. They cannot overcome the prejudice, discrimination, low incomes, and lack of education that are the underlying "causes" of ghetto unrest. At best they are complementary to programs intended to deal directly with ghetto problems. Their greatest value would be in permitting an aggressive assault on the problems of the ghetto—their role is that of a counterweight which permits meaningful and large-scale programs within *metropolitan* areas.

What form should this larger effort take? It would seem that ghetto dispersal is the only strategy that promises a long-run solution. In support of this contention we have identified three important arguments:

1. None of the other programs will reduce the distortions of metropolitan growth and loss of efficiency that result from the continued rapid expansion of "massive" Negro ghettos in metropolitan areas.

2. Ghetto dispersal programs would generally lower the costs of achieving many objectives that are posited by ghetto improvement or gilding schemes.

3. As between ghetto gilding and ghetto dispersal strategies, only the latter is consistent with stated goals of American society.

The conclusion is straightforward. When alternatives exist, and it has been a major effort of this article to show that they do exist, considerable weight must be placed on their differential impact on the ghetto. Programs that tend to strengthen this segregated pattern should generally be rejected in favor of programs that achieve the same objectives while weakening the ghetto. Such a strategy is not only consistent with the nation's long-run goals, but will often be substantially cheaper in the short run.

Alternatives to the Non-Gilded Ghetto

JOEL BERGSMAN

In addition to substantial research on the determinants of urban growth and development, Joel Bergsman is a specialist in the economics of less-developed countries: he has a long-standing interest in the Brazilian economy and has authored a number of articles and books on this subject. Bergsman is, at present, a Senior Research Associate at the Urban Institute in Washington, D.C.

WHAT DO PEOPLE mean when they talk about "ghetto economic development," "black capitalism," and related terms? How do their different goals influence the kinds of programs they like? What kinds of programs would be best for ameliorating ghetto poverty and racial discrimination?

Some of the differences on these questions clearly stem from divergent goals. But other differences seem to center on different views of the possible results of minority economic development programs. This is evident in statements that a particular program "may be desirable, but is not feasible" or ". . . but is not efficient." However, many of these disagreements *also* stem from differences in goals, values, and judgments about the basic nature of man and our society. These notes, intended as a prelude to research and to action, should also show how different goals affect which strategies are preferred, almost independently of one's view of the nature of the possibilities.

To make the picture more concrete, the first section describes three simplified packages of world views, goals, and strategies. These packages are labeled "black," "liberal," and "conservative." They are deliberately exaggerated, to show more clearly the logic which underlies the less simplistic actual views held by real people or articulated by real programs. The labels do *not* imply, for example, that I think all black people subscribe to the "black" package. The second section of the paper examines some policy issues, and a short final section is devoted to the current situation.

THREE SIMPLIFIED PACKAGES OF GOALS AND STRATEGIES

The "Black" Package · More political and economic power for poor minorities *as classes or groups* is the main goal of the "black" package. The use of this power is twofold—to choose whether or not to integrate with other groups (and if so, on what terms) and to obtain the same opportunities for jobs, housing, and so forth that others enjoy, whether the minority person integrates or not.

Those holding these goals believe that racial and ethnic separation will continue for a long time. They believe that white racial prejudice is strong and deep-seated. Their goals and strategies are designed not to eliminate, but to live with and succeed in the face of prejudice and excessive racial pride.

The means include the creation of powerful, autonomous institutions controlled by poor minorities. These institutions range from political clubs and parties to consumer associations to business firms. Economic and political power are seen as inextricably linked. The emphasis on institutions—and the disfavor of the term *black capitalism*—stem from a feeling that the development of small numbers of middle-income or even upper-income minority capitalists has had little effect on improving the economic conditions of the total minority population. The exercise of power is seen to require control of institutions, and thus voting shares in businesses, co-ops, community development corporations, or other forms "responsive to the community" are preferred to measures featuring individual gains. Development of a strong sense of racial identity and pride also figures importantly in this package. Economic efficiency is not of great concern; adherents of the package believe the goals *must* be achieved, however high the cost.

The "Liberal" Package · Equality is the basic goal of the "liberal" package. It seeks to end racism and prejudice, and thus the actions stemming from these attitudes. The insistence on equal treatment is not color blind; that is, compensatory special advantages are recognized as necessary to overcome disadvantages that groups or individuals suffer through no fault of their own.

The "liberal" does not like separatism—by whites, blacks, or anyone else. He does not like Black Power, with or without capital letters.

An assumption of the "liberal" package is that racism and prejudice can be overcome in some not-too-long time. Emphasis is on removing discrimination as a means toward equal status, where the "black" view stresses equal status first as a necessary lever for wiping out discrimination.

In contrast to the "black" view that economic and political power are inextricably linked, the "liberal" holds that the two, while complementary, may be pursued separately. When political paths are blocked, economic equality might still be pursued with good results; conversely, political power may be gained without much economic progress.

An obvious basic difference is that the "liberal" has a much larger stake in the *status quo,* and is far more wary of revolutionary change, than the "black." Thus the "liberal" programs aim more at ameliorating *results* of the *status quo*—through programs to raise income, upgrade jobs and skills, improve child development, modernize welfare programs, modify police systems, and the like—programs mostly intended to permit individuals to function better within existing institutions.

The "liberal" analyzes proposals for minority economic development in terms of over-all economic efficiency. His finding of inefficiency in plans for inducing firms to locate in ghettos bolsters his notion that separatism is bad and that dispersal should be stressed rather than subsidized ghetto development.

The "Conservative" Package · The "conservative" is found in many places. He may be an establishment figure, concerned with operation of the city government or a business corporation. Or he may be a middle-class or working-class citizen. His basic goals for the city are to increase the tax base, reduce tax burdens, and prevent disturbances; and for the corporation to encourage smooth, profitable growth in an aura of good public relations; and for himself to suppress threats to his values and his peaceful life.

This package holds that *successful* people make things work. Successful people may be of any race, but they are not poor. The poor, especially to the extent that they demand and require special public expenditures, are seen as a drag on the rest of society. (Although many segments of society benefit from and contribute to poverty through exploitation of cheap labor—including women as well as blacks, Mexican-Americans, and other minorities.)

To the "conservative," the benefits from getting rid of the ghetto appear to exceed any possible benefits of redeveloping the ghetto. Dispersing the ghetto is therefore a dominant strategy, and it is no accident that the "Negro removal" types of urban renewal and throughway clearance have been favorites of the "conservatives."

Since city or corporate power cannot remove the ghettos, the "conservative" has other strategies. These include efforts to increase the percentage of middle-class families, to stress middle-class values, and to "keep the lid on" in ghetto neighborhoods.

The "conservative" and the "liberal" are allied in preferring ghetto dispersion to ghetto gilding, and in pursuit of peace and quiet. The "conservative" is seldom on the same side as the "black"—the "conservative" may like programs to guarantee commercial loans to ghetto businessmen (especially if they stay in the ghetto), and he may like or at least tolerate subsidies to induce large businesses to locate plants in ghetto areas. Neither of these programs rates high in the "black" view. Nevertheless, an alliance of "blacks" with "conservatives" might be possible. They are each willing to live with "separate but equal" development, they each dislike welfare and paternalistic programs, and they each see the world as a pie from which they want a bigger piece. This self-interest need not create insoluble conflicts; indeed the areas of coincident self-interest are many: ghetto development would increase the city's tax base, reduce need for welfare and housing subsidies, and probably reduce crime, riots, and other antisocial behavior.

SOME ISSUES FOR STRATEGY

Individual or Community Benefits · One of the crucial issues raised by the different packages or views is the individual income-employment versus institution-community question. To what extent should programs be aimed directly at more jobs and higher wages for ghetto residents? Or should programs stress structural changes and new institutions that may benefit the minority poor only slightly in the short run?

The latter alternative—following the tenets of the "black" package—implies an acceptance of separatism. It tells the poor minorities who will continue to live somewhat separately that their long-run hope lies in controlling social, political, and economic institutions. Since integration and equal treatment will not flow from the *noblesse oblige* of the establishment, the mass of the poor minorities must develop sufficient economic and political muscle *as groups* to command equality and respect.

The individual development approach is supported by pointing to the poor minority citizens who *have* made it, and exhorting their brothers to go and do likewise.

Even the "black" accepts programs aimed at individuals—to improve skills, reduce unemployment, educate the children, and so forth. But the "black" doubts the *sufficiency* of these programs. He believes they will continue to be inadequate until poor minorities—through community development—acquire the power to alter the content and the scale of the programs.

The individual and community strategies *are* real alternatives in many ways. The minority community must compete with the establishment for the services of talented minority individuals. The two strategies compete for voters, for the attention of policy makers, and for money.

The interactions between political and economic power are pertinent here. The two kinds of power are not so intimately linked as in the "black" view—development of political power by the Irish in America, and economic power by the Jews, show this. But the extreme alternative recommendation that poor minorities concentrate all their energies on developing political institutions, and none on economic ones, is absurd. The "black" goals of economic power are not all so patently impossible or inefficient that no effort should be devoted to devising good ways to achieve them. Political power, as well as general social advancement, can be derived from economic power.

A more-or-less balanced strategy has much to recommend it. But to reject the extremes does not resolve all questions, as the debate about black capitalism illustrates. This much-praised and much maligned strategy has been defined by many of the maligners has having two elements: "black ownership of business, within the urban ghetto." Much criticism centers around the seconed element. Ghetto location is judged to imply small, unprofitable mom-and-pop stores with markets limited to poor residents who buy little.

Nevertheless, *some* ghetto businesses have been run profitably by blacks. These include not only supermarkets and other retail or distribution functions serving the ghetto market, but also "export" operations such as manufacturing and head offices of customer-located services. But more important, black capitalism is not constrained to ventures in ghettos or to serving ghetto markets.

Other criticisms, however, are leveled at the first element of the definition: black ownership of business. Andrew Brimmer, Robert Levine, and others allege that few blacks will benefit from black ownership of business wherever located, and that employment in existing institutions owned and controlled by whites offers far more promise for the poor minority masses. This conclusion follows the Berle-Galbraith views of the diffusion of ownership, the separation of ownership from control, and the supposed relative scarcity of trained and competent middle-level and upper-level management. According to this standpoint, the power, the opportunities for growth, and the economic and even the psychological rewards have passed from capitalists to technocrats.

Few would disagree that for many poor minority citizens, as for most other Americans, better jobs in existing institutions *are* the best hope. But the strong negative judgment on black capitalism seems to ignore the way power is created and used in this country. The political power of an individual is not significantly changed when his salary rises from $3,000 per year to $10,000 or even to $30,000—in fact, his political influence might actually be decreased, because he has more to lose and therefore may take fewer risks. His higher income enables him to buy more goods, but any other form of power may still be denied him. The political power of minorities as groups is not likely to be increased significantly by effecting higher incomes for, say, 10 to 20 percent of that group. Power *is* increased when a person or group gets a really large stake in one or more decision areas. Oilmen do influence our laws on income taxes and on import controls. Banks which finance exports and private foreign investment do influence our foreign policy. If poor minorities are to increase their present disproportionately low levels of power on issues which concern them (a goal not, of course, universally shared), then getting more of them into good jobs with IBM is not sufficient. They must combine to control institutions which have large stakes in relevant decisions, and whose weight will then come down on their side. Even the creation of a few thousand minority millionaires—a goal which brings automatic scorn from all sides—might possibly make a difference. Past experience does not show much solicitude of the rich for their poor brothers, but I personally would put as much—not much, but as much—trust in benefits for the poor minority masses from a few thousand minority millionaires as from a hundred thousand middle-class employees of large corporations. (This is not to overlook the direct benefits to the hundred thousand, but only to question whether this would give their minority group more power.)

Hard-Core Poverty or Less-Poor Targets · Many programs that are labeled "minority economic development" do not attack hard-core poverty. This is especially true of "liberal" and "conservative" programs. Aid to minority entrepreneurs, efforts to persuade poor minority consumers to buy minority-produced products, locating new businesses in ghetto areas, and so forth have little immediate impact on the hard-core poor. Most beneficiaries are likely to have been above or not much below the poverty line to begin with.

The most efficient way to reduce poverty may well be simply to give poor people money. But to many, poverty is much more than being financially poor. The institution-building approach aims to change and make more bearable the culture of the minority poor, their ghetto environment, and the nature of their interactions with the rest of society. This "black" approach may thus be said to be aimed at poverty, albeit more at its cultural than its economic aspects.

Ghetto "Gilding" or Ghetto Dispersal · Ghetto gilding and ghetto dispersal should not be thought of as mutually exclusive. Blacks and other poor minority groups will continue to live somewhat separately for a long time. If their neighborhoods can be improved, then they and the cities they inhabit will benefit. Of course, successful "gilding" means eliminating most of the bad characteristics that make us worry about ghettos. Park Heights in Baltimore, the Berkeley hills, and other homogeneous middle-class neighborhoods are often referred to as ghettos, but the homogeneity is voluntary and not particularly harmful. A Harlem or Bedford-Stuyvesant which was 90 percent black but had the physical, social, and economic character of Park Heights would scarcely be considered a problem.

Full ghetto redevelopment admittedly would be extremely difficult. The more successful residents tend to move away, so that an extremely rapid "big push" would be necessary to transform a ghetto area into a prosperous one with many of the same residents. This is one reason why a minority economic development strategy must have a large scope—one can conceive of a set of programs resulting in great progress for poor minorities nationally, far more readily than one can imagine transforming Hough or Harlem into a prosperous, pleasant neighborhood for the present residents.

Short of full redevelopment, however, "import substitution" can help. This strategy calls for minorities to produce for themselves certain goods and services traditionally bought from outside. Some (not all) firms which provide these goods and services will have to locate near their markets in the ghetto. This will provide employment in depressed areas, ease transport problems, and provide demonstrations of growth and success to neighborhood residents at the *places* where ghettos are.

Import substitution, nevertheless, will not be sufficient for solving the economic problems of poor minorities. Many poor black and other minorities *will* have to make it as individuals, in both black-owned and white-owned firms serving the integrated market.

Some indigenous ghetto-improvement projects, such as housing, are desirable and necessary. Some other business activities such as retail stores can be profitably located in the ghetto. On occasion wholesale, manufacturing, or service functions can be advantageously placed in ghetto areas. But for many activities ghetto location would be undesirable or infeasible. The location decision should be made on economic grounds, considering the usual factors, including the availability of transportation to outside locations for ghetto-resident workers where appropriate. This will indicate a need for at least some degree of ghetto dispersal, improvement of transport facilities, or both, à la John Kain, but probably will also indicate some profitable ghetto development.

Autarky or Economic Integration · The above discussion is closely linked to another issue: an economically autarkic, self-sufficient, separate development versus a more specialized, economically integrated kind of development. This issue is more relevant to blacks than to other poor minorities. As mentioned, a number of black-owned firms could prosper by catering largely or exclusively to black customers, and these opportunities should be developed. But achieving economic equality also requires considerable emphasis on "exports"—regional or larger markets.

The autarkic rhetoric of import substitution has caught a lot of public attention, probably because extreme versions of the idea sound so fantastically impractical. However, most "black" developers agree with Brimmer and other critics that limiting their ventures to serving only black consumers would be nonsense. Many actual programs have large export components. They are interested first and foremost in *black* development or *black* capitalism. This may have some *ghetto*-improvement aspects, and some new businesses may be located in the ghetto— but they recognize no constraint to limit activities either to ghetto areas or to black customers only. If the ghetto has functioned in a colonial role *vis à vis* the rest of the economy, and even if its future development is seen as somewhat separate, most minority developers are not interested in reducing exports—rather they want to increase exports, and to shift them from mostly low-paid labor, to goods and services to which they can contribute high value-added.

While the colony-metropole metaphor has much descriptive validity, it should not be used for advocating a pure import substitution strategy for three principal reasons. First, poor minorities are not sovereign and cannot easily promote development with tariffs, subsidies, and the like. Concerted withdrawal or redirection of buying power can do something in this direction, but is hard to sustain or generalize. Second, the intimate availability of the entire U.S. economy offers too great a potential to turn one's back on. True, there are plenty of restrictions on exports from the "colonies" as well as political repression, use of force, and the like. But with all that, the possibilities for reversing the exploitation are there, and offer great profit and growth opportunities. Third, import substitution in most underdeveloped countries has been far from a complete success. Moreover, the single most important ingredient to whatever success it has had —a large, reservable market—is not present in the case of the American minority poor.

A little-discussed aspect of the autarky-economic integration issue is the question of geographic scope. Most programs now in existence are related to specific neighborhoods or, at most, specific cities. This is understandable at the present beginning stage of these efforts. But metropolitan, regional, and national coordination probably offers great advantages, especially in political development. Expanding the scope should produce more efficient ways to do the same things now being attempted locally, and may also open up new approaches that could not be applied on a fragmented scale.

To sum up on markets, the extreme, doctrinaire views which attract so much discussion are palpably false and get little attention in actual projects. A minority market *does* exist: Minority people are consumers, and to the extent they become producers, they are also commercial purchasers. Their self-identification as members of a minority can sometimes be used to direct their purchasing power to or from a certain seller to gain certain objectives. Organized boycotts also may be a springboard for other cooperative activities. Yet the minority market has its limits; appealing to it or organizing its purchasing power is not always possible or profitable. The "$30-billion Negro" is not easily controlled in his buying habits, and in any case he is not so rich compared with the $900-billion non-Negro.

Control · Many important differences center on whether control should be "inside" or "outside" the minority community. If inside, what degree of community control? In either case, what corporate forms of control and ownership?

One of the first minority development efforts to receive favorable national attention, the Bedford-Stuyvesant program, focused much interest on the control question because branch plants of large corporations were located in the ghetto. This "control outside" kind of program has since appeared elsewhere, notably in Boston and Los Angeles. Its main thrust is to provide jobs for ghetto residents. In some cases, eventual transfer of ownership to some sort of minority control is planned. Such programs have been criticized as being less efficient and less desirable than moving the ghetto residents to where the jobs are. These programs also fail to appeal to those with the "black" goal of creating their own institutions that will not only employ poor minority workers but also provide profits (they hope) and economic and political power. With "control inside" programs, important differences arise over the degree of community control and the corporate forms. The desire for community control and the need to make a profit may create a certain conflict. To the extent that profits are required—that is, if an enterprise will not be fully or continually subsidized—real control by a large number of people may not work. "Community control" in practice usually means a combination of ultimate but remote control by a large, community-selected board of directors or stockholders, plus spreading the benefits—*not* the control—among a large percentage of the relevant population, through employment, subsidized stock purchasing, provision of social services, and the like. This spreading of benefits, like spreading control, can also create problems for the economic viability of the enterprise.

Many believe that profits can be made in minority economic development, if only constraints and discrimination are removed. Others deny this, alleging that subsidies are essential. This disagreement is hard to resolve, first because of the ambiguity of defining operationally the difference between "removing constraints and discrimination" and "subsidies," but more importantly because there is so little experience with either type of program.

Employment Policies · The employment issue is simply how hard to try to employ the "hard-core unemployed." The conflict is whether to serve individuals who need help most, or to hire the best possible personnel. The U.S. Department of Labor tries to resolve this dilemma through subsidies to firms that hire and train the "hard core." Reports of the value of the subsidies and the difficulties encountered vary.

A problem of implementation, however far one reaches for trainees, is the avoidance of dead-end jobs—creating a set of activities which provide an employment "ladder" for workers to climb.

Choice of Sector · Choice of sector—manufacturing, retail or wholesale trade, and services—can be important because of linkages. A combination of enterprises which are each others' customers and suppliers makes a lot of sense. For instance, a black-controlled bank, construction company, building supply firm, housing rehabilitation program, and carpenters' union can perhaps help each other to succeed where separately any might have a harder time. Obviously the bank must find other borrowers and other depositors, the building supply firm other customers, and so on. But a little cooperation at the start can make a big difference.

As enterprises develop these linkages on a regional or national scale, the opportunities for political-economic linkages will give added importance to choices of sector.

THE CURRENT SITUATION

The government is doing very little either to gild or to disperse the ghetto. The Office of Minority Business Enterprise was endowed with no program funds and no power of its own other than to "coordinate" government, private, foundation, and church programs. The Office of Economic Opportunity has taken leadership, through its Special Impact Programs amounting to about $30–$40 million per year, in financing experiments in community-controlled development programs in a dozen cities. This money, never adequate for more than a few experiments, now is drying up. A number of foundations are contributing money and personnel. University faculty and students also are getting involved here and there.

The people directly involved—blacks, Mexican-Americans, and other poor minorities—have been active. They know that nobody is going to "develop" them or gild their ghettos for them. But the effects of continued *and continuing* discrimination and poverty are hard to overcome. Without sovereign powers to tax, to levy import tariffs, and so forth, these "colonies" are finding that *both* massive capital inflows *and* effective will to develop are necessary conditions for rapid progress.

Thus the main constraint now seems—to me at least—to be money. Borrowed funds are increasingly available, but the owner's 10 or 20 percent, which has to be there first, is hard to come by. Also of great importance would be the further reduction of discriminatory practices.

Lurking not far behind these monetary and discriminatory constraints, however, are very real problems of ignorance about how to proceed. Given the money and opportunities, we still do not know the best ways to deal with poverty and ghetto living conditions. A number of appealing ideas are around, but they are largely unproven. Testing these experimentally—with adequate scope and funding—might well clear up many of the issues discussed in this paper, and pave the way for faster, more efficient progress.

The Economic Potential of Black Capitalism

ANDREW F. BRIMMER AND HENRY S. TERRELL

Arthur Brimmer, formerly a Governor of the Federal Reserve, is now a Professor at the Business School at Harvard University. Henry Terrell is with the Federal Reserve Board. The findings in this paper, which builds on data from the Survey of Economic Opportunity, were first presented before the American Economic Association in New York in 1969.

INTRODUCTION

IN THE RECENT PAST it has become fashionable to stress a strategy of "black capitalism" as a means of stimulating economic development for Negroes. This rather unique strategy has an intuitive appeal to varying shades of political opinion. To the black militant, it is appealing because it promises community ownership of property and an end to "exploitation" by outside merchants. The strategy is appealing to white conservatives because it stresses the virtues of private enterprise capitalism as the path to economic advancement instead of reliance on public expenditures, especially for public welfare. Since this strategy has received explicit approval and encouragement in the federal government and has led to the creation of various governmental bodies, it merits a critical examination of the contribution which it might be expected to make to minority economic development in the United States.

The selection of a strategy centering on black ownership of business enterprises raises several fundamental economic questions which this paper will attempt to answer:

What is the nature of the economic environment in which black businessmen operate?

What are the types of businesses that are likely to evolve from this environment?

What are the main economic forces at work in the national economy that are influencing the number and scale of operation of the types of firms in which black businessmen are concentrating?

Can black-owned businesses offer reasonable employment opportunities to a sizable proportion of the black population?

In terms of individual opportunities, which career path is the more promising—a career as a self-employed businessman or a career as an employed manager or official in a larger corporation? Expressed differently, which economic choice is superior—one involving investment in a business firm or one involving investment in human capital?

In general, while "black capitalism" means different things to different observers, two key elements appear to be essential to the concept: black business ownership and the location of these businesses in urban ghettoes. Nevertheless, considerable confusion has developed between the pursuit of "black capitalism" and the expanding role of Negroes as owners and operators of business enterprises. The two concepts are not the same. "Black capitalism" includes the latter as a necessary element, but is far more restrictive in terms of both geographic focus and racial identity of participation.

In contrast, the participation of Negroes in business enterprises is far broader. For instance, Negroes may well own and operate businesses outside the ghetto, competing with other firms in the same lines, taking advantage of profit opportunities (while running the same risk or loss). Moreover, Negroes could join with white businessmen either inside or outside the ghetto to launch or expand a profit-seeking venture. In assessing the potential of black capitalism we accept the two basic assumptions of black-owned businesses located primarily in black ghettoes of large metropolitan areas.

THE ECONOMIC ENVIRONMENT OF BLACK BUSINESSES

An earlier essay identified the heavy concentration of Negro businesses in the provision of personal services within the confines of a segregated market. In general, the effects of segregation were similar to those produced in international trade when a high tariff wall is erected between two countries; separate markets prevail in the two areas for items subject to tariff control.

For Negroes the greatest barrier imposed by segregation was not in the market for goods, access to which was relatively open, but in the market for personal services (such as barber and beauty shops and funeral services) and in public accommodations (such as hotels and restaurants). Consequently, a protected market evolved for the provision of these services within the Negro community.

Moreover, as one would expect, this wall of protection provided incentives for Negro professionals and entrepreneurs who began to specialize in activities servicing the Negro community. Negro professionals were highly concentrated in fields such as medicine, education, and religion—all hedged in by segregation—but all of which also enjoyed a protected market. In occupations which were dependent on unprotected national markets, Negroes were conspicuously absent.

In business also Negroes were concentrated in enterprises serving the protected Negro market. Life insurance provides probably the best example. Beginning in the 1880s, the major life insurance companies either stopped selling policies to Negroes or did so on the basis of different actuarial tables which greatly increased the cost of protection to Negroes. The result was the creation of an environment where Negro life insurance companies were able to grow and prosper. In enterprises that sold to a more general public, such as hardware and department stores, Negroes have not made much headway.

The recent progress toward desegregation in the United States (symbolized by the opening of public accommodations) has eroded the position of many Negro businessmen who were dependent on segregation to protect their markets. For instance, in many large cities (especially in the East and Midwest), most of the hotels and restaurants which previously catered to Negroes have encountered hard times, and many have actually closed their doors.

The legacy of racial segregation is of critical importance because it has shaped the economic environment in which Negro businessmen are currently operating and in which they can be expected to operate into the foreseeable future. The general economic factors determining the limited markets facing potential black entrepreneurs are rather widely known and bear only brief mention. In 1968 the median family income of Negroes in metropolitan areas was only 66 percent of that for white families, and the unemployment rate in central cities was 2.0 times greater for Negroes than for whites. The unemployment data probably understate the true magnitude of the labor market problem in urban ghettoes due to the underemployment of many urban Negroes and the discouragement effect of the high unemployment rates on potential Negro workers. Recent data from the 1967 Survey of Economic Opportunity on assets and liabilities point out a further dimension of the poverty status of urban ghettoes. The SEO data showed conclusively that the net accumulation of urban black families is significantly less than for white families; thus observed differences in income alone seriously understate the relative economic position of urban Negroes.

The general picture of the urban ghetto economy is one of low income, high unemployment, and a poor net financial position of urban Negro families. This general picture certainly constitutes a poor economic environment for business investment. A paradoxical problem is that any economic advances by urban Negro families may not necessarily improve the profit prospects for Negro-owned businesses. With increased economic status come greater mobility and more diverse tastes. As Negroes become more affluent, they most likely will prefer to consume in the more diverse national economy. Statistical evidence on the residential choices of more affluent Negro families indicates that this pattern may in fact be emerging. In 1968, noncentral city portions of metropolitan areas over one million contained 18.9 percent of all Negro families in these large metropolitan areas. The median income of Negro families outside central cities in 1968 was 18.1 percent higher than for those Negro families within central cities, suggesting that higher income Negro families are migrating away from central cities. A further problem is that economic gains by central city Negro families have encouraged large department stores to modify their merchandise to suit the tastes of their black customers.

This same type of paradox faces black entrepreneurs in their search for qualified labor. One of the serious economic constraints on ghetto development is the lack of human capital among its residents. Businessmen have difficulty finding employees with high levels of education and on-the-job work experience. The acquisition of human capital by ghetto residents will not necessarily increase the supply of qualified labor to black businessmen because many of the qualified black workers will be attracted to the higher expected returns and the greater job security in firms operating in the national economy.

One final problem facing black entrepreneurs concentrated in urban ghettoes is the impact of federally funded urban renewal programs on their very existence. One study has pointed out: "Since Negroes make up the largest percentage of persons in the low income levels, Negro-owned businesses in Negro communities undergoing urban renewal generally have high liquidation rates." These findings underscore the paradox that federal urban renewal programs may in fact be working at cross purposes with federal programs to foster black capitalism. In effect, black capitalists may suffer not only from the economic advances of Negroes but also from federal efforts to ameliorate the physical condition of core cities.

CHARACTERISTICS, EFFICIENCY, AND RELATIVE SIZE
OF BLACK BUSINESSES

Having discussed the economic environment in which black capitalists have been operating, it is important to examine the characteristics of the businesses that have evolved within this environment. Table 1 presents summary data on the categories of Negro-owned businesses in Washington, D.C., for 1967 and 1969, the largest sample currently available. These data demonstrate quite clearly that Negro businesses are heavily concentrated in services, with a secondary concentration in retail trade. An examination of the subcategories is particularly revealing. Within the main heading of services is a heavy concentration of barber and beauty shops and dry-cleaning establishments. The retail sector is composed primarily of foodstores, while the category of finance, insurance, and real estate is almost exclusively unincorporated real estate agents. The general pattern which emerges is a mosaic of small, service-oriented businesses which owe their existence to a protective barrier of segregation.

To date, little has been known about the detailed character-

TABLE 1.   *Distribution of Negro-Owned Business in Washington, D.C.*

Type of Business	Number 1967	1969	Percentage change	Distribution percentage 1967	1969
Services	1,238	1,380	+ 11.5	60.7	57.7
Barber shops, beauty salons, and beauty schools	555	595	+ 7.2	27.2	24.9
Dry-cleaning establishments	146	146	0.0	7.1	6.1
Retail	467	636	+ 36.2	22.8	26.6
Carryout shops, delicatessens, grocery stores, and restaurants	239	287	+ 21.1	11.7	12.0
Service stations	101	104	+ 3.0	4.9	4.3
Liquor stores	10	71	+710.0	0.5	3.0
Construction	119	143	+ 20.2	5.8	6.0
Finance, insurance, and real estate	84	95	+ 13.1	4.1	3.9
Real Estate	73	74	+ 1.4	3.6	3.1
Transportation	82	73	− 10.8	4.0	3.1
Manufacturing	35	41	+ 17.1	2.6	2.7
Newspaper publishers, printers, and sign shops	28	32	+ 14.3	1.4	1.3
Total	2,043	2,393	+ 17.1	100.0	100.0

SOURCE: *A Directory of Black-Owned Businesses in Washington, D.C.* (compiled by the Small Business Guidance and Development Center, Howard University, 1969).

istics of black businesses. A recent seven-city survey of 564 black-owned businesses conducted by the National Business League (NBL) in early 1968 has helped to fill this data gap. The NBL survey found roughly the same industry orientation as the Washington area displayed. Of the 564 businesses surveyed, 102 (18.1 percent) were barber or beauty shops, 82 (14.5 percent) were grocery stores or supermarkets, 54 (9.6 percent) were restaurants, 38 (6.7 percent) were laundry or dry-cleaning establishments, and 40 (7.1 percent) were service stations or auto repair shops.

The NBL survey was particularly valuable because it gathered considerable data on the various characteristics of black-owned businesses. A brief profile of the typical black business depicts a very small scale of operation. The businesses in the NBL survey averaged only 2.2 full-time employees, 1.1 part-time employees, had a mean gross income of only $19,147, and mean net profit of only $3,430. These figures show clearly that the black firms in the survey are quite small by any standards.

The NBL data also permit an elementary statistical analysis of the factors affecting the profitability of Negro-owned businesses. Multiple regression analysis suggested that total observed profits were statistically related to: (1) the size of the business as measured by the number of workers; (2) efficiency, which was measured by receipts per worker; and (3) membership in a business organization. The statistical relationship between membership in a business organization and total profits is consistent with the alternative explanation that these organizations may be of some benefit to black businessmen, or that more successful black businessmen tend to join these organizations.

A second regression equation was computed which attempted to estimate the quantitative significance of those factors affecting the efficiency of the black-owned firms. The regression analysis showed quite clearly that efficiency, as measured by profits per worker, varied closely with the absolute size of the firm as measured by its total receipts. The equation estimated that economies of scale were important, as profits per worker rose an estimated $10 with a sales increase of $1,000. This finding alone suggests that any programs to assist black business ownership should focus on relatively large-size units rather than inefficient small-scale operations.

Two other important factors which influence the profitability of minority-owned businesses but are not amenable to rigorous statistical analysis are crime and insurance. A survey taken in 1969 of the expansion plans of 100 small businesses in Washington, D.C., found that 85 percent felt it would be unwise to expand, primarily because of problems of crime and insurance. Some 92 percent of these same businesses reported that their insurance coverage for theft, loss, and fire was inadequate. The summary to the *Directory of Black Owned Businesses* cited earlier also stated: "Crime is one of the biggest problems of the black businessman today. While crime has caused some long established white businesses to change over to black ownership, the problems related to this crime appear to be no less devastating to the black owners." Although it is impossible to quantify the precise impact of high crime rates on the profitability of black businesses, the high incidence of crime in ghetto areas is certainly a factor retarding the growth of minority businesses, and this factor is clearly perceived by the businessmen themselves.

Having discussed the size and efficiency of black-owned firms, let us now compare their size to the size of businesses in the same categories as reported in the 1963 and preliminary 1967 Census of Business. Before analyzing the data in Table 2, two sources of upward bias for NBL survey data must be noted. First, the NBL data refer to 1967–1968 as base years, whereas much of the census data refers to 1963, and there has been a strong tendency for retail businesses to grow in terms of both sales and employment. A second source of upward bias for the NBL figures concerns the question asked about employment. The Census Bureau asked how many people were on the payroll at a given moment in time, whereas the NBL asked for the number of full-time and part-time employees.

The data on size of firm defined in terms of employees or total receipts show clearly that Negro-owned businesses within each category tend to be smaller. The discrepancy is particularly large in terms of sales per establishment and widens in both relative and absolute terms in the categories where average size was largest. The average foodstore in the census (the category with the largest receipts) was almost 8½ times as large as the average NBL foodstore. In barber and beauty shops, the category with the smallest average receipts, the average business in the census had receipts of roughly 1¾ times the average NBL firm.

The data on employment per establishment are not nearly as convincing in terms of relative size as the data on receipts. Negro beauty and barber shops actually tended to have more employees on average than the typical firm in the census. The fact that the size differentials of establishments are greater when measured on a receipts basis rather than on an employee basis leads to the result that receipts per employee are from three to six times as great in firms in the census as for those responding to

TABLE 2. *Selected Characteristics of Business Firms: Negro-Owned vs. All Firms* *

Type of business	Number of establishments		Employees per establishments		Receipts per establishments		Receipts per employee	
	NBL survey	Census	NBL survey	Census	NBL survey	Census	NBL survey	Census
Laundries, cleaning and other garment services	38	111,926	4.8	5.1	$14,655	$ 48,535	$3,053	$ 9,489
Beauty and barber shops	102	291,706	2.5	1.1	6,678	11,912	2,671	10,784
Gasoline service stations	40	216,059	2.3	2.7	18,065	105,086	7,854	39,480
Foodstores	82	294,243	3.1	4.9	28,258	238,752	9,115	49,116
Eating places	67	236,563	1.8	7.3	7,346	79,789	4,081	11,729
All services and retail trade	564	2,951,138	3.3	4.4	19,147	125,602	5,802	35,668

* For purposes of comparability the NBL categories had to be adjusted slightly to match the census data. The NBL category of grocery stores and supermarkets is compared to the census category of foodstores.
SOURCE: Project Outreach of the National Business League, U.S. Department of Commerce, Bureau of the Census, 1967 Census of Business, *Selected Services: United States Summary* (Washington, D.C., 1970). Data for Negro-owned firms are from NBL Survey and refer to 1968.

the NBL survey. The data in Table 2 reinforce the earlier conclusion of the inefficiency of the smaller-scale Negro-owned firms,
as the larger firms in the census tended to have higher sales per
employee, suggesting a better utilization of personnel.

Given this evidence relating to the general size and characteristics of Negro-owned businesses, it is instructive to examine
the growth trends in these areas. One of the most striking features has been the absolute decline of 6,200 in the number of
retail establishments between 1948 and 1967. This trend toward
fewer retail establishments has not persisted evenly among establishments of all sizes. Between 1948 and 1963, there was an
increase of 15,700, or 247 percent, in the number of retail firms
with sales over $1,000,000. At the other end of the spectrum, there
has been a persistent decline in the absolute number of small
retail firms. During the 1948–1963 period, the number of retail
firms with receipts under $20,000 declined by 162,000, or by 31.5
percent.

The impact of the trend to larger retail units is also demonstrated by the rise in the proportion of total receipts received by
firms with sales over $1,000,000. For all retail firms, this fraction
increased from 19.8 percent in 1948 to 36.5 percent in 1963, and
for foodstores the fraction practically quadrupled from 12.0 percent in 1948 to 46.4 percent in 1963. At the opposite extreme, the
fraction of total receipts received by firms with sales of under
$20,000 dropped from an insignificant 3.8 percent in 1948 to a
microscopic 1.5 percent in 1963.[1] These figures suggest a clear
tendency for consumers to spend a much larger fraction of their
disposable income in larger-unit stores in general, and in particular a much larger fraction of the total food budget is being spent
in supermarkets rather than in small grocery stores. These data
show clearly that the small-scale, limited-employment, Negro-
owned businesses are running counter to strong trends in the
national retail sector, where the emphasis is on larger units in
which receipts per establishment are rising rapidly.

1. These figures must be interpreted carefully. Between 1948 and 1963
the mean sales per retail establishment increasd by 99.4 percent. During this
same period the Consumer Price Index rose 27.3 percent, suggesting that
roughly one-quarter of the apparent rise in the average size of retail establishments was due to price increases while the remaining three-quarters reflect a
rising level of real sales per establishment.

THE STRATEGY OF SELF-EMPLOYMENT

The previous sections have analyzed black businesses in the context of comparable businesses in the general economy. This section will consider the broader question of the occupational choice between salaried and self-employment. The highest paying occupational category is professional, technical, and kindred workers. In the 1957–1967 decade, employment in this category rose by 52.5 percent, and the proportion of nonwhites also rose substantially from 3.8 percent in 1957 to 6.0 percent in 1967. The ability of nonwhites to gain access to the high-paying and rapidly growing professional and technical positions is an important step toward economic equality, showing that nonwhites have been able to acquire technical education to take advantage of these expanding opportunities.

The second highest-paying occupational class is managers, officials, and proprietors. Employment in this category grew a less rapid 11.8 percent in the 1957–1967 decade, and the nonwhite share increased from 2.1 to 2.8 percent. The trends affecting this second category become much clearer when the category is subdivided into salaried and self-employed. The growth trend for salaried managers and officials has roughly paralleled the trend in the professional category, with a rapid over-all growth of 73.5 percent combined with an extraordinarily rapid rate of growth of nonwhite employment. The absolute number of nonwhite salaried managers and officials tripled in ten years, and their share rose from 1.1 to 2.2 percent of the total. In the professional and in the salaried managerial occupational categories, nonwhites as a fraction of the total increased, because nonwhites were able to gain access to rapidly growing occupations faster than the national growth rate.

An entirely different picture emerges in the case of the self-employed manager or proprietor. Between 1957 and 1967 the absolute number of self-employed in the managers, officials, and proprietors category declined by 39.6 percent. In the same period, the share of self-employed proprietors who were nonwhite actually rose from 2.9 percent to 4.2 percent. In the case, then, of the self-employed proprietor, the increase in the proportion of nonwhites is not due to an ability to gain employment in an expanding area; rather it can be traced to a relative sluggishness in abandoning an area which is declining rapidly. This relative reluctance on the part of nonwhites to leave self-employment is true for both the retail and other self-employed categories. An absolute decline of 761,000 in the number of self-employed in retail trade between 1957 and 1967 coincides with the trend to fewer but larger retail establishments mentioned earlier.

The trend toward the rapid decline in the number of self-employed managers has not been without economic justification. This trend can be easily explained by the figures on earnings levels and earnings growth for the subcategories in the managers, officials, and proprietors category. The two subcategories, salaried versus self-employed, probably represent the fundamental choice available to someone with less than the human capital to become a professional or technical worker. He can either become a self-employed businessman or seek a salaried position as an official or manager with an already established business. Tabulations from the Census Bureau show that salaried male managerial workers have higher median earnings than self-employed male managers, and the rate of growth of salaried earnings has been faster than the rate of growth of earnings of the self-employed. Starting from a base which was 27.5 percent higher, median earnings of salaried male managers grew at an average annual rate of 5.0 percent between 1958 and 1968, compared to a rate of only 3.7 percent for self-employed managers. The relative growth of the salaried segment within the managerial class is clearly a logical economic response to the higher and more rapidly growing earnings in salaried *vis-à-vis* self-employment.

Economists expect a twofold relationship between earnings differentials and occupational shifts. An earnings differential is expected to induce an occupation shift to higher paying positions, and the occupational shift is expected to narrow the differential by expanding the relative supply in the originally higher paying occupation. In the case of the components of managers, officials, and proprietors, the rapid occupational shift has not reduced the earnings differential. In 1958 the median earnings of a male salaried worker in this category were $1,416, or 27.5 percent higher than for a self-employed individual. By 1968 this gap had widened to $3,252, or 43.9 percent.

Earnings data point up the economic rationale for the very rapid decline in the number of self-employed in the retail trade. This occupational choice is by far the lowest paying within the managerial category, and its median earnings declined continuously relative to salaried managers. In 1958 a self-employed male in retail trade had median earnings equal to 69.8 percent of the earnings of a male salaried manager; in 1963 the ratio had declined to 65.1 percent, and by 1968 it had declined further to 63.8 percent.

The failure of the rapid shift from self-employment to salaried employment within the managerial class to reduce the earnings gap between these two types of careers has serious implications for future employment trends. The continued large relative economic returns to salaried employment as against self-employment suggest strongly that the future will witness a further rapid exodus from self-employment to salaried employment in general, and in particular, out of self-employment in the retail trade.

The changes in relative earnings have been suggestive, but tabulations from the 1967 Survey of Economic Opportunity provide a much more complete picture of the earnings and income opportunities available to whites and Negroes. For earnings of Negro heads of families, the same pattern emerges as from the national totals. Negro family heads have high expected earnings as self-employed professionals (in large part reflecting returns to human capital) and much lower expected earnings as self-employed than as salaried managers. The SEO data are particularly important because they allow a comparison of the expected returns for Negroes as self-employed managers versus employment as craftsmen. In 1966 the mean earnings of self-employed Negro managers were only 66.4 percent as high as those of Negro craftsmen. Exactly the opposite pattern prevailed for whites, among whom expected earnings of self-employed managers were 25.2 percent higher than for craftsmen. Thus, while relative earnings of Negro craftsmen were 72.1 percent of their white counterpart, those of a self-employed Negro manager were only 38.3 percent as high as those for white self-employed managers.

The wide discrepancy between whites and Negroes in the relative earnings from self-employment as a manager or as a craftsman is explained by the fact that self-employed Negro businessmen are heavily concentrated in the poorer ghetto economy, while a Negro craftsman operates for the most part in the national economy. In a study prepared for the Small Business Administration, it was found that Negroes owned only 2.7 percent of all businesses in the survey, but owned 18.3 percent of all businesses located in ghettoes and only 0.7 percent of businesses located in the suburbs. Stated slightly differently, 33.3 percent of all businesses owned by Negroes were located in the ghetto, while only 3.2 percent of the businesses owned by whites were in the ghetto. Clearly the low-income status of the self-employed Negro manager is in large part due to his concentration in the poor economic environment of the ghetto.

The case of the Negro craftsman is completely different. Since the ghetto economy has little effective demand for his skills, he is employed primarily in the national economy, and his job rights are often protected by strong unions. The problem facing the Negro craftsman is not relative wages, since unions tend to insist upon equal wages for all members, but rather being able to obtain full-fledged membership in the craft unions with their apprenticeship requirements and seniority preferences.

The disparity in the relative rewards to Negro craftsmen compared to self-employed Negro managers is important because it points out one of the economic problems associated with maintaining a self-contained ghetto economy. It is axiomatic in economics that the real wages of labor increase directly with the amount of complementary capital. By being employed in the national economy, the Negro craftsman is working with roughly the same amount of capital as his white counterpart. The self-employed Negro manager, however, by being limited mainly to the small amount of complementary capital available from the low level of ghetto savings, will have a substantially lower expected income.

The general conclusion from this section is that self-employment in the managerial occupations offers a poor economic future for Negroes as well as whites. The relative economic rewards to Negroes of employment in salaried managerial positions

or as craftsmen are potentially much higher primarily because
these occupations permit the Negro employee to work with a
relatively large amount of complementary capital, rather than
confining himself to the capital-short ghetto.

THE EMPLOYMENT POTENTIAL OF BLACK CAPITALISM

At this point, we should pause to ask how much difference it
might make to Negroes generally if the campaign for black capitalism were to achieve even a moderate level of success. Defining success in this context is obviously difficult. One criterion (and
a measure emphasized by some of the most vigorous advocates
of black capitalism) might be the equalization of the Negro's
share of ownership and control of enterprises in all industries
across the board. In our judgment, such a standard of success is
unlikely to be attained. Instead, it seems reasonable to use tests
relating to the equalization of the Negro share of ownership and
control, by the year 1980, in those fields where they are already
concentrating.

Utilizing this criterion, we can make a rough estimate of the
employment potential for Negroes of a reasonable degree of success achieved by black capitalism. In making this estimate, the
first step was to take the total number of businesses in the United
States economy in those areas in which Negroes are concentrating
and estimate the number of enterprises which Negroes would
control if they owned the same share of each type of business as
their share in the total population (11 percent). The second step
was to estimate the total number of jobs made available by these
firms using data on the average number of jobs per establishment.
The calculations were performed under the alternative assumptions that these firms would employ at the same rates found in
(1) the National Business League sample described above, or
(2) the rates reported by all firms in the over-all census data.

The results of the calculations performed under the two alternative assumptions suggested that the total number of jobs
created in the principal lines of Negro business activity would
range roughly between 320,000 and 450,000. It was noted earlier
that these leading fields contain almost three-fifths of all Negro
businesses. Assuming that the employment prospects of the rest

of the Negro businesses were the same as in the categories identified—and assuming that they expanded proportionately—the resulting expansion would lead to the creation of between 550,000 and 885,000 new job opportunities, depending upon the assumptions regarding the NBL sample or Census Bureau employment rates.

To measure the impact of this hypothetical job creation through the expansion of black-owned businesses, these figures must be compared to the total Negro labor force expected in 1980 of roughly 11,205,000 workers. The creation of between 550,000 and 885,000 job opportunities means that these black-owned businesses would offer employment to between 4.9 percent and 7.9 percent of the total Negro labor force. Stated differently, between 92.1 percent and 95.1 percent of Negro workers would still require jobs in firms owned and controlled by persons other than Negroes in 1980.

A second and even more radical assumption regarding the success of black capitalism would be to assume that by 1980 Negro businessmen would control 11 percent of all retail and service establishments and that these establishments would offer the same job potential as current retail and service operations. Under this assumption it was estimated that by 1980 black-owned firms would offer employment to only 1,454,600 workers, or to 13.0 percent of all Negroes in the labor force. Comparing these figures to the estimated growth of the Negro labor force in the 1970s of 2,326,000 suggests that at best firms owned by Negroes could employ only slightly better than three-fifths the increment in Negro workers during the decade. Thus, in 1980 black capitalists would be able to offer employment to only a small fraction of the Negro work force, and the absolute number of Negro workers relying on employment in firms owned by persons other than Negroes would undoubtedly increase in the next decade.

In making the above calculations regarding the employment potential of black capitalism, we omitted consideration of employment in Negro-owned firms in transportation, manufacturing, and construction. This omission was not accidental; rather it resulted from the basic fact that there are few Negro-owned firms competing in these types of businesses. Since firms in these categories (and especially in manufacturing) rely on important economies of scale, it is highly unlikely that a limited localized ghetto economy could effectively support them. The feasibility of creating large-scale ghetto-based manufacturing export industries appears to be critically limited by certain adverse locational factors. The most critical locational factor is the high cost and unavailability of adequate land area in an era when "technological developments favor the use of single-story continuous process plants." In the case of construction, it should be noted that the bulk of the increase in the supply of ghetto buildings arises primarily from the conversion of existing structures and to a much lesser extent from the creation of new structures. Thus, the outlook for construction companies confined to ghetto operations is not very promising.

CONCLUDING OBSERVATIONS

The general conclusion from this analysis is that the strategy of black capitalism, as we have defined it, offers a very limited potential for economic advancement for the majority of the Negro population. The ghetto economy as we understand it today does not appear to provide profitable opportunities for large-scale business investment, and any economic advances made by residents of this marginal sector of the economy in all likelihood will not materially alter the investment prospects. This situation is in large part due to a tendency for affluent Negroes to shop in the more diverse national economy.

The strategy of black capitalism fails, however, for an even more fundamental reason; it is founded on the premise of self-employment. Our research has indicated clearly that self-employment is a rather rapidly declining factor in our modern economy because the rewards to employment in salaried positions are substantially greater. Self-employment may be the path to affluence for the fortunate few who are very successful, but for the great majority of the Negro population it offers a low and rather risky expected pay-off.

At this juncture, we would like to point out that our disenchantment with the strategy of black economic development through black capitalism is not based simply on its limited economic potential. We are also concerned that reliance on such a strategy may substitute for efforts in vital areas which are of the utmost importance to the Negro population. In the long run, the pursuit of black capitalism may retard the Negro's economic advancement by discouraging many from the full participation in the national economy with its much broader range of challenges and opportunities. A strategy of black capitalism may also prove deleterious to the Negro community because, in the words of two observers, "the programs would place those least capable of accepting risk in the position of accepting large risks." New ghetto enterprises would certainly be more prone to failure than already established firms, and their failures would leave a lasting burden on the individuals starting these firms and on those employees who had been induced to work in such enterprises rather than in businesses not dependent on the ghetto economy.

As we mentioned at the outset, we believe there is considerable scope for Negroes to make advances in the field of business. This is especially true if the effort is made through a corporate form of organization with enough capital and managerial expertise to survive the severe competition of large regional and national firms. Moreover, such efforts should be mainly outside the ghetto, and they must be in the expanding sectors of the economy (not necessarily large-scale manufacturing) if they are to have any chance of surviving. Progress in business ownership, however, is not sufficient by itself to alleviate the economic problems of Negroes and other disadvantaged groups. Efforts must be made on a variety of fronts, and the choice among the mix of potential programs must be made quite carefully. It has been with the express purpose of facilitating this choice that we have analyzed the economic potential of black capitalism.

PART FIVE   Urban Crisis and

Urban Prospect

Why Government Cannot Solve
the Urban Problem

EDWARD C. BANFIELD

*Edward Banfield, University Professor of Government at the Uni-
versity of Pennsylvania, has authored many books on urban politics. Banfield's trenchant critical views of urban public policy have
aroused considerable controversy and, in the words of one re-
viewer, earned him the appellation "the maverick of urbanology."*

BY THE SERIOUS PROBLEMS of the cities I mean those that affect,
or may affect, the essential welfare (as opposed to the comfort,
convenience, and business advantage) of large numbers of people or the ability of the society to maintain itself as a "going concern," to be in some sense free and democratic, and to produce
desirable human types. As examples of serious problems I will
cite chronic unemployment, poverty, ignorance, crime, racial and
other injustice, and civil disorder. To my mind, these problems
are of a different order of importance than, say, the journey to
work, urban sprawl, or the decline of department store sales.

What I am calling serious problems exist mainly in the inner
parts of the central cities and of the older larger suburbs. The
large majority of city dwellers do not live in these places and
have little or no firsthand knowledge of these problems; most
city dwellers have housing, schools, transportation, and community facilities that are excellent and getting better all the time.
If there is an urban crisis, it is in the inner city. The lowest-
skilled, lowest-paid, and lowest-status members of the urban
work force have always lived in the highest-density districts of

the inner city, that being where most of the jobs for the low-skilled have always been. Improvements in transportation have in the last thirty years or so hastened a process of outward growth that has always been going on. Most of those who could afford to do so have moved from the central city to the suburbs and from inlying suburbs to outlying ones. Much manufacturing and commerce has done the same thing. The inner city still employs most of the unskilled, but the number (and proportion) that it employs is declining, and considerable numbers of the unskilled are in a sense stranded in the inner city. The presence there of large concentrations of people who have relatively little education and income accounts for—perhaps I should say constitutes—the so-called urban crisis. Most of these people are black. From an objective standpoint, this is of less importance than most people suppose: If all Negroes turned white overnight, the serious problems of the city would still exist and in about the same form and degree; *it is the presence of a large lower class, not of Negroes as such* [emphasis added], that is the real source of the trouble.

Government can change the situation that I have just described only marginally; it cannot change it fundamentally. No matter what we do, we are bound to have large concentrations of the unskilled, of the poor, and—what is by no means the same thing—of the lower class in the inner parts of the central cities and the larger older suburbs for at least another twenty years. Rich as we are, we cannot afford to throw the existing cities away and build new ones from scratch. The decentralization of industry and commerce and of residential land use is bound to continue, leaving ever-larger semi-abandoned and blighted areas behind.

If government cannot change fundamentally the pattern of metropolitan growth, neither can it solve any of the serious problems associated with it. To be specific, it cannot eliminate slums, educate the slum child, train the unskilled worker, end chronic poverty, stop crime and delinquency, or prevent riots. Of course, I do not mean that it cannot eliminate a single slum, educate a single slum child, or prevent a single riot. What I mean is that it cannot put a sizable dent in the problem as a whole. These problems may all become much less serious, but if they do, it will not be because of the direct efforts of government to bring about reforms.

We cannot solve these problems or even make much headway against them by means of government action not because, as many seem to suppose, we are selfish, callous, or stupid, but rather because they are in the main not susceptible to solution.

THE IMPERATIVES OF CLASS

A slum is not simply a district of low-quality housing; rather, it is one in which a squalid and wretched style of life is widespread. The logic of growth *does* require that, in general, the lowest-income people live in the oldest, highest-density, most rundown housing, which will be nearest to the factories, warehouses, stores, and offices of the inner, or downtown, part of the central city; however, nothing in the logic of growth says that such districts must be squalid or crime-ridden.

The concept of class should be taken into account for these and certain other features of metropolitan development in the United States. Certain patterns of perception, taste, attitude, and behavior operate (within the limits set by the logic of growth) to influence the city's form and the nature of its prob lems. These patterns, no less than the logic of growth, are constraints which the policymaker must take into account and which limit what he may accomplish.

American sociologists define social class in very different ways: by objective criteria (income, schooling, occupation), subjective criteria (attitudes, tastes, values), and position in a deference hierarchy (who looks up to whom), among others. Whatever criteria are used, it turns out that essentially the same pattern of traits is found to be characteristic of the class. "All who have studied the lower class," writes Lee Rainwater, one of those who has studied it most, have produced findings that suggest a "distinct patterning" of attitudes, values, and modes of behavior. The same can be said of those who have studied the working, middle, and upper classes. Each class exhibits a characteristic patterning that extends to all aspects of life: manners, consumption, child-rearing, sex, politics, or whatever. In the United States over the past half-century these patternings have been described—although never with the completeness that an ethnographer would want—in hundreds of books and articles. By and large these many accounts agree.

Various principles have been advanced by which to rationalize or "explain" the association of the many, heterogeneous traits that have been found to constitute each "distinct patterning." Probably no one of these is best for all purposes. For the purpose here—namely, analysis of social problems from a policy standpoint—the most promising principle seems to be that of psychological orientation toward the future. Consequently, in what follows much will be made of the concepts "present-" and "future-orientation." The theory or explanatory hypothesis (it cannot be called a "fact," although there is some evidence to support it) is that the many traits that constitute a "patterning" are all consequences, indirect if not direct, of a time horizon that is characteristic of a class. Thus, the traits that constitute what is called lower-class culture or life style are consequences of the extreme present-orientation of that class. The lower-class person lives from moment to moment, he is either unable or unwilling to take account of the future or to control his impulses. Improvidence and irresponsibility are direct consequences of this failure to take the future into account (which is not to say that these traits may not have other causes as well), and these consequences have further consequences: Being improvident and irresponsible, he is likely also to be unskilled, to move frequently from one dead-end job to another, to be a poor husband and father. . . .

It is useful to employ the same principle—ability or willingness to provide for the future—to account for the traits that are characteristic of the other class cultures as well. The working class is more future-oriented than the lower class but less than the middle class, the middle class in turn is less future-oriented than the upper. At the upper end of the class-cultural scale the traits are all "opposite" those at the lower end.

Members of a "class" as the word is used here are people who share a "distinct patterning of attitudes, values, and modes of behavior," *not* people of like income, occupation, schooling, or status. A lower-class individual is likely to be unskilled and poor, but it does not follow from this that persons who are unskilled and poor are likely to be lower class. (That Italians eat spaghetti does not imply that people who eat spaghetti are Italian!)

The Upper Class · At the most future-oriented end of the scale, the upper-class individual expects a long life, looks forward to the future of his children, grandchildren, great-grandchildren (the family "line"), and is concerned also for the future of such abstract entities as the community, nation, or mankind. He is confident that within rather wide limits he can, if he exerts himself to do so, shape the future to accord with his purposes. He therefore has strong incentives to "invest" in the improvement of the future situation—i.e., to sacrifice some present satisfaction in the expectation of enabling someone (himself, his children, mankind, etc.) to enjoy greater satisfactions at some future time. Future-oriented culture teaches the individual that he would be cheating himself if he allowed gratification of his impulses (for example, for sex or violence) to interfere with his provision for the future.

The upper-class individual is markedly self-respecting, self-confident, and self-sufficient. He places great value on independence, curiosity, creativity, happiness, "developing one's potentialities to the full," and consideration for others. In rearing his children, he stresses these values along with the idea that one should govern one's relations with others (and, in the final analysis, with one's self) by *internal* standards rather than by conformity to an externally given code ("not because you're told to but because you take the other person into consideration"). The upper-class parent is not alarmed if his children remain unemployed and unmarried to the age of thirty, especially if they remain in school.

It will be seen that two features of this culture—the disposition to postpone present satisfaction for the sake of improving matters in the future and the desire to "express one's personality"—are somewhat antagonistic. Upper-class (that is, future-oriented) culture permits the individual to emphasize either theme. If he thinks that his means (money, power, knowledge, and the like) are almost certainly adequate to maintain him and his "line" throughout the future he envisions, the future-oriented individual has no incentive to "invest" (that is, trade present for future satisfaction) and may therefore emphasize self-expression. If, on the other hand, he thinks that his means may *not* be adequate (he will think this, of course, no matter how large his means if his plans for the future are grand enough), he is likely to emphasize self-discipline so that he may acquire the larger stock of means that he thinks he needs. Insofar as he chooses the expressive alternative, the upper-class individual's style of life may resemble the present-oriented one of the lower class. But whereas the lower-class individual is capable *only* of present-oriented behavior, the upper-class one can choose.

The Middle Class · The middle-class individual expects to be still in his prime at sixty or thereabouts; he plans ahead for his children and perhaps his grandchildren, but, less future-oriented than the ideal typical member of the upper class, he is not likely to think in terms of "line" or to be much concerned about "mankind" in the distant future. He, too, is confident of his ability to influence the future, but he does not expect to influence so distant a future as does the upper-class individual, nor is he as confident about the probable success of his efforts to influence it. The middle-class individual's self-feelings are a little less strong than those of the upper-class individual; he is also somewhat less desirous of privacy. Although he shows a good deal of independence and creativity and a certain taste for self-expression, these traits rarely lead to eccentricity. He is less likely than the upper-class individual to have means that he considers adequate to assure a satisfactory level of goal attainment throughout his anticipated future. Therefore, "getting ahead"—and the self-improvement and sacrifice of impulse gratification that it requires—will be more likely to take precedence over him over "the expression of one's personality."

The Working Class · The working-class individual does not "invest" as heavily in the future, nor in so distant a future, as does the middle-class one. He expects to be an "old man" by the time he is fifty, and his time horizon is fixed accordingly. Also, he has less confidence than the middle-class individual in his ability to shape the future and has a stronger sense of being at the mercy of fate, a "power structure," and other uncontrollable forces. For this reason, perhaps, he attaches more importance to luck than does the middle-class individual. He is self respecting and self-confident, but these feelings are less marked in him than in the middle-class individual and they extend to a somewhat narrower range of matters. As compared to the middle-class individual, he is little disposed toward either self-improvement or self-expression; "getting ahead" and "enlarging one's horizon" have relatively little attraction for him. In rearing his children, he emphasizes the virtues of neatness and cleanliness, honesty, obedience, and respect for external authority. If his children do not go to college, the working-class individual does not mind much. In his relations with others, he is often authoritarian and intolerant, and sometimes aggressive.

The working-class individual's deepest attachment is to his family (most of his visiting is with relatives, not friends). The sense of sharing a purpose with others is not as important to him as it is to members of the upper classes, and when he joins an organization it is more likely to be for companionship and "fun" than for "service" or civic improvement. He may vote, especially if someone asks him to as a favor. His opinions on public matters are highly conventional (it does not seem to occur to him that he is entitled to form opinions of his own), and his participation in politics is motivated not by political principles but by ethnic and party loyalties, the appeal of personalities, or the hope of favors from the precinct captain.

The Lower Class · At the present-oriented end of the scale, the lower-class individual lives from moment to moment. If he has any awareness of a future, it is of something fixed, fated, beyond his control: Things happen *to* him, he does not *make* them happen. Impulse governs his behavior, either because he cannot discipline himself to sacrifice a present for a future satisfaction or because he has no sense of the future. He is therefore radically improvident: Whatever he cannot use immediately he considers valueless. His bodily needs (especially for sex) and his taste for "action" take precedence over everything else—and certainly over any work routine. He works only as he must to stay alive, and drifts from one unskilled job to another, taking no interest in his work. As compared to the working-class individual, he "doesn't want much success, knows he couldn't get it even if he wanted to, and doesn't want what might help him get success." Although his income is usually much lower than that of the working-class individual, the market value of his car, television, and household appliances and playthings is likely to be considerably more. He is careless with his things, however, and, even when nearly new, they are likely to be permanently out of order for lack of minor repairs. His body, too, is a thing "to be worked out but not repaired"; he seeks medical treatment only when practically forced to do so: "symptoms that do not incapacitate are often ignored."

The lower-class individual has a feeble, attenuated sense of self; he suffers from feelings of self-contempt and inadequacy, and is often apathetic or dejected. In his relations with others he is suspicious and hostile, aggressive yet dependent. He is unable to maintain a stable relationship with a mate; commonly he does not marry. He feels no attachment to community, neighbors, or friends (he has companions, not friends), resents all authority (for example, that of policemen, social workers, teachers, landlords, employers), and is apt to think that he has been "railroaded" and to want to "get even." He is a nonparticipant; he belongs to no voluntary organizations, has no political interests, and does not vote unless paid to do so.

The lower-class household is usually female-based. The woman who heads it is likely to have a succession of mates who contribute intermittently to its support but take little or no part in rearing the children. In managing the children, the mother (or aunt, or grandmother) is characteristically impulsive: Once children have passed babyhood they are likely to be neglected or abused, and at best they never know what to expect next. A boy raised in such a household is likely at an early age to join a corner gang of other such boys and to learn from the gang the "tough" style of the lower-class man. The stress on "masculinity," "action," risk-taking, conquest, fighting, and "smartness" makes lower-class life extraordinarily violent. However, much of the violence is probably more an expression of mental illness than of class culture. The incidence of serious mental illness is greater in the lower class than in any of the others. Moreover, the nature of lower-class culture is such that much behavior that in another class would be considered bizarre seems routine.

In the middle- and upper-class cultures, one's house and grounds afford opportunities for self-improvement and self-expression. To the upper-class individual, it is the latter value that is usually more important: The house is the setting for and the representation of his family line ("house"). The middle-class individual is more likely to value his house for giving scope to his impulse to improve things—not only physical things (the house and grounds) but also, and especially, his own and his family's skills, habits, feelings, and attitudes.

In the upper- and middle-class cultures, the neighborhood and community are as important as the house and are hardly to be separated from it. It is essential to live where there are good schools, for otherwise the children might not get into good colleges. Other community facilites—parks, libraries, museums, and the like—are highly valued, as are opportunities to be of "service" by participating in civic organizations. This desire to belong to a community partly accounts for the exclusiveness of the "better" neighborhoods and suburbs.

To the working class, a different set of values to accord with its life style governs the choice of physical arrangements in the city. Space is less important to the working-class family than to the middle- or upper-class one. It prefers being "comfy" to having privacy; it is thought natural for children to sleep two or three to a room or perhaps even to a bed. Having neighbors—even noisy ones—down the hall or in a house that is adjoining or almost adjoining is taken for granted.

The lower-class individual lives in the slum, which, to a greater or lesser extent, is an expression of his tastes and style of life. The slum, according to the sociologist Marshall B. Clinard, is a way of life with its own subculture. The subculture norms and values of the slum are reflected in poor sanitation and health practices, deviant behavior, and often a real lack of interest in formal education. With some exceptions, there is little general desire to engage in personal or community efforts for self-improvement. Slum persons generally are apathetic toward the employment of self-help on a community basis, they are socially isolated, and most sense their powerlessness. This does not mean that they are satisfied with their way of life or do not want a better way to live; it is simply that slum apathy tends to inhibit individuals from putting forth sufficient efforts to change the local community. They may protest and they may blame the slum entirely on the outside world, but at the same time they remain apathetic about what they could themselves do to change their world.

Although he has more "leisure" than almost anyone, the indifference ("apathy" if one prefers) of the lower-class person is such that he seldom makes even the simplest repairs to the place that he lives in. He is not troubled by dirt and dilapidation and he does not mind the inadequacy of public facilities such as schools, parks, hospitals, and libraries; indeed, where such things exist he may destroy them by carelessness or even by vandalism. Conditions that make the slum repellent to others are serviceable to him in several ways. First, the slum is a place of excitement—"where the action is." Nothing happens there by plan and anything may happen by accident—a game, a fight, a tense confrontation with the police; feeling that something exciting is about to happen is highly congenial to people who live for the present and for whom the present is often empty. Second, it is a place of opportunity. Just as some districts of the city are specialized as a market for, say, jewelry or antiques, so the slum is specialized as one for vice and for illicit commodities generally. Dope peddlers, prostitutes, and receivers of stolen goods are all readily available there, within easy reach of each other and of their customers and victims. For "hustlers," the slum is the natural headquarters. Third, it is a place of concealment. A criminal is less visible to the police in the slum than elsewhere, and the lower-class individual, who in some parts of the city would attract attention, is one among many there. In the slum one can beat one's children, lie drunk in the gutter, or go to jail without attracting any special notice; these are things that most of the neighbors themselves have done and that they consider quite normal.

Although it is the lower class that gives the slum its special character, lower-class people are by no means the only ones who live in it. Some blocks may be occupied almost exclusively by the lower class, but in the district as a whole, the majority of residents may well be working-class and not a few middle-class. These are people whose incomes do not correspond to their class culture; in some cases they are the victims of bad luck— the death of a breadwinner, for example—but more often they are in the slum because racial discrimination, past or present, has deprived them of normal opportunities for education and employment.

For these working- and middle-class slum dwellers, life in the slum is a daily battle to preserve life, sanity, and self-respect. They must send their children to schools where little or nothing is taught or learned and where the children are in constant physical and moral danger; they must endure garbage-filled alleys and rat-infested halls; if they shop in nearby stores, they must pay high prices for poor selections of inferior goods (the prices are often high only for them—for the lower class, which demands credit even though its credit rating is very poor, the same prices may actually be low); they must suffer the risk of annoyance and even of serious hardship by being mistaken for members of the lower class by policemen, teachers, landlords, and others, who either cannot discern or do not trouble to look for the clues to class differences among the poor.

Although the lower-class *type* finds the slum convenient and even congenial, there are many lower-class individuals—especially women—who are ambivalent about it or who want to escape from it. By exceptional luck or enterprise now and then one does. To the normal people who live in the slum, the worst feature of life there is fear.

Within the limits set by the logic of growth, the mix of class cultures more than anything else determines the city's character and the nature of its problems. Almost everything about the city—population density, per capita income, the nature and quality of housing, the crime rate, the dropout rate, the level of public services, the tenor of race relations, the style of politics—depends in some way and to some extent upon the class composition of the population. When this changes, either in a neighborhood or in the city as a whole, almost everything else changes accordingly. And except as they are compatible with the realities of class culture in the city, the most carefully contrived efforts of public and private policymakers cannot succeed, for the mix of class cultures is a constraint as real as those of income, technology, or climate. It is necessary, therefore, to form the best estimate one can of the direction that change in the class system will take.

The mass movement from the working into the middle class and from the lower middle into the upper middle class accounts as much as anything for the general elevation of standards that makes most urban problems appear to be getting worse even when, *measured by a fixed standard,* they are getting better. The new standards are those of a higher class. It is because the process of "middle-class-ification" has given great numbers of people higher perspectives and standards that dissatisfaction with the city is so widespread. The city that was thought pleasant when most people were working class is thought repellent now that most are middle class, and it will be thought abhorrent when, before long, most are upper middle class.

The ascendancy of the middle and upper middle classes has increased feelings of guilt at "social failures" (that is, discrepancies between actual performance and what by the rising class standards is deemed adequate) and given rise to public rhetoric about "accepting responsibility" for ills that in some cases could not have been prevented and cannot be cured. In the upper-middle-class view it is always society that is to blame. Society, according to this view, could solve all problems if it only tried hard enough; that a problem continues to exist is therefore proof positive of its guilt.

In this tendency to find society responsible for all ills, including those that are a function of rising standards, two dangers appear. One is that the allegation of social guilt may lead the individual to believe that he can do nothing to help himself. The other danger is that many people will take the talk of social guilt seriously and conclude that the society is one for which they can have no respect and in which they can place no trust. Such condemnation is mainly to be expected in those sections of society—the upper classes, especially their youth—that are most alive to moral issues, and in those other sectors—notably the poor and the minority groups—that have obvious grounds for thinking themselves victims of social injustice.

THE FUTURE OF THE LOWER CLASS

So long as the city contains a sizable lower class, nothing basic can be done about its most serious problems. Good jobs may be offered to all, but some will remain chronically unemployed. Slums may be demolished, but if the housing that replaces them is occupied by the lower class it will shortly be turned into new slums. Welfare payments may be doubled or tripled and a negative income tax instituted, but some persons will continue to live in squalor and misery. New schools may be built, new curricula devised, and the teacher-pupil ratio cut in half, but if the children who attend these schools come from lower-class homes, the schools will be turned into blackboard jungles, and those who graduate or drop out from them will, in most cases, be functionally illiterate. The streets may be filled with armies of policemen, but violent crime and civil disorder will decrease very little. If, however, the lower class were to disappear—if, say, its members were overnight to acquire the attitudes, motivations, and habits of the working class—the most serious and intractable problems of the city would all disappear with it.

Some readers may suspect that when the author uses the words *lower class* what he has in the back of his mind is *Negro*. They may suspect, too, that the "real" purpose of the rather pessimistic account of the possibilities of reducing the size of the lower class that follows is to lay the basis for the conclusion that nothing should be done about any of the city's serious problems. There is, of course, no arguing with a reader who is determined to mistake one's meaning. There are lower-class people, as defined here, in *all* ethnic groups, including the Anglo-Saxon white Protestant one, and most Negroes are not improvident, do not live in squalor and violence, and therefore are *not* lower class.

Whether lower-class outlook and style of life will change—or can be changed—and, if so, under what circumstances and at what rate—are questions of great interest to policymakers. Social scientists differ as to the relative importance of "social heredity" and "social machinery" in forming class patternings of attitudes, values, and modes of behavior. Both sets of influences are undoubtedly at work and interact in complex ways; undoubtedly, too, the relative importance of these forces, as well as the nature of their interaction, differs from one group to another and from one individual to another.

The conclusion is unavoidable that for at least several decades there will be a lower class which, while small both in absolute numbers and as a percentage of the whole population, will nevertheless be large enough to constitute a serious problem—or, rather, a set of serious problems—in the city. The question arises, therefore, as to what policies might minimize the difficulties that must inevitably exist when a lower-class minority lives in the midst of an increasingly middle- and upper-class society.

When the lower class lived on farms and in small cities, its members were to some extent both held in check and protected by being physically isolated from each other. Also, there were few, if any, opportunities for easy money, and without money the lower-class person was effectively tied down. An even greater constraint on him, perhaps, was his visibility. In the slums of a big city, it is easy to drop out of sight. In a town or small city, on the other hand, there is no place to hide. The individual is known personally by the landlord, corner merchant, and policeman; he cannot escape into anonymity. In the big city he need never see the same merchant, landlord, or policeman twice. As an economist might put it, one who wants to lead a lower-class style of life has the advantage of numerous "economics of scale" in the big city.

Therefore, from the standpoint of a society that wants at once to protect lower-class people from each other and to protect itself from them, there are advantages in having lower-class people live in the town or small city, or, if they must live in the large one, in having them scattered in a way such that they will not constitute a "critical mass" anywhere. These considerations suggest that government programs (subsidies to large farmers, for example) that tend to push unskilled people off the land and out of rural areas ought to be stopped, that welfare programs should aim at making life in towns and small cities much more advantageous to the chronically poor than it is now (thereby reducing one of their incentives to come to the city), and that, within the large cities, there should be an end to that kind of urban renewal (almost the only kind in fact) the tendency of which is simply to shift the lower class from one place to another and not to dissipate it.

It might be argued that the hardest cases among the lower class ought to be treated as semicompetent (incompetents being those—for example, children, the insane, the feeble-minded —who are incapable of knowing where their own interest, not to mention the social interest, lies). Such persons could be cared for in what may be called semi-institutions—small enclaves of lower-class people who, either because they wanted help in "staying out of trouble" or because they desired certain material benefits (extra-generous allowances for housing, food, clothing, and health care) would agree to accept certain limitations on their freedom. For example, they might agree to receive most of their income in kind rather than in cash, to forgo ownership of automobiles, to have no more than two or three children, and to accept a certain amount of surveillance and supervision from a semi-social-worker–semi-policeman.

Several considerations, however, argue against semi-institutional care for the lower class. As a practical matter, it is unlikely that many of the hardest cases—those from whom society most needs protection—would choose semiaffluence in a semi-institution in preference to the life of the slum. If these hardest cases are to be controlled at all, they must be controlled totally—that is, put into prison. This approach is obviously out of the question, since "being lower class" is not a crime or committable condition and is not at all likely to be made one. The tendency, in fact, is in the opposite direction: to confine fewer and fewer of those who have been convicted of crimes or have been judged mentally incompetent.

A very important danger in such efforts to restrain the lower class is that they might be applied also to people who are *not* lower class, thus abridging the freedom of these others without justification. This danger exists in part because euphemisms— e.g., "the poor"—have collapsed necessary distinctions between the competent and the semicompetent. (The blind, for example, are often lumped together in welfare programs with the lower-class poor.) It exists also because prejudice or convenience sometimes causes caretakers to treat externals—skin color, speech ways, and so forth—as indicators of lower-class culture.

Another objection arises from the fact that at the present time (fifty or more years ago it was otherwise) most lower-class people in the large cities are black. Putting them in semi-institutions would inevitably appear to be a reflection of racial inferiority or an expression of racial prejudice. What is even more important, perhaps, is that taking the lower-class black out of the slum of the great city would tend to cut him off psychologically from the black community. It is by no means inconceivable that the "black pride" movement may engender morale in the mass of black people—morale that the lower class may in some degree share if it is in close physical contact with the main body of blacks. To be sure, one could argue this the other way, contending, first, that nothing would do more for the morale of the black community than to have the worst of the lower class removed from its midst and, second, that lower-class people are by nature of their culture immune to any moral influence from the surrounding society.

Finally, there is clearly a tension if not an out-and-out incompatibility between the goal of restraining the lower-class individual and that of stimulating him. The first calls for reducing his freedom, the second for enlarging it. If it were possible to identify persons who are irremediably lower class and to place them and them alone under restraints, this objection would not apply. In fact, there is no way of knowing which individuals would respond significantly to incentives and which would not. The danger of perpetuating and increasing present-orientedness while endeavoring to restrain it makes the whole enterprise of restraint suspect. Despite the high costs to society and to the lower-class individual himself that follow from increasing his freedom, doing so may well be the best course of action in the long run.

Challenge to Orthodoxy

RUSSELL D. MURPHY

The next two selections are taken from reviews of The Unheavenly
City. *Russell Murphy's review was published in* Trans-action.
*Murphy is Associate Professor of Government at Wesleyan Uni-
versity.*

The great tragedy of Science—
the slaying of a beautiful hypothesis
by an ugly fact.
—Thomas Henry Huxley

THERE ARE at least two ways to visualize unheavenly cities. The
most obvious of these is the image of festering urban sores, of
cities beset by physical deterioration, and by human deprivation and degradation. A second and only slightly less obvious
image is that of cities unburdened by moral posturings, of communities guided in their policy deliberations by the canons of
rigorous and systematic social analysis.

Of two images, the latter is the more appropriate summary of
Edward Banfield's *The Unheavenly City.* The book is offered
as a rigorous analysis of the current urban crisis; its central theme
is that conventional definitions of this crisis are greatly exaggerated and largely beside the point. The urban crisis, according to Banfield, is reflected not so much in the endless, dreary,
but misleading and misunderstood statistics on poverty, crime,
and social disintegration that punctuate drawing room dis-
courses on the topic. Rather it lies in the failure to examine "the
facts, however unpleasant," and more especially to apply these
facts to policy choices. Stated somewhat differently, contemporary
man, like the *philosophes* of Carl Becker's *The Heavenly City
of the Eighteenth Century Philosophers,* is less emancipated than
is commonly thought. In an era proud of its scientific methods
and analytical techniques, many of today's policy-makers, social
commentators, and political critics are still confined by the moral

prescriptions of traditional orthodox reform. This unquestioning attachment to orthodoxy and to its untested premises, Banfield argues, has led to the adoption and perpetuation of ineffective and deleterious governmental programs.

One major constraint on policy, according to Banfield, is the existence of an urban lower-class culture. In his words, this culture is characterized by an "outlook and style of life which is radically present-oriented and which therefore attaches no value to work, sacrifice, self-improvement, or service to family, friends, or community." The definition is a familiar one, for there is general agreement that the lower class is distinguished by a unique set of norms and values, among them the belief that the world is malevolent and that there are precious few rewards for personal enterprise. But in his understanding of the relationship between this culture and poverty, the author parts company with most social commentators. For Banfield, the culture is the cause, not the result, of poverty and the social pathologies associated with poverty. By contrast, the more conventional proposition holds that the culture is rooted in the existential condition of the poor. According to the latter interpretation, lower-class individuals learn that their resources and opportunities are too limited to succeed, and they respond by adopting alternative values that help them adapt to real-world conditions. Equally important, these alternative values lack what Lee Rainwater terms "full normative character." The lower class never entirely rejects the general norms of the larger society and these general norms, including the moral imperative to compete and achieve, continue to provide the canons for self-evaluation among lower class individuals.

These contrasting explanations of the lower class culture have significant policy implications. For Banfield's lower class, current social welfare policies have little positive value, predicated as they are on the assumption that, given the opportunity, people can and will invest in the future. Public schools, for example, cannot educate children when their social backgrounds have failed to instill the capacity for postponing gratifications, which is needed for academic achievement. Manpower programs are similarly hampered since the "unemployed and the intermittently employed have habits or cultural characteristics incompatible with employment in steady, high-paying jobs," specifically a difficulty in accepting "the discipline of regular work in accordance with definite work rules." Income maintenance programs, including proposals for guaranteed annual incomes, merely compound the difficulties by producing "disincentives not only to work but also to save, to learn skills, and in general to provide for the future." Indeed, so basic are the policy constraints of the lower class, Banfield concludes, that "so long as the city contains a sizeable lower class, nothing can be done about its problems"—except, perhaps, such radical proposals as the author's own humane variation on Jonathan Swift's *A Modest Proposal*—that, instead of eating their children, the poor should sell them.

Before resorting to such radical proposals, however, more information clearly is needed on the dimensions and dynamics of the lower class culture, on the characteristics of those whose world is bounded by the here and the now. Unfortunately the evidence presented in *The Unheavenly City* is largely indirect and spotty; as a result Banfield's provocative analysis is not persuasive.

To begin with, more needs to be known about how the population of our cities is distributed along the class continuum. This would tell us whether Banfield's extreme lower class, those who are totally immobilized, is a null set. Determining this will require sensitive interviewing techniques and sophisticated observation and analysis. Otherwise there is a danger that the totality of the lower-class culture will be missed. As Lee Rainwater reports in the Spring 1970 issue of *The Journal of Social Issues*, careful observation of actual lower-class behavior reveals that this behavior contradicts the norms associated with the culture, that although individuals have a distinct ideology that seemingly legitimates their deviant behavior, they really do not believe in this ideology.

Secondly, more needs to be known about the dynamics of the culture and in particular about the conditions under which movement occurs, in both directions, along the class continuum. Banfield finds no literature on this point but, reflecting on nineteenth century American experience, speculates that "those in the lower class rarely, if ever, climbed out of it." To phrase it

somewhat differently, if Banfield is correct then few if any
swamp Yankees or shanty Irish ever made it into the world of
the Brahmins or the lace curtain.

This may have been the case, though there are no firm data
to support the proposition. But even if one assumes it was the
case, the question remains as to what distinguished the rare few
from the not so fortunate masses. Similar questions need to be
posed about the contemporary urban experience. Are there, as
Banfield at one point seems to suggest, at least some lower-class
urban whites who are not descendants of an older lower-class
generation? If so, what accounts for the absorption of this group
into the present-oriented culture? More generally, given the author's admittedly speculative observation that "it is possible . . .
the old lower class produced very few descendants. It may have
died off without reproducing itself," what accounts for the current urban lower class? An obvious answer might be the immi-
gration of individuals from the rural lower class, in particular
lower-class blacks. But migration to the city would seem to be
prima facie evidence of the migrant's future-orientation, of his
hopes and positive expectations for himself and his progeny. Is
it possible, then, that the contemporary urban lower class was
not always thus afflicted, and that the city has somehow failed
in its time-honored role as the facilitator of upward social
mobility?

Finally, more needs to be known about the impact of government programs on the lower-class individual, and especially the
impact of recent efforts associated with the national war on poverty, among them such legislation as the Economic Opportunity
Act of 1964. At this particular juncture in history, however, it
would seem somewhat premature to offer any final, over-all assessment of these as social welfare efforts inasmuch as it was not
until the early part of the last decade that the country discovered rock bottom poverty. Moreover, in the short time since then,
much of the effort in the war on poverty, including the effort of
government agencies, has been devoted to what may be termed
"politicizing poverty." In this sense, the early years of the war on
poverty were devoted to something more than just social welfare
policy. They were also part of a political process concerned as
much, if not more, with the redistribution of power as with

the redistribution of income, an effort, in short, to ensure that a greater share of the nation's resources— its time, attention, and skills, as well as its money—were devoted to the stubborn and chronic problems of poverty and near-poverty. And in this important respect, the efforts have had positive implications for the poor, since the search for solutions is underway, in ways that contrast dramatically with the general complacency of the previous decade.

Banfield's "Heresy"

Theodore Marmor, author of The Politics of Medicine, *is on the faculty of the University of Chicago. His review of* The Unheavenly City *was published in* Commentary.

THE CONTROVERSY over *The Unheavenly City* was expected, and indeed it was partially provoked. Banfield seems to lead readers into distemper, the preface to his book containing the following anticipation of adverse reaction: "This book will probably strike many readers as the work of an ill-tempered and mean-spirited fellow. I would not mind that especially if I did not think it might prevent them from taking its argument as seriously as they should. I should like therefore to assure the reader that I am as well-meaning—probably even as soft-hearted —as he. But facts are facts however unpleasant. . . ."

In substance, if not in tone, *The Unheavenly City* reads like a political scientist's version of Milton Friedman's *Capitalism and Freedom*. In it, Banfield makes a number of different claims about twentieth-century urban progress, the character of America's "lower class," and the minimal, sometimes negative, contribution of public programs to urban change. He shows how urban conditions have improved in absolute terms during this century and asserts that only our "rising expectations" explain why our present circumstances are seen by some as a "crisis." Blacks have taken part in this general progress, he maintains, citing secondary evidence of the unmistakable improvement in the housing, income, health, and political patterns of black Americans. The situation of the city's least fortunate inhabitants, he concludes, is thus not all that bad.

However, Banfield claims that most of this improvement has been produced not by government policy, but by the independent play of market and social forces. It is unlikely, furthermore, that government policy can deal successfully with the one intractable problem which has resisted solution by the private sector. That is the problem of our "lower class," the group whose cultural level is as low as its income and whose inability to postpone gratification makes it stumble and fail continuously in the great American upward scramble. The "lower class" is dispro portionately black and urban;[1] it will not, like old soldiers or nineteenth-century immigrants, fade away from public notoriety. Nor will the problem of the "lower class" respond to governmental remedies.

Finally, in other essays included in *The Unheavenly City*, Banfield makes a number of separate points about housing and metropolitan growth patterns, riots and their causes, minimum-wage legislation and education policy, private wants and the public inability to satisfy them.

But if Banfield's views read like a political-science version of Milton Friedman, they have been received with nothing like the scholarly respect that Friedman regularly commands. Although Banfield has had his champions (who include James Q. Wilson, Irving Kristol, and Robert A. Nisbet) and although some of these have if anything exaggerated the excellence of *The Unheavenly City*, they have been overwhelmed both in numbers and in passion by his detractors. These latter have charged Banfield with a bewildering variety of sins: distortion by selective citation, unsound inferences, intellectual opportunism, moral insensitivity. His book has been described as "warped," "perverse," "wrongheaded," "a tract that will have unfortunate social effects."

Why has the book aroused so much emotion and so little fairminded analysis? To discover the answer is to understand why dissenting voices in the social-policy community have been subjected to intimidation and why the discussion of social policy has become so shrill an enterprise. In part, the emotionalism indicates that what Banfield has to say is significantly disturbing. His ideas about the existence of an entractably pathological lower class, for example, strike at the very basis of middle-class reform ardor. "If Banfield is right," Richard Todd noted correctly in the *Atlantic Monthly*, "the noblest efforts of the past 30 years have

1. That is to say, a higher percentage of blacks are in poverty than are in the middle or upper class; among Americans as a whole there are of course more whites than blacks in impoverished circumstances.

been wrong." This is heresy to liberals, and it is attacked as such.

Others among Banfield's critics have charged him with *academic* heresy—that is, with bias and distortion. As Robert L. Bartley summed it up in a sensible essay on the whole Banfield affair in the *Wall Street Journal*, "The ever-present insinuation [of reviewers] has been that Mr. Banfield did not follow his evidence and logic to his conclusions, that the conclusions spring first from some ulterior purpose, that he is a dishonest scholar." Thus Peter Rossi, the Johns Hopkins sociologist, described Banfield's analysis in the *Social Science Quarterly* as "intellectual opportunism" and "selective citation," and labeled the book, "a political tract, better documented than most, but a tract nevertheless." Robert Agger claimed in the same issue of the *Social Science Quarterly* that "Banfield's use of studies and events to document his theses is a not so clever but purposeful, manipulative, selective ordering of so-called fact."

The charge that Banfield is merely an apologist for the *status quo* was leveled by others. Writing in the New York *Times Book Review*, Jeff Greenfield accused Banfield of blatant political bias in a "largely theoretical tract" which "absolves institutions now in power." "Banfield," fumed Richard Sennett in the *New York Review of Books*, is ". . . an innocent, blind to the facts of class and race in America today, and taking refuge from the storms of modern events in an old-fashioned small-town mythology of class and the individual's place in history."

The Banfield controversy sharply illuminates our depressing current mode of discussing social-policy issues. First, it illustrates the habit shared by many intellectuals of dismissing claims that, even if true, might tend to weaken reform impulses. Such critics seem to believe that improvement for black Americans cannot proceed if even demonstrable falsehoods—such as that the material circumstances of blacks have been getting worse over the past decade—are laid to rest. Thus, Robert Agger warned that the fact that "Banfield is quite right in demonstrating the hopelessness of well-intended but minor reforms should lead no one to his inference and guiding postulate that 'fundamental reforms' are impossible or unwise in a free society." Agger took the anti-intellectual and rather alarmist position that "During this period of groping for new forms and new solutions, the voices of the Banfields could do damage." Peter Rossi said of Banfield, "It is all too easy to read into [his] term 'lower class' the content 'black' and to conclude that as long as we have blacks in our cities we will have problems because so many of them are incorrigibly lower class." These critics held Banfield to the position that truth and bad consequences are unheavenly partners.

Second, the reception illustrates how the scholarly community fails to assess dispassionately the *relative merits* of a book or argument. Many rejected the entire book on the basis of partial disagreement, especially on the issue of income-redistribution and its power to affect poverty. Banfield believes that welfare payments do not produce greater independence or self-reliance in the "lower-class" poor because lower-class culture amounts to a pathology that is immune to merely symptomatic treatment. "The implication that lower-class culture is pathological," wrote Banfield, "seems fully warranted . . . because of the relatively high incidence of mental illness in the lower class."

But how large is this group of the culturally poor? Banfield does not know. What is the evidence that such a group exists at all in anything but trivial numbers? Banfield is not clear. Frank Levy properly noted in remarks before the American Political Science Association in 1971:

. . . on the issue of size, Banfield is quite ambiguous. When making estimates, his numbers seem small. When discussing policy, the numbers seem large indeed. Banfield quotes with approval an estimate that 5 per cent of all city families and 15–20 per cent of all city families below the poverty line are "multi-problem" families, families who qualify as Banfield's polar case of the lower class. This suggests that the other 80 per cent of poverty families could benefit to some extent from government programs. Yet many of Banfield's verbal arguments sound almost like the opposite proportions exist.

Peter Rossi supported Levy's criticism, claiming that "there is nothing but the most fragmentary and inconclusive evidence that there is a 'lower class' which is unable to defer gratification, or plan for the future"; and he thereby concluded that Banfield builds his model of urban society in order "to support his conservative ideology."

This criticism is important and cannot be lightly dismissed by

Banfield or his defenders. Yet it does not prove that Banfield's thesis about housing patterns is false, that his views of the "costs" of rising expectations are wrongheaded, or that in general he is a Nixon lackey. He might just be wrong about income-maintenance and the definition of poverty.

The Unheavenly City is written in a cantankerous, irritating tone, and it is true that this tone may have prompted some of Banfield's critics to respond in kind. In his passion for criticizing the unreason of liberal clichés, Banfield characteristically comes on as a "soured idealist"; as the *Wall Street Journal* noted, Banfield has

an argumentative streak . . . which is not entirely unrelated to the book's reception. Even his defenders observe that he has a taste for zingy rhetoric that can invite outraged reply. His chapter on urban riots, for example, argues that a certain incidence of outbreaks was inevitable when large and growing numbers of lower-class youths became concentrated in central cities and that this was much aggrevated when political leaders started to read into outbreaks the quasi-justification of political purpose. He chose to title this "Rioting Mainly for Fun and Profit."

The fury of the liberal response to Banfield is, then, understandable and Banfield himself is not without responsibility in provoking it. Nevertheless, the entire enterprise of intellectual debate in the United States was demeaned by the reception of *The Unheavenly City*. No work by a prominent social scientist, however unorthodox, however flawed, however provocative, merits the kind of hysteria which greeted this book. In the process, another chance was lost to discuss seriously the problems of urban America and their possible cures.

Social Problems and the Urban Crisis: Can Public Policy Make a Difference?

WORTH BATEMAN AND HAROLD M. HOCHMAN

This essay, written jointly by Worth Bateman, Director of the Land Use Center at the Urban Institute, and the Editor, contains an alternative interpretation of the urban crisis and the necessary ingredients of its solution. It was first presented at the annual meetings of the American Economic Association in 1970.

FOR US, as for Banfield, the term *urban crisis* connotes a set of unwanted social and economic conditions. As Banfield is the first to acknowledge, it is disagreeable to be confronted with under-nourished and poorly educated children, dilapidated housing and abandoned neighborhoods, or rising unemployment and high rates of crime. However, while Banfield's analysis reflects concern with these conditions, it implies that the more affluent members of society can do little about them, for it sees the lower classes as enmeshed in a culture of poverty which virtually guarantees the failure of positive action programs. In a sense, Banfield's interpretation suggests that the middle and upper classes are also victims of the urban crisis; perceiving the conditions in which the lower classes live, they wish to help, but every attempt is frustrated because the patient fails to respond to treatment. In these circumstances, Banfield's counsel of resignation is a comfort to the frustrated do-gooder who can thus continue to live comfortably, though social problems remain unchanged.

Basic to our analysis, as to Banfield's, is the presumption that the urban crisis derives from the dissatisfaction of the lower classes. This dissatisfaction is based on their perception that the conditions in which they live are unacceptable in relation to what *they* would like them to be. The problem thus posed is primarily an urban one for two reasons: (1) the poor have tended more and more to concentrate in urban areas, and (2) the disparities between income and wealth are much more obvious in urban areas where the very rich and the very poor live in physical proximity. If either of these conditions did not hold, there would be no urban crisis *per se.*

Primarily, our analysis differs from Banfield's in its explanation of *why* our society has not made more progress in dealing with the crisis in urban communities. For Banfield, the "present-orientedness" of the lower classes is responsible for the failure of public policy; for us, it is the political majority that has failed, by not adopting the essential reforms in social and economic institutions. If this majority could remedy its own shortsightedness, it would recognize that such reforms are in its own self-interest. In other words, our belief is that responsibility for the urban crisis stems neither from the lower classes nor from market failure, but from the deficiencies of the process of governance itself and the systems of rights it sanctions.

DIMENSIONS OF THE URBAN CRISIS

In our view, two characteristics of our society are the heart of the urban crisis. The first is a judgment, held by significant political minorities, that the present degree of inequality in the distribution of income, wealth, and social opportunity is unjust; the second is the spillover effects of such distributional inequality: crime, family disintegration, poor education and health services, and the deterioration of the physical environment. While in themselves these problems are not peculiar to cities, the spatial concentration of people and industry which characterizes urban areas makes their effects both more acute and more apparent and, in the same time, facilitates the political organization of those who are most dissatisfied. Taken alone, however, the existence of these problems in urban areas is not sufficient to justify a diagnosis of "urban crisis." [1]

1. Thus, as we use it, the term *urban crisis* connotes something more than the fact that urban society is not a utopia, that cities are not perfect and some wants of city dwellers go unsatisfied, as they always must, because public means are constrained. Not all externalities with which cities must deal originate in distributive injustice. Simpler externalities in consumption give rise to many urban allocation problems and are, in large measure, the basis for the public provision and financing of many local public services. But such problems, in our definition, are something different from the urban

What has given the current situation its crisis proportions is that governments at all levels— local, state, and federal—have been unable to achieve a rate of progress, in dealing with distributional inequalities and their negative spillovers, acceptable to the individuals and groups pressing for social change. Discrimination in employment and housing persists; public education is in a shambles in many urban school systems; wide disparities are evident in the quality and availability of such basic public services as fire protection, police, and sanitation; the incidence of poverty is high; and for generations the distribution of income has remained much the same. Most of all, the critical divisions between rich and poor in our society have increasingly been drawn along racial lines, even though racial differences in some socioeconomic measures have narrowed. Thus, despite some well-intentioned efforts and some progress in absolute terms, the Kerner Commission's portrayal of our society as "separate but unequal" seems as accurate now as it did in 1966.

Three interacting reasons can be cited for the failure to deal decisively with these problems. First, population mobility has produced patterns of settlement in metropolitan areas (within and among jurisdictions) that are sharply stratified geographically, and therefore politically, along economic, social, and racial lines. Second, the existing distribution of public authority within the federal structure and, in particular, the division (among levels and units of government) of the fiscal power to tax and spend has obstructed political action. Finally, the political process itself has tended to cater to pluralistic and powerful special interests.

Metropolitan areas continue to collect a growing proportion of the nation's population, income, and wealth. Rising incomes in these areas are associated with suburbanization, a lateral movement which has had a distinctive racial bias. Low-income households and racial and ethnic minorities are increasingly concentrated in the central cities, with the relatively more affluent tending to the suburbs. On the one hand, this location process has increased the extent to which central city residents must bear the fiscal and administrative burdens of providing basic public

---

crisis itself and relate to it only to the extent that they interact with and exacerbate the primary causes identified in the text.

services; on the other, it has severely undercut the financial capabilities of central city governments. Central cities, without significant change in the structure of metropolitan government and its financing, can do little to deal with the distributional problems that pervade urban society and give rise to the urban crisis. Moreover, by accelerating the migration of industry and middle- and upper-income residents to the suburbs, attempts to implement a strongly redistributive central city budget or to use public expenditure patterns in such areas as education and recreation as *de facto* means of redistribution are likely to be counterproductive.[2]

While cities lack the resources and authority to deal effectively with the problems which confront them, other levels of government—state and federal—are limited in what they do by the political forces they represent.[3] These forces reflect the interests of political majorities (or majority coalitions of minorities) who reside (and vote) primarily *outside* the jurisdiction of the city. The interests of these majorities and the legislators who represent them are frequently in conflict with the fundamental structural reforms needed to deal with distributive injustice and its external effects. This is seen, for example, in the actions of state legislatures in which rural-suburban coalitions block reforms intended to ease distributional inequities in school finance, law enforcement, and health services. At the federal level, also, the Congress has been overwhelmingly effective in frustrating attempts to reconcile the distributional problems of urban areas and overwhelmingly ineffective in adapting its procedures to the demands which an increasingly diverse and troubled society place upon it. In part, as Banfield's perceptive critique of current public policy points out, this is because reasonable-sounding programs have been misguided. But much of the responsibility rests in the hands of vested interests—sectional, economic, and political—operating through the Congress or the President, opposed

2. What we refer to here—"the prisoner's dilemma" in which cities and suburbs find themselves—is well known.

3. Of course, these same political forces operate among districts and neighborhoods within central cities, but within cities the critical factor of rigid political boundaries is absent.

to distributional change or bent on diverting public resources to parochial goals through such measures as oil depletion allowances, agriculture and maritime subsidies, educational aid to federally impacted areas, the interstate highway program, and, certainly not least, many military programs.

This situation is not new. Cities have always spawned more problems than their financial resources or political authority would permit them to resolve, and state and federal governments have always been heavily influenced by interests that appeared indifferent or even hostile to the people and problems of the city. If anything, the situation in an absolute sense may now be better than before, because cities, the disadvantaged, and racial minorities have benefited from such measures as voting-rights legislation and reapportionment. Nevertheless, the situation in which the cities now find themselves is distinguished from the past by a number of factors, all of which justify a current diagnosis of "urban crisis." Our generally affluent society has heightened aspirations of all social and ethnic groups in relation to realizations, and the twin processes of urbanization and suburbanization have themselves widened the gap between actual and minimally acceptable social conditions. A series of constitutional and legislative victories have legitimized the grievances and claims for justice of racial and economic minorities. Thus encouraged, these groups have stepped up their pressure for reforms to make such legal and moral rights a reality. However, the slow adjustment of social institutions and practices, plus the inevitable effects of a heritage of discrimination and prejudice on human attributes and capabilities, have kept measurable progress well below the pace of expectations.

Thus, perceived distributive injustice, coupled with the urban concentration of those who are most dissatisfied, is what the urban crisis is all about. What triggers the crisis is a judgment that the structure of rights to property, income, and political power, and the institutions and rules determining the way in which these rights are established and enforced are inequitable and unlikely to change. Repeated frustration of attempts to change prevailing practices increases the likelihood of recourse to violence or other extralegal protest and separation (effective secession of the disaffected minorities) from the rest of society.[4] In the extreme, neither of these alternatives is likely to be successful. The threat or fact of violence to protest perceived injustice makes more likely the formation of majorities which will enforce restraints on individual freedom, particularly the freedom of those most dissatisfied with the *status quo*. This multiplies the resentment, discontent, disagreement, disorder, and repression which is already characteristic of the urban scene. Extreme separation is also not a tenable solution, though it may be advantageous for a small number of the disaffected. Unless the separatist minorities are willing to accept a permanent position of inequality (and inferiority), conflict will result. Thus, separation, as a long-term arrangement, seems unstable and unsustainable. Moreover, like other social institutions which impede resource mobility, separation is inefficient. On balance, it will reduce not only the welfare of the political majority, but also that of minorities which practice it.

CAN PUBLIC POLICY MAKE A DIFFERENCE?

Our diagnosis, if correct, suggests that the urban crisis is a crisis of legitimacy, deriving: (1) from a failure of existing institutions to produce outcomes consistently which all members of society can believe to be in their long-run interest, and (2) from a conviction that the process by which these outcomes are achieved is itself unfair. In our view, resolution of the crisis requires fundamental structural reforms in economic, social, and political institutions. The accomplishment of this objective requires that the *de facto* system of legal, political, and economic claims be acceptable to all members of society. Such consensus must develop from a conviction that the obligations and rewards

4. One side-effect of this situation is a loss of faith in the idea, basic to a free society, that rational and unfettered inquiry, given enough time, will yield a just and acceptable solution. One might argue that disadvantaged minorities themselves have never harbored any such presumption; however, it has surely been a basic premise of idealists, including students and intellectuals. To the extent that the urban crisis is manifested in violence and disdain for law, not just on the part of the disadvantaged but among some idealists at all levels of economic well-being, this belief appears to have broken down.

of a just and stable society are a matter of universal self-interest.[5]

If self-interest is narrow in scope, then the best to be hoped for is action to reduce the unwanted spillover effects of distributional inequalities that are felt by both majorities and minorities (either because of utility interdependence or because they affect individual welfare narrowly conceived). Stricter law enforcement, urban renewal, and a number of environmental programs fit this description. However, such measures are insufficient to set in motion the corrective forces needed to relieve the urban crisis because they do not come to grips with fundamental deficiencies in the "rules of the game" or "effective constitution" which govern social interaction and determine the distribution of income, wealth, and social opportunity. Use of the fiscal structure to redistribute income and wealth directly (e.g., universal income supplementation) is one way of affecting such change. In addition, other changes which govern market or nonmarket rules of the game (e.g., voting-rights reform and open housing) can in due time significantly alter the distribution of private and social claims. The latter changes, in contrast to direct action programs, need neither strain the public budget nor require periodic authorizations, or annual appropriations, and do not rely on the bureaucratic structure for success.

At a practical level, all of this suggests that civil rights legislation and enforcement, income maintenance, open housing, and programs which assure equal access to education and equal protection of the law hold much more promise for the future of a "free" and harmonious (though still heterogenous) urban society than an admixture of functional and categorical programs of limited scope. Urban renewal, the hodgepodge of *ad hoc* welfare programs now in force, and large-scale efforts to induct technological change and innovation in such areas as home construction and urban transportation are unlikely, or less likely, to make much of a dent in the urban crisis.[6]

5. Little can be gained by arguing over a definition of consensus. Surely, it seems reasonable to assume that malevolent people are not a politically relevant force. If they were, a free society could not endure. In any case, true malevolence is an uncommon condition.

6. Indeed, it is not always clear that disadvantaged families are the primary beneficiaries of programs ostensibly designed to help them or that the programs benefit the disadvantaged at all. One result of urban renewal,

Changes in "rules of the game" which are basic to the urban crisis directly modify the effective structure of property rights and the structure of claims associated with them. In conjunction with market forces, such rights and claims largely determine the long-run distributional characteristics of our society and whether they are perceived as fair or unfair.

Thus, the system of private rights to property is very much bound up with the "urban crisis," not just because the distribution of such rights is unequal and the use of resources for private gain generates some diseconomies, but because these rights are not absolute. One man's rights are often another's deprivation. The issue of fairness or distributive justice arises, thus, in any discussion of property rights because the distribution of claims, which in a market-oriented society imply political as well as economic power, derives from such rights.

For a social practice like rights to private property to be acceptable to all members of a community, Rawls has argued it must be fair, and to be fair, it must satisfy two conditions: (1) all parties whom the practice will affect must be given an opportunity to make claims on its design,[7] and (2) the practice must apply equally to all affected by it unless a deviation from equal application will benefit all concerned. This definition provides a rationale for attenuating or modifying some existing property rights through a consent mechanism (e.g., through redistributive taxation, which alters rights to earned income). It also gives the reason why society characteristically proceeds with caution in doing so. The interests of those adversely affected are crucial in determining the degree and speed with which unjust practices are changed. It is one thing to begin *de novo* to build a system of law which restricts the rights attaching to private property; it is quite another to modify existing rights, thereby changing rules of the game in midstream.

The distinction we are making here is between "payoff prob-

---

after all, has been neighborhood dissolution; another has been the opportunity for gain it presented to home-builders and land developers. Similarly, claims on the agricultural surplus are surely preferable to hunger. But are the subsidies which generate this surplus preferable to the direct income transfers which they might otherwise finance?

7. Note that this criterion provides a philosophical basis for black Americans, whose ancestors did not voluntarily opt into our society, to object to its existing system of poverty rights and prevailing distributive characteristics.

lems," which are evaluated within a given system of rules, and
"choice of game" problems, in which the rules themselves are
decided. There are two ways of viewing the proper procedures
for changing an unfair practice. They differ fundamentally on
the issue of compensation. One approach holds to the view that
the process of change requires compensation of the in-
jured party; i e, even the party now benefiting from an unfair
practice whose interests will be adversely affected by a change
in the practice. The second approach distinguishes between
those claims which are legitimate and those which are not and
holds to the view that the claims of those who benefit from an
unfair practice can be overridden. These are primarily differences in moral views. As a practical matter, compensation or
long lead times, or both, are generally associated with fundamental changes in the rules of the game.[8]

The problem of fairness in transition is, of course, less significant when the effect of rule changes on individuals is indirect,
as with congressional reform and measures designed to make
federalism more effective (such as revenue sharing or changes
in metropolitan or regional political structures). It is more significant (and difficult) when rule changes affect individuals directly (as when property rights are modified or attenuated, since
property and income attach to particular individuals) When rule
changes *do* affect property rights directly, the assurance of or-
derly transition is greater if changes are such that they can work
themselves out through market transactions. To be specific, open
housing, which is a change in market practices, is clearly preferable to a system of residential quotas or enforced and uncompensated scattered-site housing.

An instructive approach to the dilemma of constitutional
change—both in terms of the goals of change and the process for
getting there—has been suggested by Buchanan.[9] In his view,

8. Thus, for example, a community of risk-averse individuals, totally
ignorant of their future income prospects, might choose a fiscal constitution
which calls for equalizing redistribution. But immediate income prospects
are not at all uncertain in the real world and consensus on such a rule is
hardly realistic.

9. Buchanan has argued, as we have, "in fiscal theory, as in politics generally, scholars need to pay more attention to the working out of rules or
institutions through which final outcomes emerge and less attention to the
shape of these outcomes themselves."

consensus on basic changes in social institutions is more likely to be achieved if individuals have a dispassionate and detached view of their expected effects. This is true if constitutional-type changes, once adopted, do not take effect until a later point in time (say, twenty-five years), thus exempting the present generation from their effects. It may well be that we can do little to resolve the urban crisis equitably in the short run, but that in the long run, appropriate constitutional-type changes, capable of consensus, can bring about social justice and, thereby, dissipate the crisis itself. But, whatever its conceptual appeal, a delayed solution (and much less one that puts change off for a full generation) does not come to grips with the interim problem of preserving a free society in the face of what appears to be a degenerative (perhaps rapid) movement away from consensus.[10]

CONCLUSION

Reduced to its common denominator, our discussion suggests that a "solution" of the urban crisis, in the short or long run, requires that the various constituencies in our nation be able to see the kinds of constitutional-type changes described (including changes in the fiscal constitution) as a matter of their own long-run self-interest. To attain justice with fairness, what is needed is a broad moral consensus, founded in a heightened perception of human interdependence and an understanding that a just and free society are the stakes of a game which must be played out within a viable time frame.

While we interpret the urban crisis quite differently from Banfield, some of our policy recommendations are similar to his. But while Banfield, in large part, sees the crisis as deriving from the present-orientedness of the lower classes, our analysis sug-

10. The idea of postdating change is not fully consistent with the premise that all parties whom a social practice will affect must be given claims on its design. Pragmatically, however, this counterargument is less troublesome than our prior reservation, for it is not necessarily inappropriate to interpret the constitutional preferences of any given social or demographic cohort as a surrogate for the preferences of its children. The implication of Buchanan's argument, moreover, is that the realistic alternative to fairness in the future is not fairness at present, which may be unattainable in any case, but the perpetuation of legally sanctioned inequities.

gests that it is precisely the lower classes' ability to project an intolerable situation forward, together with the present-orientedness of the political majority and the political incentives of their representatives, which leads to action or inaction that exacerbates or perpetuates the crisis.

Thus, while Banfield's counsel is one of pessimism and resignation, ours is not. We believe that resolution of the crisis is possible if political majorities are future-oriented enough to adopt constitutional reforms which not only benefit the lower classes but serve the majority's long-run self-interest. If these political majorities have the foresight to adopt fundamental, constitutional-type change, fulfillment can be harnessed to hope, and an urban society that is just, humane, and truly free can be a reality.

Suggested Further Readings

Alonso, William, *Location and Land Use*. Cambridge, Mass.: Harvard University Press, 1964.

――――――. "The Mirage of New Towns," *The Public Interest*, no. 19 (Spring 1970).

Altshuler, Alan. *Community Control: The Black Demand for Participation in Large American Cities*. New York: Pegasus, 1970.

Baumol, William. "Macronomics of Unbalanced Growth: The Anatomy of Urban Crisis," *American Economic Review* 57 (June 1967).

Berry, Brian. "Cities as Systems within Systems of Cities," *Papers and Proceedings of the Regional Science Association* 13 (1964).

Bish, Robert L. *The Public Economy of Metropolitan Areas*. Chicago: Markham, 1971.

Bradford, David F., and Oates, Wallace E. "Suburban Exploitation of Central Cities and Governmental Structure," in Harold M. Hochman and George E. Peterson, eds., *Redistribution through Public Choice*. New York: Columbia University Press, 1974.

Brazer, Harvey E. "Some Fiscal Implications of Metropolitanism," in Guthrie S. Birkhead, ed., *Metropolitan Issues: Social, Governmental Fiscal*. Syracuse, N.Y.: Maxwell Graduate School of Citizenship and Public Affairs, 1962.

Buchanan, James M., "Who Should Distribute What in a Federal System?" in Harold M. Hochman and George E. Peterson, eds., *Redistribution through Public Choice*. New York: Columbia University Press, 1974.

Campbell, Alan, and Sacks, Seymour. *Metropolitan America: Fiscal Patterns and Governmental Systems*. New York: Free Press, 1967.

Chinitz, Benjamin. "Contrasts in Agglomeration: New York and Pittsburgh," *American Economic Review* (May 1961).

――――――, ed. *City and Suburb: The Economics of Metropolitan Growth*. Englewood Cliffs: Prentice-Hall, 1964.

Crecine, John P., ed. *Financing the Metropolis*. Beverly Hills, Calif.: Sage Publications, 1970.

Davis, Kingsley. "The Urbanization of Human Populations, *Scientific American* 213, no. 3 (September 1964).

Davis, Otto, and Whinston, Andrew. "Economics of Urban Renewal," *Law and Contemporary Problems* 26 (Winter 1961).

Downs, Anthony. *Urban Problems and Prospects*. Chicago: Markham, 1970.

Duncan, Otis Dudley, and Duncan, Beverly. *The Negro Population of Chicago*. Chicago: University of Chicago Press, 1957.

Fisher, Joseph L., and Wingo, Lowdon. "Directions for Metropolitan Policy," from Mark Perlman, Charles J. Leven, and Benjamin Chintz, eds., *Spatial, Regional and Population Economics: Essays in Honor of Edgar M. Hoover*. New York: Gordon and Breach, Science Publishers, 1972.

Forrester, Jay W. *Urban Dynamics*. Cambridge, Mass.: MIT Press, 1969.

Goetz, Charles J. *What Is Revenue Sharing?* Washington, D.C.: The Urban Institute, 1973.

Gordon, David M. *Problems in Political Economy: An Urban Perspective.* Lexington, Mass.: Heath, 1971

Gorham, William, ed. *Urban Processes.* Washington, D.C.: The Urban Institute, 1972.

Greene, Kenneth V.; Neenan, William S.; and Scott, Claudia D. *Fiscal Interactions in a Metropolitan Area,* Lexington, Mass.: Heath, 1974.

Hirsch, Werner Z. *Urban, Economic Analysis.* New York: McGraw-Hill, 1973.

Hoover, Edgar M. *The Location of Economic Activity.* 1948.

————. "Spatial Economics: Partial Equilibrium Approach," in *The Encyclopedia of The Social Sciences.* New York: Macmillan, 1968.

————, and Vernon, Raymond *Anatomy of a Metropolis.* Cambridge: Harvard University Press, 1959.

Jacobs, Jane. *The Economy of Cities.* New York: Random House, 1919.

————. *The Rise and Decline of Great American Cities.* New York: Doubleday, 1969.

Kain, John F. "Housing Segregation, Negro Employment, and Metropolitan Decentralization," *The Quarterly Journal of Economics* 827, no. 2 (May 1968).

Long, Norton E. "The City as Reservation," *The Public Interest,* no. 25 (Fall 1971).

Lösch, August. *The Economics of Location.* New Haven: Yale University Press, 1954.

Lowry, Ira S., et al. *Rental Housing in New York City: The Demand for Shelter.* New York: New York City RAND Institute (June 1971).

Margolis, Julius. "Metropolitan Finance Problems: Territories, Functions and Growth," in James M. Buchanan, ed., *Public Finances: Needs, Sources, and Utilization.* Princeton, N.J.: Princeton University Press, 1966.

————, ed. *The Analysis of Public Output.* New York: National Bureau of Economic Research, 1970.

————, ed. *The Public Economy of Urban Communities.* Baltimore: Johns Hopkins, University Press, 1965.

Meyer, John; Kain, John; and Wohl, Martin. *The Urban Transportation Problem.* Cambridge, Mass.: Harvard University Press, 1965.

Mills, Edwin S. *Urban Economics.* Glenview, Ill.: Scott, Foresman, 1972.

Mushkin, Selma, ed. *Public Prices for Public Products.* Washington, D.C.: The Urban Institute, 1972.

Muth, Richard. *Cities and Housing.* Chicago: University of Chicago Press, 1969.

————. "Migration: Chicken or Egg?" *Southern Economic Journal* 37, no. 3 (January 1971).

Myrdal, Gunnar. *An American Dilemma.* Rev. ed., New York: Harper and Row, 1962.

National Commission on Urban Problems. *Building the American City.* Final Report, 1969.

Neenan, William B. "Suburban-Central City Exploitation Thesis: One City's Tale," *National Tax Journal* 23, no. 2 (June 1970).

Netzer, Dick. *Economics and Urban Problems.* New York: Basic Books, 1970.

Ostrom, Vincent; Tiebout, Charles M.; and Warren, Robert O. "The Organization of Government in Metropolitan Areas," *American Political Science Review* 60 (December 1961).

Owen, Wilfred. *The Metropolitan Transportation Problem.* Washington, D.C.: Brookings, rev. ed., 1966.

Pascal, Anthony H. "The Economics of Housing Segregation," P-3095. Santa Monica, Calif.: The RAND Corporation, 1965.

_____, ed. *Thinking about Cities: New Perspectives on Urban Problems.* Belmont, Calif:. Dickenson Publishing, 1970.

Perloff, Harvey, et al. *Regions, Resources and Economic Growth.* Baltimore: Johns Hopkins University Press, 1960.

_____, and Wingo, Lowdon, eds. *Issues in Urban Economics.* Baltimore: Johns Hopkins University Press, 1968.

Pressman, Jeffrey L., and Wildavsky, Aaron B. *Implementation: How Great Expectations in Washington Are Dashed in Oakland.* Berkeley, Calif.: University of California Press, 1973.

Rothenberg, Jerome. *Economic Evaluation of Urban Renewal.* Washington, D.C.: Brookings, 1967.

Schaller, Howard G., ed. *Public Expenditures Decisions in The Urban Community.* Washington, D.C.: Resources for the Future, 1963.

Sternlieb, George. "The City as Sandbox," *The Public Interest,* no. 25 (Fall 1971).

Taeuber, Karl E., and Taeuber, Alma F. *Negroes in Cities; Residential Segregation, and Neighborhood Change.* Chicago: Aldine, 1965.

Thompson, Wilbur. *A Preface to Urban Economics.* Baltimore: Johns Hopkins University Press, 1965.

Tiebout, Charles. "A Pure Theory of Local Expenditures," *Journal of Political Economy* 64 (October 1956).

Vernon, Raymond. *Metropolis 1985.* Cambridge, Mass.: Harvard University Press, 1960.

Vickrey, William S. "Pricing in Urban and Suburban Transport," *American Economic Review* 53 (May 1963).

Webber, Melvin M. *Explorations into Urban Structure.* Philadelphia: University of Pennsylvania Press, 1964.

Wertheimer, Richard. *The Monetary Rewards of Migration within The U.S.* Washington, D.C.: The Urban Institute, 1970.

Wilson, James Q., ed. *The Metropolitan Enigma.* Washington, D.C.: Chamber of Commerce of the United States, 1967.

Wingo, Lowdon, ed. *Transportation and Urban Land.* Washington, D.C.: Resources for the Future, 1961.

Wood, Robert C. *1400 Governments: The Political Economy of the New York Metropolitan Region.* Cambridge, Mass: Harvard University Press, 1961.